Wellington's Two-Front War

CAMPAIGNS & COMMANDERS

GREGORY J. W. URWIN, SERIES EDITOR

CAMPAIGNS AND COMMANDERS

GENERAL EDITOR

Gregory J. W. Urwin, *Temple University, Philadelphia, Pennsylvania*

ADVISORY BOARD

Lawrence E. Babits, *East Carolina University, Greenville*
James C. Bradford, *Texas A&M University, College Station*
David M. Glantz, *Carlisle, Pennsylvania*
Jerome A. Greene, *Denver, Colorado*
Victor Davis Hanson, *California State University, Fresno*
Herman Hattaway, *University of Missouri, Kansas City*
J. A. Houlding, *Rückersdorf, Germany*
Eugenia C. Kiesling, *U.S. Military Academy, West Point, New York* Timothy K. Nenninger, *National Archives, Washington, D.C.*
Frederick C. Schneid, *High Point University, High Point, North Carolina*
Timothy J. Stapleton, *University of Calgary*

WELLINGTON'S TWO-FRONT WAR

THE PENINSULAR CAMPAIGNS, AT HOME AND ABROAD, 1808–1814

JOSHUA MOON

UNIVERSITY OF OKLAHOMA PRESS : NORMAN

Library of Congress Cataloging-in-Publication Data
Moon, Joshua Lee, 1972–
  Wellington's two-front war : the Peninsular Campaigns, at home and abroad, 1808–1814 / Joshua Moon.
    p. cm. — (Campaigns and commanders)
  Includes bibliographical references and index.
  ISBN 978-0-8061-4157-2 (hardcover) ISBN 978-0-8061-9224-6 (paper)
  1. Peninsular War, 1807–1814—Campaigns. 2. Wellington, Arthur Wellesley, Duke of, 1769–1852—Military leadership. 3. Peninsular War, 1807–1814—Great Britain. 4. Great Britain—Politics and government—1789–1820. I. Title.
  DC231.M498 2011
  940.2′74—dc22   2010026445

Wellington's Two-Front War: The Peninsular Campaigns, at Home and Abroad, 1808–1814 is Volume 29 in the Campaigns and Commanders series.

The paper in this book meets the guidelines for permanence and durability of the Committee on Production Guidelines for Book Longevity of the Council on Library Resources, Inc. ∞

Copyright © 2011 by the University of Oklahoma Press, Norman, Publishing Division of the University. Paperback published 2023. Manufactured in the U.S.A. All rights reserved. No part of this publication may be reproduced, stored in a retrieval system, or transmitted, in any form or by any means, electronic, mechanical, photocopying, recording, or otherwise—except as permitted under Section 107 or 108 of the United States Copyright Act—without the prior written permission of the University of Oklahoma Press.

To Christine

beat navy!

Contents

List of Illustrations	ix
Preface and Acknowledgments	xi
Introduction	3
1. Roots of the Struggle: The Campaign of 1808	13
2. A Second Chance: Wellesley's Return to Iberia in 1809	26
3. The Trials Begin: The Campaign of 1809	37
4. Waning Support: The Defense of Portugal, 1809–1810	54
5. The Crucible: Masséna's Invasion of Portugal, 1810–1811	71
6. The Tide Turns: The Pursuit of Masséna, 1811–1812	92
7. Exploitation: The Burgos Campaign, 1812–1813	122
8. Opportunity Arrested: The Campaign of 1813	149
9. The Final Act: The Invasion of France, 1813–1814	186
Conclusion	213
Appendices	
A. Cabinet Positions with Strategic Responsibility, 1808–1814	223
B. French Army Commanders in Spain, 1810–1813	225
C. Chronology of the Peninsular War	227
Notes	231
Bibliography	267
Index	275

Illustrations

FIGURES

Administration of the British Army, 1808–1814	4
William Grenville, 1st Baron Grenville	83
Richard Colley Wellesley, Marquess Wellesley	84
George Canning	85
André Masséna, duc de Rivoli, prince d'Essling	86
Henry Bathurst, 3rd Earl of Bathurst	87
Robert Stewart, 2nd Marquess of Londonderry (Lord Castlereagh)	88
Robert Jenkinson, 2nd Earl of Liverpool	89
Robert Dundas, 2nd Viscount Melville	90
Arthur Wellesley, 1st Duke of Wellington	91

MAP

The Iberian Peninsula, 1808–1814	xiv

Preface and Acknowledgments

This book found its origins in a famous 1812 letter credited to the Duke of Wellington. Addressed to the "Esteemed Gentlemen in Whitehall" for "elucidation" of his purpose for "dragging an army over the barren plains" of the Iberian Peninsula, Wellington asks, "[Am] I to train an army of uniformed British Clerks in Spain for the benefit of the accountants and copy boys in London, or am I to see that the forces of Napoleon are driven out of Spain?" Anyone who has ever walked a battlefield can appreciate the anger and despair in Wellington's words. No commander should become hindered on the war front by the political and military mechanisms on the home front. Although no archival proof of Wellington penning that letter exists, the questions it raises beg further examination.

The Duke of Wellington's military campaigns in the Iberian Peninsula have attracted the attention of scholars and soldiers for two hundred years, but no study sheds ample light on the problems Wellington encountered having to fight not only the French, but also an unforgiving military and political bureaucracy at home and abroad, which, subject to public opinion and an often hostile press, struggled to formulate a clear and decisive strategy for victory. This book aims to fill this gap in academic inquiry by examining Wellington's campaigns from 1808 to 1814 in light of the strategic, operational, and often political impediments he encountered on the home front while liberating the Iberian Peninsula from French control.

The unceasing and generous assistance of several people and institutions made the completion of this work possible. Most important, I would like to thank Donald Horward. A consummate scholar, teacher, and friend, his presence dominates the field. I am immensely proud to have studied under his tutelage, and I owe an immeasurable amount of gratitude to him and to the Institute of Napoleon and French Revolution at Florida State University. I would also like to thank the late Ben Weider, George Knight, and Skip Vichness. Their generosity made it possible for me to travel to the United Kingdom to conduct the archival research necessary to write this book. I am also grateful to all the professors who have helped me over the past several years, particularly Jonathan Grant, Edward Wynot, Joseph Richardson, Patrick O'Sullivan, and Jim Jones. All are great examples of the experience and professionalism found at Florida State University. I would also like to thank colleagues and fellow Seminoles John Severn, Kevin McCranie, Lt. Col. Brian DeToy, Maj. Jason Musteen, Kenny Johnson, Alexander Mikaberidze, Jackson Sigler, Jolynda Chenicek, and the late Richard T. Herzog for their mentorship, friendship, and scholarly advice.

I owe a great deal of gratitude to Chuck Rankin, Bobbie Drake, Connie Arnold, Emily Jerman, and copyeditor Melanie Mallon of the University of Oklahoma Press. They have made this process rewarding and fun. I am also indebted to Gregory J. W. Urwin and the Campaigns and Commanders series advisory board for their vote of confidence. Collectively, they saw the merits of this project and had the audacity to place it alongside the many great works of that prestigious press.

A special measure of gratitude goes to Gen. Robert Doughty, Col. Lance Betros, Col. Mat Moten, Col. Ty Seidule, and Col. Gian Gentile at the United States Military Academy, and Gen. Jeffery Underhill, Col. Rick White, Col. Roger "Rooster" Brown, and Col. Anthony "AC" Shaw. I have had the distinct honor to serve with these men over the past several years, and all have graciously granted me the time to pursue this project. I would also like to thank my brothers in arms who have pulled their fair share of my weight while I worked. Most important thanks go to my former office mate at West Point, Lt. Col. Mike McDermott; and in the USPACOM J393 BMD "Pit,"

I would like to thank Jim Fletcher, Ed Stikeleather, Dave Barden, LCDR Chris Adams, Lt. Col. Jade "JOJ" Norstrom, and Lt. Col. "Sven" Holmquist.

I owe special thanks to the librarians who have assisted me throughout this process. At Florida State's Strozier Library, I would like to thank the head of Special Collections, Lucy Patrick, and her staff. At West Point's Cadet Library, I would like to thank the head of Special Collections, Suzanne Christoff, and her staff. An extra measure of gratitude goes to Deborah DiSalvo at West Point's ILL Department.

I also received invaluable assistance from many people in Britain. Foremost, I would like to thank Col. John Hughes-Wilson and Col. Sean Lambe. Both outstanding officers embody the finest traditions of the British army's untiring service and fidelity to their queen and country. For his invaluable commentary and overall contribution to our understanding of the complexities of nineteenth-century Spain, I would like to thank Charles Esdaile. I also need to thank Christopher Woolgar and Karen Robson of the Hartley Library at the University of Southampton and David Rimmer and his staff at the County Gwent Record Office, in Cwmbrân, Wales, for their help and generosity.

I am also grateful to Frances Woodard of Huntsville, Alabama. Her love for the Iron Duke shines forth in the help and guidance she has graciously provided me throughout this process. As her husband, Charles Woodard, would attest, this was not the first time her wisdom and keen eye has helped an aspiring scholar.

I am particularly grateful to my parents, Col. John and Sandra Moon. I could not have written this book without your guidance and friendly encouragement. Thanks for your help and most importantly for the example you have always set for King, Kelly, and me.

Above all, I would like to thank my beautiful wife, Christine, our two sons, Jackson Lee and Preston Alexander, and our beautiful twin girls, Vivienne Marie and Olivia Grace. They have loaned me to this project for several years and every day gave me the love and support I needed to get through this process. They are the love of my life and the reason I serve my country.

My final thanks are reserved for Sir Arthur Wellesley, the Duke of Wellington. As he might say, "Three cheers for His Majesty followed by bayonet charge!"

The Iberian Peninsula, 1808–1814 (Reproduced courtesy of John Gilkes)

Wellington's Two-Front War

Introduction

In the spring of 1808, Britain faced a strategic dilemma. Since the beginning of the Revolutionary Wars in 1793, Britain had organized four unsuccessful coalitions against France. The army had suffered major defeats in the Low Countries in 1793 and 1799, and apart from a minor victory at the battle of Maida in July 1806, had never defeated a standing French army on the Continent. Unfortunately, the British government could not rely solely on the Royal Navy to defeat France. By 1808, the French emperor, Napoleon Bonaparte, had allied with Eurasia's other great land power, Russia, establishing the Continental System to embargo British goods. In response to these setbacks and to demonstrate their resolve to their allies and against Napoleon, Britain sought an opportunity to employ its army to break Napoleon's European hegemony.[1]

In 1808, such an opportunity presented itself. In the spring, Napoleon replaced the Spanish monarch with his brother Joseph. When the Spanish people revolted against Joseph, and the Spanish government requested British military and economic assistance, the British government agreed to intervene. In June 1808, the cabinet turned to a very young general officer, Sir Arthur Wellesley, who had forged several successful campaigns in India yet was unproven against the French. In July, Wellesley departed Cork for the Iberian Peninsula with ten thousand men. After landing in northern Spain, he assessed that strategic circumstances favored action in Portugal, not Spain;

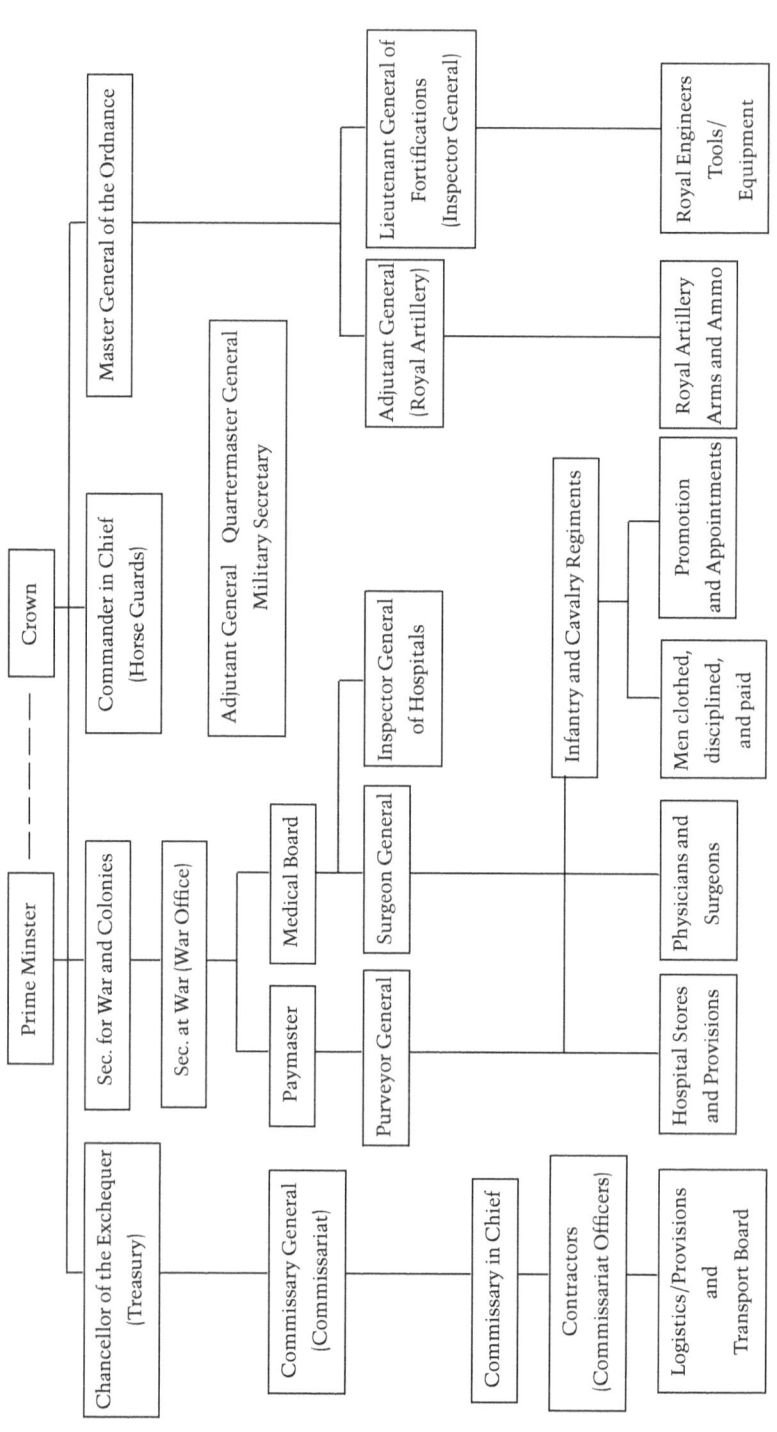

Administration of the British Army, 1808–1814. Based on the chart in Stephen G. P. Ward, *Wellington's Headquarters: A Study of the Administrative Problems in the Peninsula, 1809–1814* (Oxford: Oxford University Press, 1957).

therefore, in August he landed north of Lisbon. In doing so, Wellesley began a campaign that not only changed the course of Britain's war with France but also ushered in a new period of continental commitment for the British army.[2]

During the following six years, Wellesley, later the Duke of Wellington, and his allied army fought tenaciously against not only the many French armies sent to drive them into the sea, but also the harsh Iberian environment. Extreme temperatures in the summer and winter, rugged or nonexistent infrastructure, disease, and desertion all took their toll, yet Wellington never lost sight of his objective: to drive the French out of the Iberian Peninsula.

To understand the roots of Wellington's challenge, it is necessary to analyze the confusing hierarchical relationship that Wellington maintained with the various offices that governed the British army. Wellington's difficulty was founded in Parliament's large bureaucracy designed to preserve tight constitutional control over the British army.

The rationale for this structure dated to the seventeenth century. Before civil control of the military began, several English monarchs had used the army to ruthlessly enforce their writ. Parliament ultimately gained control of the army and established strict measures for its size and use, leaving to the Crown only internal control, such as training, officer promotion, and disciplinary enforcement. Parliament wielded the real power by deciding the army's size, deployment, and, most important, its budget. To reaffirm its power, Parliament passed the Annual Mutiny Act, renewing its military control each year. For the next two hundred years, Parliament and royal powers over the army remained separated.[3]

In the eighteenth century, a series of wars considerably increased the size and expenditure of the army. For example, prior to 1760, the army's budget rarely exceeded 10 percent of the national budget. Yet during the Seven Years' War, the army consumed almost 45 percent of the government's budget. By 1793, the army rivaled the Royal Navy in expenditure. This trend continued during the Napoleonic wars as the army became ruinously expensive for Britain. In 1805, Parliament was informed that during the previous year the navy had cost more than £11.75 million, the army just under £15.75 million. The Ordnance Board added to that total by another £3.5 million. Compare those figures to the national gross revenue of £40.7 million, and the army absorbed nearly 40 percent of the nation's budget. While Parliament struggled to limit the size and budget of the army, the monarchy sought to maintain order and discipline within the ranks of an ever-growing yet decreasingly professional army.[4]

By 1788, the army's size had increased beyond the king's ability to manage it effectively, and he created the office of commander in chief to assist him in directing his ground forces. Despite his lofty title, the commander in chief possessed very little power and wielded no strategic or operational control over the army. The duties and responsibilities were largely dependent on the energy and political background of the man who occupied the position. From 1798 to 1822, the king's second son, Frederick Augustus, the Duke of York, held the office. He served in this position during the entire Peninsular War with only one break in service, from March 1809 to 1811, when his father replaced him with Sir David Dundas. Despite a poor combat record in leading troops, the Duke of York was an excellent administrator, and many of his reforms, including the reduction of commission purchase and the standardization of tactical drills and maneuvers, were paramount to the British army's success in the peninsula.[5]

In addition to serving as the king's liaison to the army, the Duke of York also presided over the Horse Guards, a branch of government consisting of several military offices that combined to serve as the army's personnel headquarters. Divided into three departments, the Horse Guards included the army's adjutant general, quartermaster general, and military secretary. While the adjutant general controlled discipline, training, military regulations, and applications for leave of absence, the quartermaster general was responsible for transferring and quartering British troops in Ireland and Britain.[6] In 1795, the Duke of York, to facilitate the commander in chief's oversight of the army list and to communicate with expeditionary force commanders, established the office of military secretary. Often referred to as the patronage secretary, the military secretary, by nature of his relationship with the commander in chief, wielded enormous influence in recommending promotions in the infantry and cavalry branches and in appointing general officers to serve on expeditionary force staffs. The two men who served as military secretary during the Peninsular War were Col. James Willoughby Gordon (1808–1809), and Col. Henry Torrens (1809–1814). In 1809, the entire staff of the Horse Guards numbered only thirty-two men.[7]

Despite his leadership of the Horse Guards, the commander in chief had no influence over the army's financial administration, nor did he have the authority to appoint officers in the Royal Artillery and Royal Engineers. These duties were the prerogative of the master general of the ordnance and the secretary at war.[8] An oddity, unique to the British army, was that the master general directed the artillery and engineers. The office was reserved for a senior army officer; consequently, he was the only active military officer to serve in the cabinet. Although he was not generally consulted on questions of strategy, his primary responsibility was to ensure that both the army and the navy received the necessary armaments for deployments. Because the artillery and engineers fell under the jurisdiction of the Ordnance Board, they were not considered part of the army command structure. As the commander in chief controlled promotions within the infantry and cavalry, the master general supervised all promotions within the army's technical branches.[9]

As the commander in chief governed the army for the Crown, the secretary at war regulated its administration for Parliament. Appointed by the prime minister, the secretary at war was usually a junior ranking politician who served outside the cabinet, presiding over the British government's largest department, the War Office. Because of the importance of his position, the secretary at war remained politically neutral, and his portfolio did not change hands when a cabinet was replaced. He presented annual estimates of troop strength and disposition, and he authorized all monetary expenditures for the army, which included regimental accounts. He also coordinated all troop movements within Britain and Ireland and further ensured that no units were mobilized during an election. To facilitate his complex task, he employed over 120 clerks in the War Office, which by numbers alone was far greater than the size of both the Foreign Office and War Department combined.[10] Despite its manpower, the War Office was notoriously inefficient. It struggled to keep pace with the increased demands of administering an army engaged in a global war against France. An example of the immensity of this task is found in a letter from Lord Palmerston, secretary at war during the Peninsular War, to his sister: "In the War Office, there is an immense number of backlogged army accounts unsettled, and [every day] more and more [delinquent accounts] accumulate."[11]

Strategic planning and policy powers belonged to the secretary for war and colonies. By far the most influential cabinet post during the Peninsular War, the secretary for war was the prime minister's principal military adviser and supervised the War Department. Responsible for conducting most communications with British commanders, the secretary for war and colonies approved all strategic and operational deployments of British troops, including issuing and deploying reinforcements.[12] (For a list of the principal cabinet positions and office holders during the Peninsular War, see appendix A.)

Three additional offices not included in the army's direct administration played crucial roles in determining Britain's war strategy, but they also added to the army's confusing command and control structure. The first was the office of the foreign secretary, who, with the help of his many ambassadors and ministers' plenipotentiary serving abroad, conducted negotiations with Britain's allies on multiple subjects, including financial subsidies and strategy. During the Peninsular War, the foreign secretary's magnified and ill-defined role often overlapped with that of the secretary for war and caused difficulty both in the cabinet and at the front.

Two additional offices that helped determine strategy were the first lord of the Admiralty and the chancellor of the Exchequer. Because of the geography of the Iberian Peninsula, the first lord of the Admiralty assumed primary importance; it was his responsibility to provide and maintain vital naval and transportation support for Wellington's army. However, the naval bureaucracy was larger and more ponderous than that of the army. Furthermore, because the Royal Navy had always been considered Britain's senior service, Wellington's command of all British forces in the peninsula caused great friction. This fact was not lost on Wellington, who, prior to departing for the peninsula in 1808, defended the army's role in a continuing rivalry with the Royal Navy for prominence and purse. Speaking in the House of Commons, Wellington stated "that although the Royal Navy was the characteristic and constitutional force of Britain . . . the army was the new force which arose out of the extraordinary exigencies of modern times."[13] While Wellington's comments may not have made him popular in the Admiralty, he was fortunate to serve with two admirals in the peninsula who understood the difficulty of his task. These men, admirals Sir Charles Cotton and George Cranfield

Berkeley, consistently extrapolated their orders from the Admiralty Office to support Wellington and his army throughout the war.[14]

The last cabinet office that had a major impact on the course of the war was the chancellor of the Exchequer, or treasury secretary. The chancellor served in the cabinet and formed the nation's fiscal policy. As the head of the Treasury, he had an enormous impact on the supply of money for the army. In addition to these duties, the chancellor, by a quirk in the system, administered the army's commissariat, or commissary general. The commissariat was expected to organize, procure, and supply the army's logistics needs, which it did for Wellington's army through civilian commissariat officers. Because of the difficult logistics during the Peninsular War, the commissariat officers played a vital role in procuring and purchasing supplies for the army from the local Spanish and Portuguese population.[15]

Certainly not diminished in the army's command structure was the office of prime minister. Operating as the head of government, the prime minister's official position was, among other important matters, the first lord of the treasury. In this capacity, he greatly influenced the army's budget, which had a significant impact on the war in the peninsula. However, like most men in government offices, the specific duties of the prime minister were loosely defined, and his relationship with commanders, like Wellington, was largely based on his interaction with the secretary for war and colonies. All three prime ministers who served from 1808 to 1814 represented the conservative Tory Party (see appendix A).Throughout the war, the opposition party, the Whigs, maintained a constant vigil over these Tory cabinets. Led by men such as former prime minister Baron William Grenville, the Whigs frequently used the British press as well as parliamentary debates to attack Wellington, his brothers, Richard and Henry, and their strategy in the peninsula.[16]

Politics aside, the overwhelming significance of Parliament's bureaucratic control of the British army is typified by Wellington's having to seek the approval of at least five government offices just to conduct the daily administrative and tactical operations necessary to fight a war. A simple request for reinforcements required the correspondence and approval of no fewer than six cabinet ministers and the commander in chief. Within the cabinet, these would include the prime minister, the secretary for war and colonies, and the foreign secretary to shape the foreign policy objectives and to approve dispatching additional troops after conferring with the Spanish and Portuguese governments. The master general of the ordnance would be consulted to supply the artillery and ammunition for the expedition and to approve the deployment of any artillery and engineers. The first lord of the Admiralty would be asked to requisition the appropriate number of transports and to coordinate the Royal Navy's assignments, and the chancellor of the Exchequer would be forced to organize the commissariat for logistics support. Outside the cabinet, the commander in chief was required to consult the army list to recommend which units were fit for service and to name an appropriately senior commander to lead the mission. Finally, the secretary at war would be responsible for coordinating all paperwork to process the soldiers to their ports of embarkation. This all took time, a commodity that the field commander had in short supply.[17]

Such an inefficient organization could only be justified to ensure constitutional safeguards against the Crown's military usurpation. The problem was that in the British army's bloated governing structure, there were simply too many offices with no single direction to provide expeditionary commanders, like Wellington, with the efficient and timely support required to fight Napoleon's marshals, who operated with fewer restrictions and more resources.

Expeditionary commanders had the added burden of administering their own staffs. If communicating their needs through London was hard, doing the same within their own staffs was worse. Of the eight primary officers who served on Wellington's staff, seven answered directly to their superiors in London, not to Wellington. The chief of artillery and engineers reported to the master general of the ordnance; the chief commissariat to the chancellor of the Exchequer; the quartermaster general and adjutant general to the Horse Guards; and the surgeon general, apothecary general, and paymaster general to the secretary at war. The only member of Wellington's staff that fell under his direct authority was the military secretary.[18]

Even members of the British government in London viewed the system as inefficient. In 1810, a Whig leader, Charles Grey, wrote the military secretary at the Horse Guards to recommend altering the army's clumsy command structure. The former first lord of the Admiralty argued that the structure be changed to "bring under one direction all the various departments of the [army] to prevent the [confusion] of several offices which had always produced delay and great infuriation of the public interest." To accomplish this task, Grey proposed the creation of a Board of War.[19]

Grey's idea was never formally considered, but it did highlight the serious flaws in the British army's governing structure. He saw that in its quest for separation of powers, Parliament had created a confusing and unnecessary division of powers and responsibility that violated simplicity and unity of command. No one understood the implications of the system's weaknesses more than Wellington. After the Peninsular War ended, he testified before a commission, "The Commander-in-Chief of the British Army cannot at this moment move a corporal's guard from London to Windsor without going to the civil department for authority."[20]

In addition to fighting against the bureaucracy, Wellington had to guard against established regulations that determined promotion and command within his army. On a summer evening in 1826, at a dinner party in London, the "hero of Waterloo" expressed to some friends his less than favorable opinion of the office that governed the army's internal regulations: "I can't say that I owe my successes to any favor or confidence from the Horse Guards. They never showed me any [confidence] from my first day I had commanded to this hour." Reflecting on the Horse Guards removing him from command of the British Expeditionary Force to Portugal in 1808 in favor of two more senior general officers, he stated, "They removed me because [the Horse Guards] thought very little of anyone who had served in India. An Indian victory was not only [grounds for no confidence], but it was actually a cause of suspicion."[21]

Wellington, who had been chief secretary of Ireland in Parliament prior to his command, felt the Horse Guards disapproved of him also because of his close political connections with several high-ranking cabinet ministers of the time, such as the secretary for war, Robert Stewart, and Viscount Castlereagh, who led the fight for Wellington's nomination to command. Wellington declared, "because I was in Parliament, and connected with people in office, I was a politician and a politician never could be an effective soldier. Moreover [the Horse Guards] looked upon me with a kind of jealousy, because I was a lord's son, *a sprig of nobility*,' who came into the army more for ornament than use." Wellington concluded his stinging remarks by stating that the Horse Guards "could not believe that I was a tolerable regimental officer. I have proof that they thought I could not be trusted alone with a division, and I suspect they still have their doubts whether I know anything about the command of an army."[22] At the time of his remarks at the dinner party, no one in Britain questioned Wellington's service record or his ability to command an army. As the man who helped defeat Napoleon at Waterloo, Wellington had become a national hero. At the time of his appointment to command the Peninsular Expedition in 1808, Wellesley had not only commanded more British troops in the field than any other active general officer, but also possessed the finest combat record in the British army.[23] Nevertheless, the rules of the service dictated that the most senior officer command, and therefore Wellesley was superseded by two general officers who were senior to him in age and service but not in competency or ability. The labyrinth of regulations that governed the army of the day had grave implications for the British campaign in Portugal in 1808 and would be the starting point for a long and unforgiving second front for Wellington and his men in Iberia.

1

ROOTS OF THE STRUGGLE: THE CAMPAIGN OF 1808

We are going to hell by another road.
Wellington to his brother William Wellesley-Pole, 24 August 1808

In early August 1808, Wellesley and his force were landed by the Royal Navy at Modego Bay in Portugal and immediately went on the offensive. Wellesley combined his force with the five thousand British troops commanded by Maj. Gen. Brent Spencer and defeated the French at Roliça, on 17 August, and four days later at the battle of Vimeiro.[1] During the two-week campaign around Lisbon in 1808, Wellesley's army inflicted over three thousand French casualties and captured most of the enemy's artillery. Thus, Wellesley established himself as the youngest lieutenant general in the British army to lead a major expeditionary force against the French on the European continent, and he became the first British general since the Duke of Marlborough to achieve a significant victory.[2]

Despite his victories at Roliça and Vimeiro, Wellesley's campaign of 1808 was a formative lesson to the young general on how not to conduct a campaign. Within hours of Wellesley's victory at Vimeiro, he and his army were denied decisive victory by the imposition of a more senior general officer, Sir Harry Burrard, who had been dispatched from London to replace him. Although Burrard's replacement of Wellesley was in keeping with tradition, the timing and effect was nearly disastrous for the British expedition to Iberia. In fact, the application of seniority dates by the Horse Guards and Wellesley's inability to influence the men sent to his army would plague him for the rest of the war.

In the seniority-date system, all promotions and appointments for command in the infantry and cavalry branches above the rank lieutenant colonel were based entirely on seniority, which was dictated by the date a man achieved the rank of lieutenant colonel After attaining this rank, a man would become a general officer if he lived long enough. No British general officer, despite his competency or lack of it, could be expected to serve under another officer whose date of rank to lieutenant colonel was one day later than his own.[3]

Wellesley, who had been promoted to the rank of lieutenant general on 25 April 1808, was relatively low in seniority. In fact, of the more than 130 lieutenant generals on the army list in 1808, Wellesley was fourth from the bottom.[4] Despite this, he benefited from close political connections with the secretary for war, Viscount Castlereagh, and the foreign secretary, George Canning. Wellesley had served with both men in Parliament, and when he had publicly announced that he desired a command, Castlereagh had given him command of the British Expeditionary Force to Iberia in June 1808.[5]

At that time, British intelligence sources had estimated the French troop strength around Lisbon to be approximately five thousand men.[6] Castlereagh thought Wellesley's force combined with Major General Spencer's troops were sufficient to expel the French army from Portugal. In mid-July, however, two pieces of critical intelligence changed the government's calculations. The first was an updated report from Spencer estimating Gen. Andoche Junot's strength in Portugal as actually over twenty thousand men. More important, Sir John Moore's force of eleven thousand British troops returning from a disastrous expedition to Sweden was available for duty.[7] Although Sir John Moore outranked Wellesley, George Canning disliked him. Therefore, the Horse Guards scrambled to find a suitably senior officer to lead the force in Portugal. That no other British general officer possessed either Wellesley's or Moore's combat record was immaterial.[8]

The decision to deny Moore command in the British army demonstrates one of the great peculiarities of the British system. Although the Horse Guards recommended names for command, the nominations were always subject to personal and political vetting.

In an age of personality-driven politics, the most capable man did not always get the job. Canning carried enough political influence to remove Moore's name from consideration. To placate Moore, who felt as though he should command the army, the Horse Guards were forced to locate another officer who outranked Moore and had an understanding of the strategic and political situation in the peninsula. With few alternatives, the Horse Guards selected Sir Hew Dalrymple. As the governor of Gibraltar, Dalrymple posed no political threat to the administration and was thirteenth in terms of seniority; Despite Dalrymple's forty-five years in the army, however, he had served only one year in the field and had no experience commanding a large army in battle. But political affiliations and personal relationships won out, and Dalrymple was approved for command. In fact, because of Dalrymple's service as governor of Gibraltar, the cabinet felt he possessed a high level of insight concerning peninsular politics and diplomacy.[9]

Time was an issue, however. By the time Dalrymple received news of his appointment reached the field, the tactical situation in the peninsula would have certainly changed. Therefore, the Horse Guards required another officer to serve as an interim commander until Dalrymple arrived, one who outranked Moore yet could serve as second-in-command to Dalrymple. This officer would also have to reach the peninsula on short notice.[10]

Of the seventy-four officers who appeared in the army list between Dalrymple and Moore, only thirty-one were considered for the job. Of these, only one officer, Sir Harry Burrard, who was commanding the First Guards in London, had a good relationship with Moore and would not personally offend the general by his selection. As with Dalrymple, Burrard's command experience was limited. His only active service was against the French in Flanders in 1796, and during that expedition he had never commanded more than a brigade. Nevertheless, the Horse Guards, motivated by political considerations and the restrictions of seniority, viewed Burrard as the only officer who would deploy in time to prevent a union between Moore and Wellesley and keep Moore from taking command in the field. It would prove to be a disastrous decision.[11]

On 15 July, only two days before Wellesley would depart England, Castlereagh notified him that despite his faith in Wellesley's ability, he would be relieved from command in the peninsula. Castlereagh claimed, "I shall rejoice if [the command] shall have fallen to your lot to place the Tagus River in our hands, [but] I have no fear that you will do yourself honor and your country service [by following Dalrymple and Burrard's orders]."[12] Wellesley's answer was courteous and respectful: "All that I can say on the subject is, whether I am to command the army or not, or am to quit it, I shall do my best to insure its success; and you may depend on me. . . . I shall not hurry the operations, or commence them one moment sooner [so] that I may acquire the [greatest opportunity for] success."[13] In a letter to a friend, however, Wellesley hinted at his resolve to prove the government wrong. "The government has taken the alarm and ordered about [15,000 reinforcements] with several general officers, more senior to me [to include] Sir Hew Dalrymple to command the whole army. I hope that I shall have beaten Junot before any of them arrive, and then the government can do as they please with me."[14] In a letter to his older brother and confidant William Wellesley-Pole, the young general expressed his true dejection about being relieved before he had the chance to demonstrate his competence: "I do not know what the government propose to do with me. I shall be the junior of all the lieutenant generals and [therefore will be placed in] the most awkward situations in the world, which is to serve in a subordinate capacity in an army which one has commanded. . . . I think they had better order me home."[15] Despite his anger, Wellesley understood and accepted the established regulations that dictated the government's action. He feared that the government's decision to replace him during a campaign not only would violate the army's continuity of command, but would have adverse effects on the overall operation. Confirmation of those fears came shortly.

As the cabinet had planned, the first of the two more senior generals to arrive and replace Wellesley was Sir Harry Burrard. He had been dispatched with orders to take control of Moore's ten thousand men, proceed to Portugal, and assume command from Wellesley pending Dalrymple's arrival. Wellesley was aware of Burrard's instructions, but he was uncertain when Burrard would arrive. True to his word, Wellesley did not wait. He organized his army, and on 8 August he went on the offensive, taking care to leave behind instructions for Burrard's arrival, including a detailed report of the friendly and enemy tactical situation and a proposed course of action for Burrard to follow. In his assessment, Wellesley suggested, "If, however, the command of the army remained in my hands, I should certainly land the corps which [is now under your orders] at Mondego, and should move it upon Santarém River. Upon landing, aggressively march into the enemy's rear to prevent the French from escaping."[16] Although Wellesley knew that he could not order Burrard, he hoped that Burrard would at least heed his advice and allow Wellesley to retain command until the campaign concluded. He would be disappointed. Wellesley's plan was too aggressive, and his instructions were written for an aggressive officer who Wellesley hoped trust his judgment. Burrard was neither.

Arriving off the coast of Portugal on the evening of 20 August with 10,000 men, Burrard did not land until mid-morning of the next day. Despite Wellesley's instructions, Burrard spurned any suggestion to move his troops to the rear of the French formation. Instead, a cautious Burrard sent for reinforcements. He ordered Sir John Moore, whose troops had landed to the north, to begin marching south. His reluctance to march his men immediately cost the British any chance of a decisive victory. Had Burrard maneuvered to the rear of the French, while Wellesley applied pressure with his seasoned troops, the British could have decisively crushed the French. Instead, Burrard moved slowly, and in accordance with his orders from London, rode to meet Wellesley and relieve him from command.

By the time Burrard found Wellesley, the battle of Vimeiro was almost over. The last of the French attacks had been defeated, and Wellesley proposed an aggressive pursuit. Burrard relieved Wellesley and rejected the younger general's motion. Wellesley pleaded with Burrard, "Sir Harry now is your chance. The French are completely beaten; we have a large body of troops that have not yet been in action. Let us move on the right with the troops on the road to Torres Vedras. You take your force here straightforward; I will follow the French with [my troops] on the left. We shall be in Lisbon in three days!"[17] Unwilling to risk the fruits of the victory, Burrard ordered Wellesley to suspend offensive action until Moore's reinforcements arrived from the north. In his dispatch to Castlereagh, he mentioned nothing about preventing Wellesley from pursuing the French: "On my landing this morning, I found that the enemy's attack had already commenced.... I was fortunate enough to reach the field of action in time to witness and approve of every disposition that had been made. Sir Arthur Wellesley's comprehensive mind furnishing a ready resource in every emergency rendered it quite unnecessary to direct any alternative [plan]."[18]

Wellesley wasted no time dispelling Burrard's record of events. In a letter to Castlereagh, he questioned Burrard's indecision: "Sir Harry Burrard will probably acquaint you with the reasons which have induced him to call for Sir John Moore's [10,000 men] . . . [Despite being opposed] by not more than 12,000 to 14,000 Frenchmen, [I do not agree with the decision to] halt here till Sir John's corps shall join [us]. You [must understand], that this [decision] is not in conformity with my opinion, and I only wish Sir Harry had landed and seen things with his own eyes before he made it."[19] The next day he followed his letter to Castlereagh with a more direct attack on Burrard's indecisiveness: "If we do not move on . . . we will be poisoned by the stench of the dead and wounded, or we will starve, as everything in the neighborhood is already eaten up."[20]

Despite his demotion, Wellesley insisted that the British troops remain loyal to him, not Burrard: "The army are delighted that they gained [this] victory under the command of their 'old general.' I still command the army, as all the department heads will not go to [Burrard] for orders."[21] Wellesley's comment about the loyalty of the army remaining with him was important. Although it was the right tactical decision to leave Wellesley in the field after replacing him, it clearly broached unity of command; the loyalty of the officers and men was assuredly divided.

Wellesley's frustration and the confusion grew worse. On the next day, 22 August, Dalrymple arrived from Gibraltar to replace Burrard. Like Burrard, Dalrymple favored caution. Wellesley disagreed. He sensed that the French were beaten and vulnerable. He desperately wanted to pursue and destroy Junot's retreating army, to secure the security of Portugal with a treaty dictated on Britain's terms. Later that afternoon, Junot dispatched Gen. François Kellermann to negotiate a cease-fire agreement with the British. Kellermann initially approached Wellesley with his terms because he knew that Wellesley had been responsible for the campaign; however, Dalrymple refused to allow Wellesley to negotiate with Kellermann.[22] Within a few minutes, Dalrymple requested Burrard and Wellesley to join him in the negotiations. Kellermann proposed an immediate cease-fire leading to a convention for the French evacuation of Portugal. He wanted the British to embark the French army, with its Portuguese loot, in British ships for the return to France. Not wanting to squander the hard-fought victory, Dalrymple agreed to these terms. Wellesley objected.[23]

In a letter to Castlereagh, Wellesley expressed his displeasure at Dalrymple's actions and the contents of the convention, which, despite his signature, he opposed: "Although my name is affixed to this instrument, I beg that you will not believe that I negotiated it, [or] that I approve of it, or that I had any hand in wording it. It was negotiated by [Lieutenant General Dalrymple] himself. . . . I object to its verbiage. I object to the indefinite suspension of hostilities, [which] ought to have been for forty-eight hours only. As now, the French will have forty-eight hours to prepare for their defense, after Sir Hew [negotiates an] end to the suspension."[24] Wellesley was also concerned about the army's new command structure: "I will not conceal to you that my situation in this army is a very delicate one. I never saw Sir Hew Dalrymple till yesterday; and it is not a very easy task to advise any man on the first day one meets with him. [In addition, Dalrymple] must at least be prepared to receive advice." Concerned that Dalrymple deliberately avoided his advice concerning the cease-fire agreement, Wellesley declared, "[The fact that] I have been successful with the army and [the commanders and staff] don't like [going] to anybody else for orders or instructions upon any subject is another awkward circumstance which cannot end well; and to tell you the truth, I should prefer going home to staying here." Wellesley concluded his letter by stating, "I only beg that you will not blame me if things do not go on as you and my friends in London wish they should."[25]

As always Wellesley was much more direct to his brother. Concerned about the political ramifications of an agreement he signed but did not agree to, he told Pole, "I wish that I was away from this army. Things will not flourish as we are situated and organized and I am much afraid that my friends in England will consider me responsible for many things over which I have no power." Fearing that the ministers in London blamed him for the stipulations of the cease-fire agreement, Wellesley attacked Burrard and Dalrymple for their refusal to listen to him, then openly questioned their competence: "It is quite ridiculous, but there is not one of them capable of commanding the army and at this moment it rests with me. In the mean time we are going to Hell by another Road. The French are fortifying trenches ... and we shall have to conquer them again.... [Dalrymple] has no plan, or even an idea of a plan, nor do I believe he knows the meaning of the word plan."[26]

Despite Wellesley's insistence that he disagreed with Dalrymple and Burrard over the cease-fire agreement, he made the mistake of signing it. It was a decision he would regret.

News of the agreement, which would be referred to as the Convention of Cintra by the British papers, reached London on 17 September and had a disastrous effect on British morale, completely overshadowing the gains of the campaign. The Whigs attempted to destroy the credibility of the ruling Tory Party by using the Convention of Cintra to demonstrate the government incompetence. The most popular tool for opposition criticism was the *Morning Chronicle*. Since its inception in 1769, the *Chronicle* had increased its circulation steadily, and by 1808 the paper was delivered to more than seven thousand homes, second in popularity only to the *Times*. Due its extensive coverage of Parliament, the *Chronicle* was perhaps the most popular in Westminster.[27]

The Tory cabinet sought to minimize Wellesley's role in the agreement, but the British press singled him out for his involvement. On 21 September, the *Chronicle* took its first steps in what would become a six-year campaign to discredit Wellesley and the government:

> Who in the absence of all evidence would believe that Sir Arthur, a Minister of State, highly and powerfully connected, of a family certainly not distinguished for the meek submissiveness of their tempers, having just resigned the command of an army, which we are told in the course of four days won two battles, would in the compliance of Sir Hew Dalrymple, a person whom the world scarcely heard of, involuntarily subscribe an instrument [which at once] dishonored himself and his country? Had he not approved of [the Convention] we are convinced that he would have rather cut off his right hand [or perhaps] he would have submitted to have been shot in front of his camp rather than sign it and stoop to such ignominy.[28]

The attacks worsened, directed also at the Wellesley family and the cabinet:

> If the Wellesley family must be employed, for God's sake, let it henceforth be in regulating the Dublin Police or guarding the residence of the Irish Clergy. ... Whether it shall turn out that our commanders have done their duty or not, and whatever may be the result of a trial, the Ministers also must assume a heavy responsibility. ... If the generals exculpate themselves it can only be by showing that they were starved into submission ... and if the army was not provided sufficient stores, Ministers must answer for it. ... If on the other hand, the Generals are tired and condemned it will still be for the Ministers to explain why they selected Officers for commands so unworthy of being entrusted to them.[29]

In a related attack the *Chronicle* insinuated that the entire episode was the fault of the army bureaucracy:

> How does it happen that our military expeditions hardly ever succeed, and our naval enterprises almost never fail? Our armies are commanded by the same men who man our fleets—our soldiers fight just a bravely as our sailors, and we have gained victories on land as well as by sea, but still our objects never are accomplished. We must look for the cause of this striking contrast in the constitution of the two services, and as long as money can purchase the rewards of merit or political influence defrauds professional distinction of its proper recompense, it is to be feared that we all have a perpetual recurrence of the same or similar disasters. And if this is really the cause of our military miscarriages, it will avail us but little on any great emergency to behead a minister or shoot a general, because the root of the evil will always remain, and respecting the present misfortune with the government.[30]

The public outrage concerning the Convention of Cintra was too much for the government to ignore, and within weeks it recalled all three general officers to England. Wellesley arrived on 4 October and immediately began his defense. Despite the press attacks against him and his family, he remained outwardly resilient. In a letter to his friend the Duke of Richmond, Wellesley wrote, "You will readily believe that I was much surprised when I arrived in England to hear the torrents of abuse with which I have been assailed. I have been accused of every crime, except cowardice. I have not read a written word on either side [of the issue] and I do not mean to authorize the publication of a single line in my defense."[31] Underneath the tough exterior, Wellesley was concerned for his future and quickly left London for the relative safety of Ireland, where he resumed his duties as chief secretary.[32]

Upon the urging of his brothers, Wellesley returned to London to face his critics and a board of inquiry. The board investigated the Convention of Cintra and for three months heard the testimony of all three officers. In January 1809, it concluded its investigation and released its findings. In keeping with a long-standing unwritten bureaucratic rule, no one was held accountable: all three officers were exonerated, and no punitive actions were recommended.[33] The press was furious. Even the *Times*, a conservative bastion, attacked the decision by questioning the board's politically motivated verdict: "The Board of Inquiry's [findings on the Convention of Cintra] gave no opinion. The Board tells us that they based their decision on the 'fitness' of the Convention, and they declared that 'no further military action (court martial) should be taken against the officers because they acted with fitness and zeal,' Figs ends and fiddlesticks!"[34]

Despite their exoneration from criminal charges, all three generals faced public humiliation and ridicule. However, the majority of blame and public scrutiny focused on Dalrymple, who subsequently retired from the service. Wellesley wasted little time resuming public life and returned to the House of Commons. Nevertheless, the constricting seniority regulations had nearly sowed the seeds for political and military disaster.[35]

Unfortunately for Wellesley and the British army, the adverse effects of officer seniority were not the only problems encountered during the campaign of 1808. The army also suffered from logistical shortages, which were the direct result of poor planning and the army commissariat's misunderstanding of the importance of a new logistics requirement in the peninsula. The most severe of these problems occurred due to shortage of contracted civilian transportation for the army's logistics and artillery wagons.

Prior to the British experience in the Peninsular War, the commissariat had relied primarily on contracted civilian transportation to move the army's supplies and artillery. Although reliance on horse-drawn carts and carriages had been effective in the British army's previous campaigns in the Low Countries, the system struggled to meet the army's requirements in the peninsula. Because the majority of the roads in Spain and Portugal were too crude and poorly maintained to support heavy wagons, the most effective means of transporting supplies was ox carts. Despite their sloth, ox carts, with their solid wood wheels, were more durable than horse-drawn carts and could carry more weight. Therefore, the procurement of ox carts and contracted drivers became crucial to any logistics system in the peninsula.[36]

The commissariat also did not effectively plan for political and diplomatic considerations that would prevent the British army from augmenting its traditionally large depot-style supply system by "living off the land." The army had to maintain good relations with the Spanish and Portuguese governments and placate the civilian population, from whom the basic supplies would be requisitioned. Wellesley understood that a hungry peasant quickly turns into an active insurgent, and he strictly forbade the forceful requisition of supplies. His army required a more robust logistics structure than any British army had ever needed. Prior to his departure, Wellesley had envisioned a system of multiple magazines and depots that could be resupplied from the sea. His commissariat officers would be responsible for the Herculean task of transporting supplies from ports to the army at the front. He also recognized that it would take time to build such a system and to procure adequate numbers of ox carts and drivers. In the interim, he would still require the draft horses of the British and Irish commissariat to provide for his immediate transportation requirements.[37]

Unfortunately for Wellesley and his troops, the Treasury shipped an insufficient number of animals to the peninsula. As a result, Wellesley was grossly unprepared to move his men, materiel, and artillery. In a letter to the secretary for war, he wrote, "I have had the greatest difficulty in organizing my commissariat for the march, and the department is very incompetent." Wellesley was particularly angry because prior to embarking for the peninsula, he had left specific instructions with the Exchequer to requisition and deploy the correct number of horses. However, because the chancellor of the Exchequer answered directly to the prime minister, Wellesley appealed to Castlereagh for assistance: "The [commissariat] deserves your serious attention as the existence of the army depends on it functioning properly, and yet the people who manage it are incapable of managing anything outside of a counting house."[38] To make matters worse, Wellesley discovered that most of his cavalry, 390 dragoons, and virtually all of his artillery had been deployed without their horses. At issue was the perception of the master general of the ordnance that horses could not be transported by sea without losing their physical fitness. Therefore, instead of the best horses, the master general and the commissariat purposely chose to deploy no horses, or the poorest conditioned mounts available. To Pole Wellesley complained, "I think [master general] Lord Chatham will repent that he did not allow me to have the appropriate number of Artillery horses. . . . We ought to have the best horses the army could afford, instead of the worst."[39]

Fortunately for Wellesley, a detachment of the Irish commissariat arrived in Portugal with their horses, good mounts but too few to meet the army's requirement, even when combined with the number of horses purchased from local merchants. In fact, after purchasing all available horses from Portuguese merchants, Wellesley could mount only 240 of his 390 dragoons, and he was still desperately short of artillery horses. This shortage forced Wellesley to leave a portion of his invaluable artillery in staging areas. Angry that a deliberate, financially driven decision made in London, despite his recommendations, would affect his campaign, Wellesley wrote to Castlereagh, "I [will have] to leave [General] Spencer's [artillery] behind for want of means for moving them, and I should have been obliged to leave my own [artillery], if it were not for the horses of the Irish Commissariat." The Irish contingent might have provided the added support because he was one of their countrymen. Nevertheless, to prevent the mistake in the future, Wellesley cautioned Castlereagh, "Let nobody ever prevail upon you to send a corps to any part of Europe without horses to draw their guns because it is not true that horses lose their condition at sea."[40]

Wellesley's complaints about lack of horse transport became public knowledge through the publication of his dispatches in the newspapers. Castlereagh responded to Wellesley's complaints by stating that one hundred of the Irish horses had been in good enough condition following Wellesley's campaign to be selected by Sir John Moore to continue the fight in Spain. In addition to defending the quality of mounts, Castlereagh was quick to point out that Wellesley should not have complained about the number of horses that were deployed, because "it was a debatable question whether an army was useless without horses at all." Castlereagh concluded his rebuttal of Wellesley by citing two examples in which the British army had recently been successful with a limited number of horses: "In Egypt in 1801, the British had but 150 horses [and were successful] and in Holland in 1807, under General Abercrombie, [the army] had none at all."[41] Despite his use of humor and history, Castlereagh's comments did little to answer Wellesley's appeal for support or assuage his burden.

Despite Wellesley's problems with the ministry, several successful aspects of his initial campaign bore favorably on the prospect of future peninsular operations. Unfortunately, very few of these had any bearing on the conduct of the cabinet; most were the result of cooperation between Wellesley and the commander of the Royal Naval squadron off the Tagus, Adm. Sir Charles Cotton. Wellesley's coordination with Admiral Cotton's naval forces ensured Wellesley's unbroken line of supply and communication, preventing a French escape. By blockading Lisbon Harbor and the Tagus River, Cotton also prevented the French forces from receiving needed supplies. Wellesley capitalized on the operational and strategic advantages provided by the Royal Navy, and his 1808 campaign ushered in a new era of cooperation between the two services.[42]

Despite Wellesley's success on the battlefield, the campaign of 1808 had been of only limited success. Hopelessly mired by logistics and the fallout of the Convention of Cintra, Wellesley became a casualty of the system of which he was certainly a product. While he had earned the right to command the initial troops in Portugal, the timing of his relinquishment of command to two generals who arrived after combat operations had begun was nearly catastrophic. By signing the Convention of Cintra, Wellesley also jeopardized his future service to his country. Fortunately, help from his family and his political association with Canning and Castlereagh would have an enormous impact in the coming months, and he would be given another opportunity to test his mettle against the French in Iberia.

2

A Second Chance: Wellesley's Return to Iberia in 1809

> Your Majesty's servants have not been unmindful of the inconvenience that might arise in case any increase of this force, from Sir Arthur Wellesley being so young a Lieutenant General.
>
> Castlereagh to King George III, 26 March 1809

The decision to send Wellesley back to the peninsula in April 1809 was the most important decision the British government made during its twenty-two-year struggle against France. However, the credit for this decision was not the cabinet's alone. In fact, Wellesley's return to Portugal was nearly scuttled by the same suffocating regulations that had ultimately led to the Convention of Cintra the previous year. His appointment to command the army was also the result of Sir John Moore's death and a nearly disastrous fracture in Anglo-Spanish relations. It was made at a time when England questioned its future commitment to the peninsula and instead decided to pursue another disastrous military adventure in the Low Countries. These events and the decision to nominate Wellesley to command the army in 1809 stemmed from the strategic situation and issues the British government faced at the time.

After the French armies in Portugal had returned to France in October 1808, the remaining British forces in Portugal had been divided. The majority of troops were placed under the command of Sir John Moore in northwestern Spain, where it was hoped that Moore's army would become the hammer the British government would use to smash the French armies in Spain against the anvil of armed Spanish resistance. The remaining British troops waited in Lisbon pending the arrival of a new commander. Unfortunately for Moore, the difficulty of coordinating his advance with the unreliable Spanish proved too great.[1]

While Britain continued the war with its new strategy, Napoleon was also on the move. In November 1808, he led the *armée d'Espagne* across the Pyrenees into Spain, where he defeated several Spanish armies and occupied Madrid on 2 December. After he reinstated his brother Joseph on the Spanish throne, Napoleon again turned to the task of destroying the British. In December, he ordered "the hero of Austerlitz," Marshal Nicholas Soult, to destroy Moore's army.

Confident that the situation in the peninsula was stabilized, Napoleon returned to Paris to counter an increasingly volatile diplomatic situation with Austria. Meanwhile, Moore's British army retreated in disarray north to the Atlantic coast. By withdrawing, Moore hoped to save his army and preserve future British options in the peninsula.[2] Soult gave Moore very little time. The French marshal pursued Moore's fleeing army to the coastal city of Coruña. Moore was killed fighting a battle to cover his army's evacuation on 16 January. His loss was not in vain as the majority of his men escaped capture by evacuating aboard transports. Nevertheless, the evacuation of the British army from northern Spain would influence British strategic alternatives.[3]

With Moore dead, command of the remaining British troops in Portugal fell to Lt. Gen. Sir John Craddock, who had arrived in Portugal on 13 December and inherited a difficult task. He faced the immediate prospect of Moore's evacuation as well as an unstable diplomatic situation in Lisbon. With fewer than five thousand British troops to counter a French advance that was sure to follow the British evacuation from Coruña, Craddock repositioned most of his troops into several fortresses outside the capital. Anticipating evacuation orders from London, Craddock's troops prepared for possible embarkation from Lisbon. The Portuguese Regency Council regarded Craddock's actions as deserting the cause, and violence ensued, during which several British soldiers were murdered by Portuguese civilians.⁴ The British government dispatched John Villiers to Lisbon as minister plenipotentiary and Maj. Gen. William Carr Beresford to command the Portuguese army and to help Craddock stabilize the situation.⁵

Marshal Soult took advantage of the upheaval and invaded Portugal. In February and March, Soult moved his troops through Portugal's northern provinces and occupied the coastal city of Porto. With the French in possession of Portugal's second largest city, the security of Lisbon was unstable. With only five thousand British troops to prevent the French from occupying the capital, the British cabinet contemplated three strategic alternatives.⁶

Craddock's army could evacuate Lisbon and be deployed somewhere else, possibly in Spain, and open a new front against the French. However, this course of action was unpopular because Anglo-Spanish relations were poor. Before the evacuation of Coruña the opposition party had favored an Anglo-Spanish War; after Coruña, few felt that the Spanish were capable of shouldering the cost of victory. As with Cintra, the press was instrumental in turning public support for the war by questioning its price in manpower and financial support. The pitiful condition of the remnants of Moore's army that had returned to Portsmouth and Plymouth in late January and early February 1809 did not help the government's cause. The cabinet had attempted to prevent the return of Moore's army to England in favor of landing it in another location, such as Cadiz or Gibraltar; however, the condition of the army necessitated its return to England. The sight of the British dead and wounded and the sheer magnitude of the army's loss of manpower and materiel outraged the British people. The *Times* reported,

> Now indeed the miseries of war have been brought home to our own doors. The scenes [in Plymouth and Portsmouth] are beyond any pen to describe . . . the wounds of the many men some of whom have never been dressed while others are dying for want are everywhere. While no less than 900 women have landed, all ignorant whether their husbands are alive or dead. In Plymouth, every house has become a hospital, every family has taken in a sick or wounded person, notwithstanding these exertions, great numbers are dying every day and all business gives way to the calls of suffering humanity.⁷

The newspapers further inflamed the situation by publishing French army bulletins from Madrid, which declared: "Thus the British failure and evacuation at Coruña terminated the English Expedition to Spain. After having fomented the war in this unhappy country, the English have abandoned it. . . . The English have gained nothing from their expedition into Spain but the hatred of the Spaniards and disgrace."[8] Witnessing the destruction of Moore's army and reading the French newspapers caused many to question whether the war in Spain was worth the cost. It also brought the reality of the Peninsular War to the British public for first time.

However, it was the reaction of the Spanish government, following the British evacuation of Coruña, that ended the possibility of repositioning Craddock's army in Spain. In February, the Spanish refused British troops entry to the island fortress of Cadiz, which angered British lawmakers and caused a severe backlash in the British press. An anonymous contributor in the *Times* argued that the preservation of Spain would be a "lost cause" if the Spanish government refused British military assistance. He also referred to Spain as "a sinking country which providence has determined its ruin and annihilation." He advocated for Spanish acceptance of British aid: "We English are ready to assist you [the Spanish] in your glorious undertaking, provided you will permit us to do so with a fair and responsible prospect of success. [We will provide you with] arms, money, clothing, etc . . . but we cannot expose our military and political credit unless you will permit us to employ them as we think efficaciously for the general cause. You shall have troops which are now ready to embark for your coasts, the moment you will by your own exertions hold out a prospect of successful cooperation." The author was equally critical of the British government, which he felt had allowed the Spanish diplomatic situation to spiral out of control.[9] As a result of the opposition attacks, the Spanish rebuff at Cadiz, and low public support for the Spanish cause, the cabinet chose not to land more troops in Spain.[10]

Another British option was to abandon the peninsula completely in favor of providing increased subsidies to continental allies or to open a second front in the Low Countries. However, several events between December and March prevented the cabinet from immediately pursuing this course. The first was Austrian rearmament and the prospect of a renewed Franco-Austrian war. In December, the

Austrians, through a secret diplomatic memorandum, made it known to the British Foreign Office that it was rearming and desired another front against Napoleon. However, due to monetary constraints, the Austrians could not complete their mobilization until late spring 1809, and to field its initial army of four hundred thousand men, the Austrians requested a subsidy of nearly £2.5 million. To maintain its army during a protracted war against the French, the Hapsburgs requested an additional £5 million per year. The cabinet was stunned by the enormity of the Austrian request. Not only was it more than any previous continental grants, but £5 million per year exceeded all past appropriations combined. In its reply, the Foreign Office informed the Austrians that the British could not deliver aid on such a scale. The Foreign Office suggested "the Austrians look to its own people and resources to prosecute the war against France, [because Austria's only hope to succeed] was if there existed a universal determination to prosecute the war in their country." They also pointed out, "Britain was already helping Austria's cause by fighting a war against Napoleon in Spain."[11]

While debate raged concerning continental strategic options, the cabinet faced an internal struggle for power between Canning and Castlereagh. Unhappy with his decreasing role in strategic matters, Canning began to plot against Castlereagh. Although this situation would not publically surface for several months, the cabinet faced increased scrutiny over a political scandal that involved the Duke of York and a former mistress, Mary Anne Clarke. The crisis stemmed from allegations that she had accepted bribes from army officers in exchange for promotions. The Duke of York was implicated. In response to the political crisis concerning his son, King George III, without the cabinet's knowledge, removed the Duke of York as commander in chief in favor of Sir David Dundas. Although the allegations against the Duke of York went unsubstantiated, the scandal covered the newspapers and dominated the debates in Parliament for nearly three months. The king's actions also angered many in Parliament, who felt the Duke of York had escaped legitimate censure. While the government's credibility was attacked for not punishing the Duke of York, the growing rift between Canning and Castlereagh was more significant, and both events diverted the cabinet's attention from focusing on a grand strategy for Britain in the peninsula.[12]

Forced to make an ad hoc decision, Castlereagh contemplated a third option: reinforce troops in the peninsula, which was widely unpopular, and plan for renewing the war in the Low Countries in support of Austria. Castlereagh's dilemma was that many in government believed that Portugal could not be held without a significant British troop presence in Spain. As Anglo-Spanish relations deteriorated, and without a clear place for Britain to focus its effort, Castlereagh began planning a major operation in the Low Countries. His decision was also based on finance. Under pressure to reduce extraordinary expenses and due to an increasing difficulty to procure gold and silver, Castlereagh wagered that sending a large proportion of Britain's "disposable force" to the Low Countries would not only decrease overall expenditures, but would also be less expensive than sending it to the peninsula. The problem was Spanish and Portuguese merchants were reluctant to accept bills, and due to exchange rates on specie, it was hoped that any force sent to the Low Countries would be able to obtain supplies and money at a low, local rate or requisition supplies for itself. Wellesley disagreed with any operation in the Low Countries and wrote a convincing memorandum that dispelled the belief that Portugal could not be held without Spain. He also presented a cost-effective alternative to raising the appropriate number of troops in the peninsula to achieve victory. In his March letter to Castlereagh, Wellesley defined Lisbon, not Cadiz, Gibraltar, or any other strategic location, as the key to winning the war in the Iberian Peninsula. He also stated that Spain and Portugal were linked not only by geography, but also by ideological similarities against the French. He felt that despite Napoleon's control over Spanish cities, the French would suffer from strategic consumption and find great difficulty in successfully occupying Portugal with fewer than one hundred thousand men.[13]

Wellesley's assertions rested on a two-pronged strategy that he felt safeguarded Portugal from a successful invasion. The first tenet in Wellesley's plan was to transform the Portuguese army into a powerful ally that would bear a greater portion of the fighting. He argued that the Portuguese army should number at least thirty thousand regular troops and should be augmented by an additional forty thousand militia. To equip that number of men, Wellesley called for approximately £1 million. He also argued for additional political assistance to aid Portugal in its defense. Wellesley recommended that the Portuguese army be placed under the command of British officers. To circumvent the logistical difficulties he had experienced in 1808, Wellesley insisted, "the staff of the Portuguese army, the commissariat in particular, must be British." Wellesley also recommended "that the current British force should be immediately reinforced with companies of British riflemen [as well as] 3,000 British or German cavalry." These reinforcements would form the core of an Anglo-Portuguese army that he believed could defend Portugal from any French invasion from Spain. Wellesley pressured the cabinet by estimating that the total cost for a year's fighting in Portugal would not exceed £1 million and stated that the war in the peninsula could be continued against France in the peninsula, for a fraction of the cost of fighting elsewhere. Wellesley's memorandum, combined with recent reports from General Craddock that upgraded his strength to nearly twenty thousand men, bolstered the cabinet's confidence.[14] Castlereagh agreed with Wellesley's assertion that Portugal was worth the effort but made the fatal mistake of continuing to plan a major invasion in Holland in support of Austria, which not only diverted valuable resources from the peninsula, but from its outset was mired in logistical delays that ultimately caused its failure.

With the decision of where to go decided, the question remained: which general officer would command the allied army? While Canning and Castlereagh jostled for control of the cabinet, both men knew that Wellesley was the obvious choice for command. Fortunately for Wellesley, they also nominated Wellesley's older brother Richard, the Marquess Wellesley, to lead Britain's diplomatic effort in Spain. Richard had made his reputation as the governor general of India from 1797 to 1805, and with Arthur's help had implemented an aggressive policy of expanding British control. Richard was a sound choice for the post, and his appointment as "special ambassador" to Spain was virtually unchallenged in Parliament. Unfortunately, the same confidence in Arthur's appointment was not widely shared; some in government felt that the more senior Craddock should retain the command.[15] For two weeks, the question remained unsettled. However, on 26 March, Castlereagh wrote the king to inform him that he nominated Wellesley to command the British Expeditionary Force to Portugal. In his letter, Castlereagh was cautious of the king's reluctance to approve the appointment of junior ranking general officers over their superiors: "In submitting [the nomination of Sir Arthur Wellesley] your Majesty's servants have not been unmindful of the inconvenience that might arise in case any increase of this force, from Sir Arthur Wellesley being so young a Lieutenant General, but they humbly conceive that your Majesty's service without prejudice to the claims of the distinguished officers in [the British army] who are [more senior] may have the benefit of Sir Arthur's [leadership] where he has been successful."[16]

Castlereagh's nomination allowed for the king to appoint a more "senior officer" to command the expedition should the need arise. As it was unlikely that substantial reinforcements would be sent to the peninsula, Castlereagh wrote, "It shall appear to Your Majesty proper to confide [the responsibility of the army] to a general officer of higher rank." The king's was predictably concerned about "so young a lieutenant general holding so distinguished a command while his seniors remain unemployed." In response to Castlereagh's statement concerning his option to appoint a more senior officer at a later date, the king added, "the claims of [officers who outranked Wellesley] could not with justice be set aside."[17]

The king was not alone in his criticism of Wellesley's nomination. In Parliament, the Earl of Buckinghamshire defended General Craddock's right to command the Anglo-Portuguese army. While he admitted that Wellesley's military record was exemplary, Buckinghamshire observed the embarrassment that "such a gallant and distinguished officer [as Craddock would feel by] being replaced by an officer with less seniority." He reminded the House of Commons that they were also replacing an officer whose actions during the Portuguese regency crisis in January had drawn the government's praise. Buckinghamshire ended his defense of Craddock by despairing that, "just as [Craddock] had gained the opportunity for military glory he was to be removed from command by a more junior officer."[18] Despite criticism, the king approved Wellesley's nomination. In early April, Castlereagh informed Wellesley that he had been appointed to the command and that Wellesley would replace Craddock in Portugal, who in turn would be promoted to take command of the garrison at Gibraltar.[19]

The news delighted Wellesley; however, two problems were quickly apparent. The first involved a confusing set of instructions that presented him with conflicting strategic priorities. Castlereagh's initial instructions to Wellesley were clear: "The defense of Portugal you will consider as the first and immediate object of your attention." They granted Wellesley unprecedented operational flexibility: "His Majesty, leaves it to your judgment to decide, when your army shall be advanced on the frontier of Portugal, how your efforts can best be combined with the Spanish as well as the Portuguese troops in support of the common cause."[20] Castlereagh's subsequent instructions, however, contradicted his initial orders and forbade Wellesley from moving his army into Spain "without the express authority of your government." In a clear move to avoid another Moore-Frere debacle and to force the Spanish to request British military assistance following their rebuke of the British at Cadiz in February, Castlereagh instructed Wellesley, "Should the enemy penetrate in towards Cadiz, it is not improbable that the reluctance of the Spanish government to admit a British force into Cadiz may yield to the sense of immediate danger. Should such a change in sentiment take place, every effort should be made to assist in the preservation of that important place. [Therefore,] you should detach an adequate force immediately, notifying me the amount of such force, so that measures may be adopted for replacing that Corps in Portugal."[21]

That the last set of instructions not only was a clear diplomatic ploy to tempt the Spanish into requesting British assistance but also gave him authority over any British representative to the Spanish junta. Since it was never his intention to send forces to Cadiz or any other Spanish city, Wellesley concentrated on liberating Portugal and limiting the repercussions of relieving Craddock.

Wellesley remembered the dangers of substituting commanding officers during a campaign. Therefore, he told Castlereagh that he would not replace Craddock if one of three conditions had taken place prior to his arrival: British forces had conducted a successful defense of Lisbon; the army had already been forced to evacuate Lisbon; or the army had been "so far engaged in a scene of operations as to render it doubtful that the command should devolve upon another." Wellesley also informed Castlereagh, "In the event of General Craddock's success in any repulse of the enemy, I could not reconcile it to my feelings to [replace] him."[22] In addition to the problems it would create for command and control, Wellesley also feared dissension from Craddock's loyal officers, who might resist a new commanding officer's orders. Wellesley concluded, "The decision of this delicate question must in a great measure rest with me, and I hope that I have fairness and firmness to decide it according to the best of my judgment."[23]

After recognizing the validity of Wellesley's argument, Castlereagh amended his initial instructions: "In the event of finding Sir John Craddock's command engaged in the field, which is by no means improbable, His Majesty trusts that the same feelings of zeal for his service which induce this suggestion on your part will determine you to place yourself under the orders of Sir John Craddock until His Majesty's further pleasure is known."[24] Two days later, Castlereagh urged Wellesley to keep the details of his initial instructions secret until he could verify the tactical situation in Portugal. Castlereagh also cautioned Wellesley not to identify future problems in his official dispatches that could be settled through their private correspondence, "because the remainder of the cabinet felt themselves [obliged] to form an opinion upon the subject" and would cause "considerable delay and inconvenience."[25]

Relieved to have been given a second chance but uneasy with Castlereagh's struggle to formulate clear instructions, Wellesley had even less faith in the capabilities of Craddock and the admiral commanding the Royal Navy in Portugal, George Cranfield Berkeley. From Portsmouth, he wrote to his brother concerning the tactical situation he felt likely to inherit in the country: "The course will be this, either Admiral [Berkeley] will write to General Craddock that he can no longer remain in the Tagus with the King's ships; or General Craddock will write to the admiral to know whether he can embark the Army to which the Admiral will answer he can not.... And then the Army will probably evacuate before I even get there.... So far I shall be lucky in being out of the scrape; and I only lament that I did not go to Lisbon two months ago."[26]

Wellesley was wrong, particularly in his assessment of Admiral Berkeley. Berkeley, who had replaced Admiral Sir Charles Cotton in January 1809, understood the complexities of joint operations and proved to be invaluable for Wellesley's future operations.[27] Nevertheless, Wellesley feared the worst and was no doubt relieved to find that Craddock's army had not been forced to evacuate Portugal. Upon landing, Wellesley wrote Castlereagh, "I arrived to find that Sir John Craddock had moved up the country to the north with his troops and I consider the affairs in this country to be exactly in the state in which I found them [in 1808]." Wellesley also informed the secretary for war that because the French had not engaged Craddock, he would, "as soon as he could communicate with the general," assume command of the army, which he did on 25 April.[28]

Despite the smooth transition, the sequence of events that preceded the change of command typified the cabinet's struggle to formulate and execute a clear strategy. In the wake of the disasters at Coruña and Cadiz, the cabinet must ultimately be given credit for not abandoning the peninsula altogether. However, in three months, the Foreign Office had jeopardized its diplomatic relationship with Spain, and in doing so, threatened its alliance with Austria by postponing payment of much-needed subsidies. It had also decided to undertake a much larger operation in the Low Countries. All of these decisions would have a dramatic effect on Wellesley in 1809. Furthermore, Wellesley's insistence, not the War Department's grand strategy, would ultimately convince the government that Portugal was worth the risk. Although the decision to dispatch Richard to Spain was insightful and helped Wellesley, Castlereagh's initial instructions forbidding Wellesley's advance beyond the frontiers of Portugal, and his subsequent orders to do so only if the Spanish requested assistance, were contradictory and at best reflected domestic political concerns, not a clear-cut foreign strategy. In the end, the decision to send Wellesley back to the peninsula was the most important decision the government could have made to preserve its hard-fought gains there, and it ensured that Britain had its most capable, albeit not senior, soldier to lead its fight against Napoleon and France.

3

THE TRIALS BEGIN: THE CAMPAIGN OF 1809

> I act with a sword hanging over my head.
> Wellington to John Villiers, 2 January 1810

After assuming command of the British army in April 1809, Wellesley surveyed the disjointed operational situation and took action. While his army was not immediately threatened, the presence of two French armies within several hundred miles caused him concern. To maintain the operational initiative and provide time to build his logistics base in Lisbon, Wellesley decided to take his army on the offensive. He believed that the greatest threat came from Marshal Claude Victor's corps in Spain. However, to attack Victor would consume invaluable time coordinating with the Spanish, so Wellesley instead decided to attack Marshal Soult's army, then occupying the important Portuguese city of Porto to the north.[1]

After consolidating his army in Lisbon, Wellesley marched north to surprise the French. On 12 May, he reached the southern bank of the Douro River, opposite Porto, only to find that the French had destroyed the main bridge across the river. Forced to improvise and aided by the citizens of Porto, British troops crossed the river in boats and defeated a rear guard on 13 May. For several days, Wellesley's army advanced northeast in pursuit of Soult's forces. Finally, the exhausted French abandoned their artillery and heavy wagons for speed. Wellesley cancelled the pursuit five days later. During the campaign,

Soult lost nearly 1,800 men and 70 pieces of artillery. Wellesley's casualties throughout the operation were only 123 killed, wounded, or missing.[2]

While Soult continued his hurried withdrawal into Spain, Wellesley turned his attention south, toward the army of Marshal Victor, who had seen an opportunity to reposition his army during Wellesley's pursuit of Soult begun moving his forty-six thousand troops toward the Portuguese border. Although Victor's troops presented a threat to the security of Lisbon, Wellesley delayed his march until he received a shipment of money from England to pay his men. In late June, Wellesley resumed his march to meet the French. Conditions were difficult on the men and horses; the heat and deprivations of food and supplies took their toll. Wellesley halted his army several times to rest and to receive needed supplies and reinforcements, which were transported to him by the navy to the ports. They were then uploaded onto civilian-contracted, flat-bottom boats that could transport the supplies up the Tagus, ninety miles farther. Throughout the course of the war, Wellesley relied heavily on the navigable portions of the Tagus and Douro rivers. The rivers were also vital for the movement of the sick and wounded as transportation by roads in ox carts was slow and produced unneeded suffering.[3] Wellesley also delayed his march to coordinate his advance with the Spanish general Don Gregorio Cuesta, who agreed to combine his forces with Wellesley to fight the French.[4]

On 27–28 July, the combined Spanish and British armies fought the first major battle of the war against Napoleon's brother King Joseph and Marshal Victor at Talavera. During the battle, the majority of Spanish troops fled the battlefield. Despite being abandoned by the Spanish, Wellesley's British troops fought a bloody battle and repulsed the French advance on Portugal. Demoralized, the French withdrew toward Madrid. Wellesley's army was also in dire condition. It had suffered nearly 25 percent casualties during battle, and under the threat of being outflanked by French reinforcements, which were converging west of Talavera, Wellesley withdrew his army toward the Portuguese border. Despite having defeated two French armies and successfully defended the Portuguese frontier, Wellesley could not exploit his victories. His army was exhausted and required rest. The oppressive heat had taken its toll, and more British troops fell to dysentery and disease than to French musket or artillery fire.[5]

Wellesley's army also suffered from a shortage of gold and silver shipments from England, which Wellesley required to pay his men and buy supplies. While British officers often received their pay in half coin and half paper, the troops were paid exclusively in coin. Therefore, without frequent shipments of gold and silver, the army could not operate efficiently. Wellesley knew the dangers of an unpaid army and did not have to search far back to find an example. A year earlier, Sir John Moore, prior to his army's retreat to Coruña, had appealed for money to pay his men and buy supplies. In November 1808, Moore had told Frere, "We are in the greatest distress for money. I doubt if there is any [money] to pay the troops their subsistence."[6] Two weeks later, Moore informed Castlereagh, "I am without a shilling of money to pay [the troops], and I am in daily apprehension that our supplies will be stopped. It is impossible to describe the embarrassments we are thrown into from the want of [money]."[7] Rampant desertion and breaks in discipline plagued Moore's retreat, and while lack of pay was certainly not the major cause for his withdrawal and eventual defeat, his situation was made worse by lack of money.

Wellesley had similar difficulties during the outset of his campaign. After his victory over Marshal Soult at Porto, Wellesley wrote to Villiers to complain about the conduct of his unpaid soldiers after the battle: "I have long been of the opinion that a British Army could bear neither success nor failure, and I have proof of this opinion in the recent conduct of the soldiers of this army. . . . They have plundered the country most terribly, [and their conduct] has given me the greatest concern." He continued, "We are terribly distressed for money. I am convinced that 300,000 [Spanish] dollars would not pay our debts; and two months pay is now due to the army." The conduct of the British soldiers would never satisfy Wellesley, and later in the war, he would describe the men in his army as the "scum of the earth." He had good reason to complain. Drawn from the lowest classes in society, the British soldier was aggressive and stubborn in battle whether in victory or defeat. While Wellesley admired their courage, he feared that his unpaid soldiers' actions after the battle of Porto threatened to jeopardize the army's favorable status in Portugal.[8]

Wellesley also depended on shipments of gold and silver to meet his logistics requirements. Unlike the French army, which subsidized its requirements by foraging the farms and countryside, Wellesley's army paid gold or silver for most of its supplies. Wellesley hoped that the local population would support the British effort with not only supplies, but intelligence as well.⁹ With good reason, Wellesley linked the morale of his army and his declining logistics situation with the government's ability to procure the money he required and concluded with a broad attack on the cabinet, which he felt had not done enough to improve his overall situation: "I suspect the ministers in England are very indifferent to our operations in this country."¹⁰ At the focal point of Wellesley's frustration was the man responsible for providing gold and silver to the army, the chancellor of the Exchequer, William Huskisson.¹¹

Shortly after his return to Portugal, Wellesley requested major financial assistance. On 5 May, he gave Huskisson an assessment of the monetary situation in Portugal: "I promised to let you know the state of our money concerns in this country and I am concerned to have to give you so bad an account of them." Instead of the £400,000 that Wellesley expected to find in British accounts, he received only £100,000. To make matters worse, it was mostly in Spanish coins, not Portuguese dollars or gold or silver, which required cumbersome conversion. Wellesley dispatched a ship to carry the majority of this money to Cadiz for exchange. Left with only £10,000 and the "monstrous demands" to procure additional supplies, Wellesley marched north against Soult.¹²

In outlining his mounting monetary deficiency, Wellesley reminded Huskisson that his army's budget was approximately £200,000 per month. Of this, Wellesley estimated that nearly £50,000 a month would be required just to pay his troops; settling accounts with the Portuguese Regency Council would use another large percentage. The remainder would be used by the commissary general to purchase supplies and to pay local merchants for their services. Wellesley also announced that his annual budget would be approximately £2.5 million per year. Although this figure was well over the £1 million he had estimated in his initial proposal, he promised Huskisson "he would attempt to keep the army's expenses as low as possible." To regularize his financial position, Wellesley requested that Huskisson send £100,000 to his army immediately and to follow that shipment with recurring monthly shipments of usable currency, which would prevent the expensive and time-consuming task of converting Spanish gold coins in the money markets of Lisbon, Cadiz, or Gibraltar. Wellesley had no reason to doubt that his pleas for support would be answered. After all, the government was saving millions of pounds by waging war directly in the peninsula rather than providing subsidies to allies.[13]

Nearly two weeks after his initial letter to Huskisson, Wellesley's army had received neither money nor news from England concerning payment. To make matters worse, the local merchants who had supplied his army since its arrival demanded payment for their goods and services, and British soldiers began to loot and plunder. The journal of a commissary officer assigned to the 14th Dragoons of the King's German Legion describes the challenges of supplying the army on the march:

> 21 May . . . After dinner I went to General Payne, who was commading the cavalry, and reported myself. . . . I told him with all due respect, but quite frankly, that I hoped his reproaches were not directed against me, for I had only been appointed commissary to the 14th Dragoons when the regiment had already been two days on the road; that my mule had been stolen from me on the journey, which was not my fault. . . . It was impossible to send provisions after a regiment of light cavalry which was pursuing the enemy night and day at such speed across the mountains and over impracticable roads. I also said that I thought I had done my utmost, and that it was not right to expect too much of a commissary, who, like myself, had been left with no money, no assistance, and no office. I added that if failure there had been, it was due to my superiors, and not to me. "Very well," he replied, "then I forgive you, but in that case allow me to sh—and spit on your Commissary General who is squatting comfortably in Porto, while he leaves us here to starve!"[14]

As the number of debts increased, and with no news of relief, Wellesley bullied the wealthy wine merchants of Porto into lending money to pay his men and purchase much needed supplies. News of the loan traveled quickly. In Lisbon, the Regency Council responded to the complaints of several of the wine merchants, who claimed that Wellesley had forced them to lend him the money. The council complained to Villiers about "Wellesley's severe conduct" and demanded an explanation. Villiers immediately solicited the general's response.[15]

In his answer, Wellesley explained that the £10,000 loan was only temporary and that it had been solicited from the merchants voluntarily. He also defended his actions on the basis of his army's requirements: "After the battle of Porto, it was presented to me that the merchants and [local government] of Porto were not unwilling to assist by a loan of money. . . . We being at the time in need of everything, particularly shoes, and not having one farthing I obliged them." However, Wellesley's story of the events was not accepted in Lisbon, where his forced loan drew the Regency Council's wrath. At issue were Wellesley's threats:"If the [merchants] refused to assist the [British army] after all we had done for them, the world, when the story should be told, would not believe it." Wellesley concluded his defense by stating: "I believe I did shame them into lending us a sum of money . . . after all, the sum was not more that £10,000, and this is what the [Portuguese government and merchants] call 'severe'? I really believe the merchants will receive much more than that in return because I saved the wine orchards from the French for which the merchants and Portuguese government will receive a hundred times the amount [of the loan]."[16]

Angry that the liberation of Porto was not appreciated in Lisbon, Wellesley concluded his correspondence with a despairing remark about future relations: "If I had waited to attack Soult until I had a sufficient amount of money to render this loan unnecessary, for which I may, the next time my assistance is wanted, the expense of the support of this army will be ten times the amount I took."[17]

The situation embarrassed Wellesley and forced him to write Huskisson, "the distress of which I gave you a sketch in my last letter has been aggravated by its continuance." Wellesley estimated that his army owed at least £300,000 to various Portuguese merchants and that additional bills were accruing daily. Despite these shortfalls, his greatest concern was that his army had not been paid.[18] In a letter to Castlereagh, Wellesley described the problems of controlling an unpaid, ill-disciplined army, "The men behave terribly ill. They are a rabble that cannot bear success any more than Sir John Moore's army could bear failure. I am endeavoring to tame them, but if I cannot succeed I [will] send one or two corps home in disgrace. The men plunder in all directions."[19] The situation grew worse. In a letter to Villiers, Wellesley warned "that his Army had even plundered the Portuguese people of their own livestock for the sole purpose of selling the animals back to the people again." In order to circumvent this practice, Wellesley asked Villiers to request a proclamation from the Regency Council "forbidding the Portuguese people from purchasing anything from the soldiers of the British Army."[20]

Wellesley issued general orders aimed at restoring the discipline of his army and the trust of the Portuguese people. In his instructions, Wellesley declared, "The commander of forces is concerned about the conduct of his troops. Not only have outrages been committed by the entire army, but there is no description of property that belongs to Portuguese citizens which hasn't been plundered by British soldiers whom they have received in their homes." Wellesley ordered noncommissioned officers to supervise each squad; these sergeants "would be responsible for the conduct of the men they were assigned, even where they slept." Wellesley also prohibited stragglers and forbade the seizure of hospital and supply carts for the purpose of carrying personal baggage and equipment.[21]

Wellesley also suffered from incompetence or worse in the civilian commissariat. At the top of the list was the senior commissary officer in Lisbon, John Rawlings. Rawlings's plan to supply the army with Portuguese dollars exchanged for British imports appeared feasible, but Rawlings deceived Wellesley by exaggerating the demand for British goods in Lisbon. However, because Rawlings did not fall under Wellesley's chain of command, the general was powerless to take any punitive action against him. Instead, Wellesley could only complain to Rawlings's superior, William Huskisson. In his letter, Wellesley asked Huskisson, "Where is the trade which is likely to supply a demand for bills in the amount of £2 million per year? In short, Mr. Rawlings has given you an erroneous view of the state of the money in this country."[22] Rawlings was not replaced. Instead, the incident marked yet another embarrassing example of Wellesley's inability to control the conduct of government officials sent from London to support his army.

The money shortages had strategic implications for the campaign as well. In mid-June, Wellesley wrote Castlereagh for help, circumventing Huskisson: "I think it proper to draw your attention [to] the want of money in this army. The troops are nearly two months in arrears, and the army is in debt a sum amounting to not less than £200,000." Wellesley requested that the government send a lump sum of £100,000 immediately. Wellesley repeated the requests he had made of Huskisson, that £200,000 a month be shipped to Lisbon for the next several months; otherwise, he stated, "the operations of the [British army] would be cramped for want of money."[23] Although his request was well beyond the Treasury's capacity, Wellesley was not bluffing. He delayed his march south against Marshal Victor until he received a shipment of money to pay his debts. In a letter to Villiers, Wellesley wrote, "I have received authority to extend my operations beyond the provinces immediately adjacent to the Portuguese frontier. I should begin immediately but I cannot venture to stir without money. . . . We are in over head and ears in debt everywhere and I cannot venture into Spain without paying what we owe, at least in this neighborhood, and giving a little money to the troops."[24]

On 15 June the shipment Wellesley had dispatched to Cadiz for exchange arrived in Lisbon. Ten days later, the money reached the British army in the field. Wellesley paid his troops the arrears and began his march. After a nearly three-week wait for pay, an angry Wellesley informed Huskisson that his army had endured "great distress because of the lack of money" and that the money he had recently received had only been enough to pay his army for their arrears. With only £30,000 to continue his operations, and unable to pay his debts to the Portuguese, a frustrated Wellesley lashed out at Huskisson by questioning London's resolve to support the war: "It will be better for [the ministry] to relinquish their operations in Portugal and Spain if they cannot afford to carry them on." Wellesley also informed Huskisson that several commissariat officers stationed in Lisbon were not fulfilling his expectations. While he acknowledged their relative inexperience, he questioned their intelligence: "I am not without grounds of complaint of the [commissariat officers'] want of intelligence. Most of them are incapable of managing anything short of a counting house."[25]

Wellesley's pleas to Huskisson did not fall on deaf ears. Unfortunately, the minister was under considerable pressure to fund a global war that was quickly devouring the country's resources. In his mind, the war was a costly error that would eventually destroy Britain's economy. Huskisson communicated his opinions by circulating an influential memorandum that expressed his view on finance and a recommendation for Britain's strategy in the war. He condemned the cost of a protracted war that the British people would not support: they would "not make the sacrifice, in terms of paying taxes, necessary to wage a lengthy war." Huskisson also questioned conducting an offensive war against the French by noting that previous "men who decided strategy," mainly William Pitt, had opted for one of "defensive warfare." Britain "ought to confine its exertion to the maintenance of maritime superiority and to the defense of its empire abroad, not engage in a costly war in the Peninsula."[26]

Huskisson had two primary concerns. The immediate problem was finding the large amounts of gold and silver bullion required by Wellesley's army to wage war. He estimated the expense of maintaining a forty-thousand-man army in the peninsula as not less than £2.5 million per year, of which more than half would be an extraordinary expense.[27] He also estimated that an additional £1.5 million would be required to support the Portuguese and Spanish armies. These sums, added to the nearly £1.7 million required to aid Sicily, meant that a protracted war would cost Britain nearly £6 million a year. Because of Napoleon's Continental System, Huskisson argued, Britain could not rely on procuring large sums of bullion unless it began using its resources to find and secure new trade partners, possibly in America: "I wish to be understood as entertaining strong doubts whether it will be practicable to provide the money to [Spain and Portugal] for any length of time when we can obtain very great facilities for procuring bullion in America and [Spain and Portugal] can only be given upon any permanent or productive scale by opening to us the trade of the continent."[28]

His second concern was the cost of the war and the effect extra taxes would have on the British people. To pay for a protracted war, Huskisson claimed, the government would require a £22.5 million loan, and the interest associated with such a loan would amount to £1.35 million per year. These totals would require the government to approve new taxes, which he felt the common British citizen would not pay. Huskisson supported rapprochement with France to end the Continental embargo of British goods instead of seeking the people's approval for taxes. He stated that "many burdens and obstacles, both in Parliament and the country would be softened by a system of rapprochement. And I must fairly state that if the war should continue for many years it would scarcely be possible to provide new taxes to meet even this diminished scale of expenditure." As a testament to Huskisson's influence within the government, the prime minister forwarded his memorandum to King George III. The king responded to Huskisson's arguments by stating that "he had long seen with concern the increased expenses of the war and he had felt the necessity of reducing them."[29]

As Huskisson at the Treasury continued to look for a long-term solution, Castlereagh came to Wellesley's assistance. Castlereagh relayed Huskisson's concerns that "the scarcity of specie has become the subject of much anxiety [in England]." Nevertheless, Castlereagh notified Wellesley that a shipment of £230,000 had been sent to "relieve [his] present wants." He explained that the government could not afford to send any more in the near future; only £100,000 could be sent to Portugal; and "until a new shipment of dollars arrived from South America (the period of which was uncertain)," Wellesley would have to work closely with the commissary general to economize for as long as possible. Due to extraordinary expense, maintaining an army on the continent cost more than three times as much as keeping the same force in Britain, as paying and supplying troops there did not rely on shipments of bullion. The situation was even more exacerbated for Wellesley as the same problem did not exist for the navy. Navy crews often went years without pay and were only paid in ports where the ships were commissioned. Therefore, in terms of bullion, the peninsular army was much more of a drain on the nation than the navy.[30]

Whitehall's restricted finances had enormous implications on Wellington's campaign of 1809—they had delayed his advance south but also prevented him from supplying the Spanish vital logistics support. Fortunately for Wellesley, the ministers obtained just enough money to continue the campaign. Nevertheless, the general knew that this struggle was not over. He rationalized that the cost of the war was insignificant compared to the gains Britain incurred, not only with its strategic position but also with its continental allies, by fighting and killing French troops in the peninsula. To the cabinet's credit, the prospect of victory in 1809–10 was grim, and therefore their parsimonious approach was certainly understandable. Austria had again been defeated and the cumulative pressure caused by the Russian and French alliance and Napoleon's Continental System had taken a large toll on the economy. Wellesley's army was Britain's last remaining hope on the continent, and the cabinet faced the realistic prospect of many more years of expensive continental commitments. Therefore, many in London did not share Wellesley's optimism, as could be seen with an emerging pattern. As long as he was victorious, financial support continued, but as soon as doubt began to creep into the politicians' minds about the safety or well-being of the army, Wellesley's financial support would again surface as an issue. Nowhere would this become more apparent than in the defense of Portugal in 1810–11.

Another problem Wellesley encountered during the campaign of 1809 was the growing wave of political opposition directed at him. In fact, opposition to Wellesley and his conduct of the campaign had begun almost immediately after the battle of Porto in May. In Parliament, the opposition leader questioned the magnitude of Wellesley's victory and called it "a ridiculously magnified affair of a rear-guard."[31] In a letter to Villiers, Wellesley responded to his critics at home: "I believe it will be very difficult to satisfy the people [of England] and the government is so weak that they are afraid to take the lead and to guide public opinion upon any subject. I am very indifferent what the opinion is of our operations. I shall do the best I can with the force given me, and if the people of England are not satisfied, they must send somebody else who will do better."[32]

Criticism of Wellesley would get worse in the British press. The catalyst was the publication of letters in the British newspapers from disgruntled officers who served in Wellesley's army. These men, whom Wellesley referred to as "croakers," had an enormous influence on public and subsequent political perception of the war. Because the British public had an insatiable appetite for negative war news, the press frequently published these letters. Following the battle of Porto, Pole warned his brother of the impending attacks in the press: "You will see the tone of which the newspapers [describe] your operations. The *Times* as usual takes the lead in the abuse of you. It is abominable and the [actions] of the press to depreciate all officers in circumstances as you are perfectly diabolical."[33] In the mentioned report, a "croaker" described Wellesley's operations as "snail paced" and he claimed that he "could do more damage to the French army with one brigade, than Wellesley's entire army affected."[34] The *Times* agreed: "We are sorry to say that the affairs of our army in Portugal emerge into notice only as cause of regret. . . . What are we doing there? What has been done since the dispersion of Soult's rear-guard in early May? We know we have a gallant army, and an active general at the head of it, but are they both possessed with one of Mr. Ambassador Frere's periodical fits of imbecility?"[35] While he was outraged by the press reports, Wellesley was even more aggravated with the cabinet, which had not supported him by responding with a rebuttal.

There was good reason for Wellesley's anger. In the wake of the decline in public support, Castlereagh questioned Wellesley's execution of the campaign, claiming that Wellesley's decision to cancel the pursuit after Porto had hindered the success of the operation. Wellesley told his brother that Castlereagh expected too much of his army: "Lord Castlereagh says all was not done which was expected.... From the force I had and the force opposed to me what right had they to expect that I should do so much? I have never yet had 20,000 men in Portugal and of these I was obliged to leave 5,000 men in Lisbon. [After augmenting the Portuguese with two thousand British troops] I had less than 13,000 men for the operation against Soult."[36] At issue for Wellesley was Castlereagh's practice of combining the number of Portuguese troops with the British troops and thereby overstating Wellesley's real troop strength to Parliament. Wellesley objected to this because he felt that despite their bravery, the Portuguese troops in May 1809 were not fully trained, and therefore their numbers could not be realistically added to his strength. As proof, Wellesley referenced the lack of respect French officers had for the Portuguese soldiers. After interviewing several captured French officers, Wellesley declared that the French "don't care a pin for thousands of [Portuguese troops] and never resist the chance to charge them ... like dogs chasing hares." Wellesley also claimed that Castlereagh should have been more pleased with the results of the Porto campaign and the subsequent pursuit: "Under all these circumstances, the defeat of Soult ought to have been more than Lord Castlereagh, as it was certainly more than I, expected or even held out."[37] Wellesley had justification for his concern; and Pole was quick to confirm Castlereagh's remarks: "Your letter has grieved me more than it has surprised me for I have had too many proofs of the mode and manner in which Castlereagh leaves [generals] in the lurch or rather should I say deceives himself about the [strength of their force] and supplies. My surprise on such objects is out of the question."[38]

The ramifications of negative press coverage were too much for Wellesley to bear alone, and they began to take a toll on the young general. To protect his military and political reputation, Wellesley informed his brother that he would in the future use their private correspondence as his outlet for the truth. His private letters would "show [his brother] exactly what he did; what he intended to do and what the motivations behind his actions were." He hoped that his brother "would then be able to set people right and if he thought it necessary and would be able to defend him in respect to the reports which even if they were not circulated, were countenanced by the Government."[39] Pole agreed and told his brother that he would use the information in their future correspondence to defend him "in case any disaster happened to Wellesley or his army, God forbid."[40]

News of the battle of Talavera reached London on 14 August 1809 and changed not only the attitude of the British press, but also the nature of political opposition. The *Times* reported that despite suffering nearly five thousand casualties, the battle of Talavera had been a "glorious event that demonstrated the native energy of British valor."[41]

As the newspapers reported the battle of Talavera as a victory, Wellesley's popularity rose. Parliament, not surprisingly, followed their example. The House of Commons voted to give Wellesley its "thanks" and approved a measure to grant Wellesley peerage and a title. With Wellesley unable to select his title personally, the task fell to Pole. In a letter to his brother, Pole explained the care he took in selecting it. He explained, "After ransacking the Peerage [tables] and examining the map, I selected the title of Viscount Wellington of Talavera, Baron Douro of Welleslie." Wellesley-Pole explained that he selected the town of Wellington because it was "located not far from Welleslie," the place of their family name. In addition, Pole hoped his brother "would not think that there was anything unpleasant or trifling in the name of Wellington." Pole concluded that "he hoped he would not be hanged for the arrangements he made in respect to his brother's new title."[42] Wellesley praised his brother: "I am very much obliged to you; I could not have picked a better name if we had discussed it twenty times."[43] After acknowledging his brother's letter, Wellesley began to use the new title, Wellington, in all his letters and correspondence.

In private, many questioned the high number of casualties at Talavera. In a letter to his former military secretary at the Horse Guards, the Duke of York remarked that "the battle of Talavera seems to have been very severe and though it has returned honor to [the

British army], the battle has cost us very dear."⁴⁴ Wellington was also concerned about the high number of British casualties, and in a letter to his brother he lamented, "How I shall be abused [by the government and press] for our loss [of men]. . . . I was hit but not hurt and I had my coat shot through. Almost all the staff officers are wounded or have had their horses shot. Never was there such a murderous battle!"⁴⁵

Despite his concern, Wellington was not vilified in the newspapers following Talavera. "The nation is delighted," wrote Pole, who nevertheless offered some criticism of the Wellington's public dispatches, which were frequently printed in British newspapers: "Your [public dispatch] of 29 July [following the battle of Talavera] is admirable, but I have one fault. You are not saying enough in praise of your officers nor do you go sufficiently [in detail] about the numbers of your prisoners. I think you are always particularly bold or cold in praising the artillery. I heard that [Brigadier General Howarth, commander of the artillery] had two horses shot from under him. This might be thrown in and would have gratified his friends [in Parliament.]"⁴⁶

Pole believed Wellington could abate the negative attention he had received from the government and newspapers by embellishing his victories, giving more credit to government officials, and praising certain subordinates who enjoyed Parliament's patronage. Pole (who had a genuine understanding of public relations) also asked Wellington to portray the war in a more patriotic manner. Wellington reluctantly agreed: "I beg you to tell Lord Mulgrave [the secretary of the Admiralty] how much obliged to him I am for all his kindness and support." Regarding his subordinates, Wellington was unwilling to praise them when he felt it was not deserved. He told his brother, "As for Lord Howarth, I might as well claim the credit for the loss of his horses myself. As Howarth was standing on the hill which I had occupied for most of the battle when a shell burst killing two of his, and a great number of other people's horses which were standing behind it. I said as much about Howarth as he deserves, for I believe myself lucky if he does not get me into a scrape yet."⁴⁷

Although Wellington's spirits were temporarily raised, news from the Low Countries quickly abated any cause for celebration. The ill-fated Walcheren Expedition, which had set sail in July on the same day that Wellington had fought the battle of Talavera, concluded as a military and political disaster for the Duke of Portland's ministry. The expedition failed its military objective of supporting the Austrians against the French, and it drained England's strategic manpower and gold reserves.[48]

The political fallout of the Walcheren disaster raised questions in England about the strategy in the peninsula. In December 1809, the Common Council of the City of London called for an inquiry into the Talavera campaign, which touched a raw nerve in Wellington by evoking memories of the Convention of Cintra.[49] He told Liverpool: "I cannot expect mercy at their hands, whether I succeed or fail; and I should fail, they will not enquire whether the failure is owing to my own incapacity, to the blameless errors to which we are all liable, to the faults or mistakes of others.... Or to the great power and abilities of our Enemy. In any of these cases I shall become their victim; but I am not to be alarmed by this additional risk, and whatever be the consequences. I will continue to do my best in this country."[50]

A resolute Wellington responded to the council's inquiry by telling Wellesley-Pole, "I see that the Common Council are to have me again *en Spectacle* at Chelsea; but that shall not prevent me from endeavoring to give the French another beating."[51] To Villiers, he wrote simply, "I act with a sword hanging over my head."[52] Wellington frequently used exaggerated language and expressed himself in vehement terms, but with the memories of the Cintra board of inquiry still fresh, his concern was undoubtedly genuine.

He had good reason to be worried as he came under attack in the House of Commons. In the wake of the council's assertions, Sir Edward Milton attacked Wellington for his decision to venture into Spain and to fight such a costly battle. He also argued against issuing the nation's thanks by stating "what thanks would Parliament bestow on an admiral who first ran his fleet on the rocks and shoals and then evidenced great skill and ability in getting them off again?" Milton argued that Wellington's actions at Talavera were remarkably similar in that "the general had imprudently brought his army into a critical situation, was forced to give battle, and was attacked by the enemy." According to Milton, Talavera was "a decisive victory followed by a precipitous retreat." Furthermore, he declared that Wellington had fought the battle "merely for peerage and a title." Milton asserted that Wellesley had purposely excluded information in his dispatches to the government concerning the capture of nearly 3,500 men, which were left in the British hospital after the battle. The member of Parliament concluded that the whole Talavera campaign was "wrapped in mystery," and that while he would give his thanks to the brave officers and soldiers of Wellesley's army, he would not vote his thanks to Wellesley.[53]

Milton was not alone in his criticism. Even the venerable Gen. Banastre Tarleton, veteran of the American War of Independence, objected to Wellesley's advancement in peerage: "The Merit of Lord Wellington is still unequivocal. Why, in cases of failure, should the merits of the officer not be enquired into as a matter of course, as in great measure, [is] the plan in the navy? I blamed Lord Wellington, when he was in this house, for the Convention of Cintra. I now blame him for this rash advance in Spain."[54]

As the Whigs continued to combine the government's failure in the Walcheren Expedition with Wellington's operations, his assessment of the political situation became pessimistic. He told Liverpool, "I am convinced that the Government cannot last."[55] A month later he told a subordinate, "The government is terribly weak, and I think it probable will be beaten upon the Walcheren question. It is impossible to say what will be the consequence. I think the King may be able to form a government without having recourse to Lord Grenville; but there will be no strength in that government and the members will have no satisfaction in conducting public affairs."[56]

Despite his reservations about the strength of the government, the new viscount Wellington realized that in the future he would have to write more politically attuned dispatches to garner public and political support for his campaign in the peninsula.[57] To receive financial and political support from home, Wellington would have to not only continue to win on the battlefield, but also counter the fickleness of British public opinion. As an aristocrat, he harbored no illusions about the capricious public. As quickly as the press reporting Talavera as a victory had garnered support for the war, a defeat in the press could turn the "mob of London" against him. Not surprisingly, Wellington's private letters reflected his frustration and exposed a vulnerability that even the French forces arrayed against him could not reveal. When published, Wellington's letters fueled the opposition and exacerbated his problems in the peninsula.

Wellington's tactical and operational decisions were not affected by public opinion polls at home because his army had more pressing concerns. The failed Walcheren Expedition had sapped his troops of badly needed supplies and reinforcements; his army required rest;

and there was still no word on new shipments of money to pay his men. The summer campaign of 1809, while successful, left Wellington with many questions. However, one fact remained certain: his troops could march and fight, and their bravery continued to give Britain its last realistic hope of victory on the Continent.

4

Waning Support: The Defense of Portugal, 1809–1810

> The troops are improved in health and I hope we shall do tolerably well, even when Boney comes to drive us into the sea.
>
> Wellington to Wellesley-Pole, 4 January 1810

Following the battle of Talavera, Wellington withdrew his army toward the Portuguese border. He established his headquarters in the fortress of Badajoz and patiently observed the activities of the French and Spanish armies. At the same time, Napoleon, after his victory at Wagram, developed a strategy to drive the British army from Portugal. With 360,000 men deployed for the subjugation of Spain in the fall and winter of 1809, Napoleon labored to organize a striking force to launch another invasion of Portugal.[1]

Well aware of Napoleon's intentions, Wellington faced his own problems. His army numbered only 26,000 British and Portuguese troops, and many were sick or wounded. Nevertheless, his greatest concern was the Spanish. Throughout the fall of 1809, the cabinet had pressured Wellington to provide military assistance to the Spanish and dispatched his brother Richard to garner needed support. Richard arrived in Cadiz in August and became a staunch advocate of Spain's potential as an ally, but he also recognized that the Spanish would require British support and Wellington's leadership to achieve success.² Wellington emphatically declined, telling Castlereagh he "felt no inclination to cooperate or join the Spanish Army again." Since the battle of Talavera, Wellington had condemned the conduct of the Spanish troops by stating that whenever they fight the French, "they make a practice of running away, throwing off all arms and accoutrements, and clothing only to reassemble in a state of nature."³ Privately, he condemned their conduct even more. Wellington told Pole, "The Spanish troops will not fight; they are undisciplined, they have no officers, no provisions, no magazines, no means of any description. If we enter into cooperation with them, the burden of the war will fall upon us and with us will rest the disgrace of its certain and unavoidable failure."⁴ The problem was two-fold. First and most important, the Spanish required extensive logistics support that Wellington and the British could not provide. Struggling to pay and supply his own army, Wellington could not take on the task of supplying the Spanish armies. In contrast, Wellington praised the Portuguese troops and appealed to Castlereagh to supply Marshal Beresford and the Portuguese army with "the ablest officers that England could afford." Wellington felt that the Portuguese army could form the nucleus of his army and thereby decrease Britain's burden.⁵

The second problem for Wellington was the unwillingness of the Spanish to accept his advice. Despite his warnings, they went on the offensive against the French. On 19 November, a French army of thirty thousand defeated a Spanish army of fifty thousand at the battle of Ocaña. The defeat was followed by another at Alba de Tormes on 28 November. Disasters for the Spanish, costing more than twenty thousand casualties, the defeats left the fertile land near Andalucia vulnerable for invasion. In January, King Joseph Bonaparte and his chief of staff, Marshal Soult invaded the province and occupied the cities of Cordoba and Seville. The French pursued the Spanish government to the fortress of Cadiz, in southern Spain, where their advance was halted on the island fortress's isthmus. Unable to break through the stout resistance, the French laid siege to the city for the next two years. As these events unfolded, Wellington incensed the Spanish by remaining stationary behind the protection of the border, planning for the defense of Portugal.⁶

The foundation for Wellington's strategy was the transformation of Lisbon and the surrounding areas into a well-defended sanctuary where Wellington could protect his troops and resources. It was a bold yet skillfully conceived plan that relied on the limitations of the French supply system to maintain large armies in one place in the peninsula. Wellington estimated that for the French to invade Portugal successfully, they would have to assemble an invasion force of nearly one hundred thousand men. Therefore, Wellington planned a multilayered defense of Lisbon that exploited the limitations of French logistics.[7]

His strategy consisted of three critical tasks. The first was to implement a scorched earth policy in the areas through which the French were expected to march. By destroying all sources of food, Wellington knew any French invasion attempt, if not immediately successful, would suffer from critical shortages of food and supplies. The second task was to mobilize the *ordenanza*. These bands of Portuguese militia would dramatically increase the number of men-at-arms, and they would help isolate the invading army by preying on French couriers, supply convoys, and stragglers. The third phase was to build a series of defensive fortifications, called the Lines of Torres Vedras, that stretched from the Tagus River, north of Lisbon, to the Atlantic Ocean, a distance of nearly thirty miles.[8]

In a memorandum about his intent for the fortifications, Wellington stated, "the great object in Portugal is the possession of Lisbon and the Tagus River. All of our measures must be directed [to the defense] of this object." Wellington also planned for the contingency that his defensive system might not work and that the British army would be forced to evacuate the country. He instructed the engineer officer in charge of constructing the fortifications, "there is a second object connected with the first . . . the embarkation of the British troops in case of reverse." Wellington identified several suitable evacuation points.[9] As he planned for Lisbon's defense, Wellington wrote Castlereagh concerning Napoleon's strategy for the upcoming year: "Napoleon is reinforcing his armies in Spain. You may depend on it. He and his marshals are desirous of revenging upon us the different blows we have given them, and when they come to the Peninsula, their first and great object will be to get the English out."[10] Wellington had reason for concern because the French victory at Wagram and subsequent armistice freed French troops for action in the peninsula. In October, Wellington traveled to Lisbon to conduct a reconnaissance. En route, he received unwelcome news from London that the Portland ministry had fallen from power.

On the heels of the Convention of Cintra disgrace, the future of the ill-fated Walcheren Expedition had sharpened the rivalry between Canning and Castlereagh. Their tempers were also flared by the ill-defined and overlapping functions of the foreign secretary and secretary for war. Castlereagh had been the expedition's architect and chief proponent and faced public and political humiliation when the expedition failed. Adding to his misery was news that Canning, in a power move to form his own ministry, had undermined Castlereagh by circulating secret pamphlets concerning the Walcheren Expedition to influential members of Parliament. To preserve his honor, Castlereagh challenged Canning to a duel, which resulted only in a wound to George Canning's thigh but it killed the cabinet's chances of surviving the Walcheren crisis. After the duel, Portland, whose health had begun to fail, resigned, and King George III asked the Tory Party leader and chancellor of the Exchequer, Spencer Perceval, to form a new government. Perceval accepted the task and immediately requested Canning's assistance. A slighted Canning declined and resigned his post. Several other ministers, including Huskisson, also resigned in protest against a coalition government. With an impending inquiry into the Walcheren Expedition and a budgetary shortfall, the Whigs also declined to join Perceval. Instead they hoped to establish their own government when Perceval's cabinet collapsed.[11]

Britain's new prime minister faced a grim situation. Parliament was scheduled to convene in January, and he knew that the Whigs would use the failure of the Walcheren Expedition to attack his new cabinet's war policies.[12] Therefore, to gain political leverage in the House of Commons, Perceval appointed moderate yet experienced politicians to his cabinet, including Wellington's eldest brother, Richard, as foreign secretary. Richard's brief post in Spain had helped Wellington's cause at a difficult time, but Perceval's appointment of a new secretary for war, Robert Banks Jenkinson, Lord Liverpool, would have the greatest impact on Wellington and his strategy during the next several months.[13]

The political upheaval in London did not ease Wellington's burden. In a letter to Pole, he stated, "all of these events are unfortunate, and the government is gone, but that is not the worst of it. [The cabinet's collapse] will confirm in the minds of all men, the despicable opinions which they have had of public servants of the state."[14] Furthermore, Wellington had little faith that the new cabinet could match the intellect and aggressiveness of its predecessor. He told Pole, "It appears to me scarcely possible to form a government that shall do the business of the House of Commons without the assistance of both Canning and Castlereagh." Wellington also attacked the party-based political system, which he felt had turned the loyalty of the people against the war: "I never felt any inclination to dive deeply in party politics, because I believe the misfortunes of the present reign of George III, to include the loss of America, and the success of the French Revolution were to be attributed in a great degree to the spirit of party in England. . . . The feeling I have for a decided party politician is rather that of contempt than any other and I am certain that his wishes and efforts for his party frequently prevent him from doing which is best for the country." Wellington concluded, "The current situation would be better served if all of the political parties in Parliament would unite to support the [cabinet] against the Jacobins." He pledged his support for the new cabinet on the grounds that "he did not conceive that he ought to embark in politics to such an extent as to preclude his serving the country under any administration that employed him."[15]

Nothing could have been further from the truth. Wellington was a much more political general than he claimed. After all, nearly every member of his family was involved in politics, and he would not have attained his command had it not been for his political ties to Canning and Castlereagh. Nevertheless, his criticism was valid because the cabinet had not contributed the resources necessary to win the war in the peninsula before launching the ill-fated diversionary attack at Walcheren. Although not openly critical of the Walcheren Expedition, Wellington must have felt that those resources were wasted. Furthermore, the collapse of the cabinet increased his burden of planning for the upcoming campaign. He had to gain the confidence of a new group of politicians, and he recognized that Whig pressure to minimize Britain's financial and military commitments in the peninsula would take its toll on the inexperienced Perceval cabinet. Over the next several months, he attempted to reassure Liverpool that his defensive plan for Portugal was sound, but Liverpool was understandably anxious, which led Wellington to further question his government's resolve.

Two months before taking office, Liverpool had rightfully written Wellington to assess the strategic situation. Liverpool was aware of Wellington's plans to defend Lisbon by a series of defensive lines, but he was skeptical that Wellington's strategy would succeed without Spanish assistance. Therefore, he asked Wellington four direct questions.[16] The first and second questions related to the Spanish. However, Liverpool's last two questions indirectly questioned Wellington's defensive plan for Portugal. He asked, "If a serious attack is made upon Portugal, what is the present prospect of successful resistance, and could the army be evacuated if the French invaded the country first?"[17] Wellington calmly refuted Liverpool's concern: "I do not think the French will make an attempt to capture Spain until they invade Portugal." He also told Liverpool that he did not believe the French "had the present means to invade Portugal." However, if they did, they "could be successfully resisted."[18] Two weeks later, Wellington requested increased financial support of the Portuguese government to raise an army: "During the continuance of this contest, which must necessarily be defensive on our part, and in which I may fail, I shall be profoundly abused and in the end, I may lose the little character I have gained, but I shall not act fairly upon the government if I did not tell them my real opinion, which is that they betray the honor and interests of this country [by not] continuing their efforts in the Peninsula."[19]

While he calmly refuted Liverpool's concern in public, privately Wellington resented Liverpool's pessimism. In a letter to Pole, Wellington declared, "I think it is probable that some of the wise gentlemen in the [London] debating society will attack many of my measures [concerning defending Portugal and not aiding the Spanish]. And I am drawing up a memorandum which I will send you in which I refer to the official documents from which you can get the truth on everything."[20] Wellington sent Liverpool a comprehensive situation report in the wake of a cautious letter from Liverpool that warned, "You are aware that it must be our policy to remain in Portugal as long as we can remain there without risking our army. But we must secure the return of the army if a serious attack is made by the French upon Portugal."[21] Liverpool's concern for the safety of the army was understandable; as the secretary for war, he was responsible for Britain's strategy, and he alone faced the critics in Parliament. However, Liverpool compromised his credibility by suggesting obscure operations in Spain.

In his orders, Liverpool told Wellington that instead of committing all of his men to the defense of Portugal, he should also explore the possibility of deploying British troops to the Spanish provinces of Catalonia, Aragon, or Valencia to lead uprisings against the French. Liverpool did not have reinforcements to send for these missions, nor did he suggest where Wellington could find the men for the task. Instead, Liverpool's only justification for the plan was that he thought "the Aragonese were universally admitted to be the most warlike people in Spain, and the Catalonians and Valencians the most industrious and active." Accordingly, Liverpool wrote, "It must be obvious that you have it in your power to employ a limited movable corps on the coasts of Catalonia and Valencia."[22]

Liverpool's proposal was poorly conceived and reflected his lack of understanding of the complexities of waging war in the peninsula. Wellington must have questioned what a "limited movable corps" was, but more important was the question of who would provide command and control or logistics support for these decentralized operations. Liverpool also failed to recognize the difficulty associated with conducting decentralized offensive operations in Spain during defensive preparations of Portugal. Wellington never seriously considered Liverpool's proposal to scatter his already overstretched forces, although he did assign a token liaison officer to explore the possibility of conducting such operations. Nevertheless, the proposal was a distraction and clearly demonstrated Liverpool's struggle to formulate and issue clear guidance.[23]

News of the Spanish defeats at Ocaña and Alba de Tormes ultimately forced Liverpool to accept Wellington's defensive strategy and temporarily abandon the idea of inciting resistance in remote Spanish provinces. He asked Wellington, "When will the Spanish be cured of fighting battles under circumstances when nothing but disaster can be expected? His Majesty is not inclined to impose any restriction upon you to conduct which may prevent your undertaking any operation . . . which may appear advantageous to the general cause."[24] Liverpool also instructed Wellington that because of "the [recent] difficulties [concerning] all operations of the Spanish Army, His Majesty would be unwilling to see the [British] army advanced beyond the frontiers of Portugal and the Spanish Provinces immediately joining it under any circumstances."[25] Wellington had already issued orders to concentrate on Portugal.[26]

Wellington's army reached Lisbon in early January 1810. He knew that time was limited before Napoleon would begin organizing his forces to invade Portugal. So he resolved to settle his debts with the Portuguese government and begin constructing the defensive Lines of Torres Vedras.[27]

Meanwhile, Liverpool and the cabinet were subjected to incessant questions about the war. At the top of the opposition's agenda was the decrease of pecuniary aid to Portugal. The *Chronicle* took the lead and openly asked Liverpool, "Are the English people to overlook the dilapidated resources of the country, and the wanton and inglorious sacrifice of its gallant defenders in the pestilential marshes of Walcheren and Estremadura?"[28]

By the fall of 1809, it had become clear that Portugal would require an increase in the subsidy if it was to maintain an active role in its defense. The twenty thousand troops Britain had agreed to support did not constitute even one-half of the Portuguese army when complete, and the subsidy provided for these men did not cover one-half of their expenses. Furthermore, costs were expected to increase as efforts were mounted to bring the army to full strength, and an additional expense of £130,000 would be incurred to raise the pay of Portuguese officers. Moreover, the Portuguese militia, which numbered more than fifty thousand, played an important role in garrisoning the fortresses, thus freeing first-line infantry for active service.[29]

In view of Portugal's financial difficulties, Wellington recommended to Liverpool that Great Britain either grant the Portuguese £300,000 for the establishment of depots or agree to support an additional ten thousand troops, at an estimated £250,000. In all, Wellington requested £980,000 for the Portuguese subsidy. He justified his request by noting that the transfer of the Brazilian trade from Portugal to Great Britain had reduced Portugal's customs revenue while greatly enriching England.[30]

There were two problems with the subsidy arrangement. When Great Britain first agreed to support a certain number of Portuguese troops, specific regiments had been selected as the recipients of this aid. However, this arrangement existed only on paper, since funds and supplies were distributed to the Portuguese army with no differentiation between subsidized and unsubsidized units. The costs for the support of these units had been estimated when they were incomplete, numbering only seventeen thousand, not thirty thousand. Therefore, Wellington's 1809 estimate was roughly half of what the Portuguese required. The Portuguese Regency Council minister of defense and marine, Dom Miguel Forjaz, caught Wellington's error, and throughout the winter and spring of 1809–1810, he lobbied Villiers and the ambassador in London, Domingos de Sousa, for a loan.[31]

In early December, Wellington told Liverpool that the Portuguese government was £980,000 in debt and required immediate help. In a letter to the minister plenipotentiary in Lisbon, John Villiers, Wellington declared, "If I had asked [the government] for £900,000, I should not have got a shilling, and I think it more than probable that I shall get the £300,000 besides the pay of the [British] officers [which command their army]. The only resource that remains is to prevail upon the English Ministers to assist Portugal—with what? Not the amount of the deficit, for that they cannot do, but with as large a sum as I think they have at their disposal, which if will not [cure] everything, will be of some use."[32]

There were two primary reasons for the government's reluctance to provide more support. First, the Walcheren Expedition had drained its gold and silver bullion reserves. Second, Napoleon's embargo of British imports had forced the British to search for new sources of bullion in the unpredictable American markets. Moreover, there was great Parliamentary opposition to sending money to Wellington for the Portuguese. In the wake of Napoleon's victory at Wagram and an anticipated French invasion of Portugal, many felt that any amount of money sent to Wellington or Portugal would be wasted. The primary advocate for this position was Huskisson's political ally George Rose, who argued in November, "To carry on the [Peninsular] War under the present scale of expense with the ordinary means of the country or anything approaching to it is utterly impossible . . . . It follows therefore of absolute necessity that unless our expenses can be greatly reduced, [the British people] cannot continue to exist long as an independent nation . . . I repeat with a clear and strong conviction that the salvation of the Empire depends upon our expenditure being effectively reduced."[33]

Gen. Henry Ferguson, an independent politician who had served in the peninsula in 1808, did not favor the measure. He declared that he did not believe there were thirty thousand Portuguese troops in the entire country "worthy enough to stand in battle against the French." He also stated that despite the "valor of Marshal Beresford and the British troops which commanded them," the Portuguese troops were not disciplined enough to fight the French and would "scatter" if seriously threatened by French troops[34] Another member of Parliament joined Ferguson, arguing that "arming 30,000 Portuguese troops would be of no use," and "it would probably have been better, if not a single English regiment had ever been sent to the Peninsula, [because] it reinforced to the Spanish and Portuguese people, to look toward the English people [for assistance] and not to themselves."[35]

Despite these obstacles, Liverpool supplied Wellington with £980,000 to support thirty thousand Portuguese troops, a sum that included £100,000 to pay the British officers in Portuguese service and £130,000 for the Portuguese officers' pay raise. Liverpool also informed him that he would dispatch £300,000 to cover the expenditures of the British army but warned him that, "the expenditure of [Britain] has become enormous and if the war is to continue we must look to economy. I do not believe this country has ever made a greater effort to afford the military and financial aid for Portugal and Spain. [The Spanish and Portuguese] should be sensible of [Britain's exertion] and should feel the necessity of making extraordinary exertions for their own support."[36]

Liverpool's apprehension was undoubtedly the result of political opposition, but it also stemmed from corruption in the Portuguese government: "[The British government] is naturally anxious to know with some certainty that [it will receive its] money's worth. It is very desirable that the sums advanced by Great Britain for the Portuguese force should be applied directly to defraying the expenses of [the Portuguese force] and should not pass circuitously through the hands of the Portuguese Government by which we may not be certain that it was not diverted to other purposes."[37] To assist Wellington in managing the new subsidy arrangement, the Foreign Office dispatched Charles Stuart in January 1810 to replace John Villiers as minister plenipotentiary to Lisbon. Fortunately for Wellington, Stuart sympathized with his difficulties, and he worked tirelessly to solidify the Anglo-Portuguese alliance. Despite Stuart's work in Lisbon, disagreements over the subsidy would continue for the remainder of the war as the Portuguese, primarily through Forjaz, complained to Wellington and the ministry that the amount of aid was never enough. The Portuguese continued to lobby for £2,190,000, or the cost of maintaining an army of fifty thousand men and forty thousand militia in the field. The problem was compounded by an acute specie shortage that affected Wellington as well as the Portuguese.

Stuart bolstered Anglo-Portuguese relations by increasing the proportion of subsidy provided in the form of grain and other foodstuffs.[38] Stuart also calmed the government's concern about corruption in Lisbon.[39]

Prior to Stuart's arrival, however, Wellington told Liverpool that the £300,000 would not fully provide back pay for his men or cover his debts: "The Portuguese people are tired out by requisitions not paid for, and nothing can be procured without ready money." Unfortunately, these concerns were secondary to the effect of an unpaid British army. Wellington feared the worst: "The conduct of the British soldiers is infamous.... The [commissariat] has never brought up a convoy of money that [the troops] have not robbed the chest.... I have never halted the army for two days that I have not been obliged to assemble a General Court Martial, and at this moment there are three trials for soldiers guilty of wanton murders."[40] In March, Wellington declared, "The constitution and the whole system of discipline, efficiency and equipment of the British Army depend upon regular payments.... If [the soldier's equipment and provisions] cannot be paid for, the soldiers will take them without payment."[41]

Political opposition had made Liverpool fixated on risk and finances and not the potential for victory. He again questioned Wellington's plan, this time doubting that the two primary Portuguese fortresses protecting Lisbon, Santarém and Peniche, would hold up to a full-scale French invasion. The origin of his fear was the late Sir John Moore's assertion in 1808 that Portuguese fortresses were vulnerable.[42] Liverpool proposed that Wellington move his army to the Spanish fortress of Cadiz: "There can be no doubt but in [England] a higher value is set upon Cadiz than upon Lisbon. Is it not true that Cadiz and some part of southern Spain might be defended if Portugal was lost, but Portugal could not be defended if Andalucia were in French possession?"[43] Furthermore, he wrote, "I should apprise you that a considerable amount of alarm exists within this country respecting the safety of the British Army in Portugal. I have no difficulty in stating that under all circumstances you would rather be excused for [evacuating] the army a little soon than by remaining in Portugal a little too long." However, Liverpool contradicted himself by stating, "I do not mean by my observation that you would be justified in evacuating Portugal before it is attacked, but whenever [the

French do attack] the chances of a successful defense are considered here by all persons, military as well as civilian, so improbable that I could not recommend a desperate resistance." Liverpool also suggested evacuation points for Wellington to consider as well as instructing him that if his army was forced to evacuate, he should proceed to either Gibraltar or Cadiz, not return to England.[44]

Yet again, Liverpool's indecision and lack of faith upset Wellington. Although he had previously expressed confidence in Wellington's strategy, Liverpool's dispatches were filled with ambiguity and questions about the security of the army. Wellington struggled with Liverpool's anxiety and attempted to ascertain what his mission was. He asked, "From your letter I understand that if there exists a military necessity for it, I am to evacuate the country, and if not I am not to evacuate the country; which means that I am not to be frightened away by a force which I do not consider superior to my own, or if the enemy invades this country with a force less than that which I should think so superior to ours, should I fight a battle to save the country of Portugal?"[45] Wellington was genuinely confused, and for good reason, since Liverpool's letters posed several important questions and offered very few answers. First, how large must the French army be to render evacuation necessary? Second, should Wellington fight a major battle before he boarded transports? And last, who was responsible for making the final decision to evacuate or fight?

While struggling to determine answers, Wellington refuted Liverpool's proposal concerning new evacuation sites: "I cannot embark [from where you suggest] without uncovering Lisbon, and since Lisbon is the primary [communications and supply] objective it is useless for me to consider the embarkation points you have proposed." Furthermore, Wellington told Liverpool that he had been misinformed about the various sites: "I think you have received your information... from some of those persons in government who have never considered the subject, and probably have never even looked at either place."[46] Wellington also cautioned that if he was forced to evacuate the army, he "felt a little anxiety to go like gentlemen, out of the hall door, particularly after the dispositions we have made to do so, and not out of the back door, or by the area."[47]

Wellington attempted to relieve Liverpool's concern about Portugal being indefensible:

> I have a great respect for Sir John Moore and his opinions . . . however my opinion is that as long as we shall remain in Portugal, the contest must continue in Spain. The French are most desirous that [the British] should withdraw. To force us out, the French will have to employ a very large force, and I doubt whether they can bring that force to bear upon Portugal without abandoning other objects and thereby exposing their whole fabric in Spain to great risk. If the French invade Portugal, and do not succeed in forcing us to evacuate, they will be in a very dangerous position, and the longer we are able to resist them, the more they will suffer materially in Spain.[48]

Wellington had strategic reservations about abandoning Lisbon in favor of Cadiz: "First, I do not think it quite clear that [the British army] will be received in Cadiz." Second, if the British abandoned Portugal, he believed that "the French would seize Lisbon the next day." If that happened, Wellington feared that the border fortresses of Ciudad Rodrigo, Almeida, Badajoz, and Elvas would fall within a short time. Without the security of the Portuguese fortresses or the presence of the British army in Portugal, "the whole French army would attack Cadiz, probably before the island could be fortified as it ought to be."[49] In a letter to his brother, Wellington was more direct about Liverpool's plan: "I doubt whether the French are sufficiently strong enough to force us out of the Peninsula. More so even than our Ministers are confident that I will lose the army. However I am in no scrape at all and if [William Pitt] was alive or if there was anything like a government in England or any public support remaining [for the war], Napoleon Bonaparte would repent his invasion of Spain."[50]

He added, "The French will not be able to [invade Portugal] until the end of June, and then if we are not destroyed for want of money, which is now pinching us greatly, we shall be much stronger than we are now." Wellington concluded his letter with a condemnation of his government in London, "It appears to me that [the British government] has lost its spirit . . . at the moment we most want it and that [the government] are more concerned about shillings and sixpences instead of opposing the enemy as the circumstances of the world enable us and as we ought to oppose him."[51]

Wellington's greatest fear was that if his army fought and lost, his government would withdraw completely from the peninsular struggle. The confirmation came from his brother: "I understand your instructions direct you to not risk your army. I hope in God that you will strictly obey them—for be afraid. In the present state of public [opinion] with respect to the war and of the [weakness of the cabinet] that if you fight a bloody battle and afterwards evacuate Portugal—you will not be safe." Pole also warned that cabinet members "are completely paralyzed [with anxiety] and nobody in government seems to think of action." The former Treasury secretary William Huskisson and his supporters advocated rapprochement with France: "The whole cry [in Parliament] is peace and ceremony. Huskisson has done infinite mischief by his statement respecting our finances and too much weight has been given to his authority. If Huskisson's principles are acted upon, it will mark the end of [Britain] as a great and warlike nation."[52]

A frustrated Wellington told Liverpool, "I am willing to be responsible for the evacuation of Portugal. Depend upon it, whatever people tell you that I am so desirous as they imagine of fighting desperate battles, if I was, I might fight one any day I please." However, he concluded with an appeal for Liverpool's confidence: "I am perfectly aware of the risks that I run personally.... All I beg is that if I am to be held responsible, I may be left to [the] exercise of my own judgment and I ask for the fair confidence of government upon the measures which I am to adopt."[53] However, in a letter to the commander of the Royal Navy squadron supporting his troops, Admiral Berkeley, Wellington complained, "The government is terribly afraid that I shall get them and myself into a scrape. But what can be expected from men who are beaten in the House of Commons three times a week? A great deal could be done [in Portugal], if there existed in England, less party, more public support and if there was any [resemblance of a strong] government."[54] Wellington told his brother, "I think that the Government and country are going to the devil as fast as possible." He added, "I expect to hear every day that the mobs of London are masters of the country."[55]

Some of Liverpool's apprehension can also be credited to Wellington. Throughout the winter and spring of 1810, Wellington never fully disclosed the extent and strength of his defensive preparations. As a result, many in London, including Liverpool, had no appreciation of the depth of the fortifications, nor were they completely assured that Wellington would complete the defensive lines in time. Wellington's rationale for keeping the construction progress and details of the lines a secret was his mistrust of the British press. While the press was at best a double-edged sword that had saved him after Talavera, the British newspapers were also one of Napoleon's best sources of intelligence because they frequently published his dispatches and the letters of officers who served on Wellington's staff. Wellington had been aware of the danger for some time, as evidenced by his memorandum of March 1809. Nevertheless, he had been unable to stop the flow of information to the press.[56] In November 1809, Wellington informed Liverpool, "In some instances the English Newspapers have accurately stated, not only the regiments occupying a position but the number of men fit for duty of which each regiment was composed. This intelligence must have reached the enemy at the same time it did me, and at a moment which was most important that he should receive it."[57] As proof, Wellington reported that the *Times* published his initial plans of the army's operational depots:

> The newspapers have recently published an account of the defensive positions occupied by the different English and Portuguese Corps which certainly conveyed to the enemy the first hand knowledge of them.... [One article] described the line of operation which I should follow in case of an occurrence, the preparations which I had made for that operation, and where I formed my magazines. It is not necessary to inquire in what manner the newspapers acquire this information, but if the editors feel an anxiety for the success of the [British] military operations, they will refrain from giving this information to the public, as they must know that their papers are read by the enemy.... I can only assure you that it will increase the difficulty of operations in this country.[58]

Liverpool assured Wellington that his office had not provided the information to the newspapers; rather, letters from the "croakers" on Wellington's staff were provided to the newspapers for publication. Liverpool credited Brigadier Charles Stewart, Castlereagh's younger brother, with the information on the embarkation sites. Liverpool suggested that Wellington issue a general order threatening to stop the post: "You are perhaps aware that Sir John Moore on one occasion actually stopped the post. I know very well such a measure could not be continued for any length of time, but at a critical period of the campaign, I should not hesitate to carry it out . . . for a time, if it should appear to be necessary, and at all events the apprehension of it would make officers more cautious in what they wrote."[59] Wellington declined: "I am sure you do not expect that I or any other officer in command of a British army can pretend to prevent the correspondence of officers with their friends. It could not be done if attempted."[60] An infuriated Wellington wrote, "As soon as an accident happens, every man who can write, and has a friend who can read, sits down to write his account of what he does not know."[61]

While Wellington struggled to limit the flow of operational information from his staff to the newspapers, the press, with less information to report, invented stories by manipulating information contained in Wellington's dispatches. The resulting forgeries nearly devastated public opinion. In August 1810, the *Times* reported that Wellington had fought a battle that never took place. The newspaper went so far as to claim that "in his victory," Wellington suffered over eight thousand casualties.[62] Wellington was outraged by the actions of the press and by the unknown party that had forged his letters. In December he wrote a close friend, "It makes one sick to hear the statements of supposed facts, and the comments upon supposed transactions, [which never took place] here which only serve to keep the people of England in a state of constant alarm and anxiety." In the same letter, Wellington joked about the speed at which the forged information had traveled to the French in the peninsula: "Unless the French received them by flying pigeons, or if they had the best [postal service] in Europe . . . my dispatch [of the 14th of October] is manifestly forged."[63]

Powerless to stop the information leaks to the press, Wellington resolved to make their task more difficult by limiting the details of his operational plans in his official dispatches. The result proved to be both positive and negative. The British papers remained uninformed of the extent of Wellington's plans and strategy; however, Wellington remained the target of politicians, who throughout the campaign expected the French to drive him into the sea. In retrospect, censoring his dispatches may seem overcautious, because the commander of the French invasion force received virtually no intelligence from Paris during the invasion of 1810–1811. However, there was no way for Wellington to predict the ineffective state of French intelligence.

His decision to keep those in London uninformed about the extent of his defensive preparations, at the cost of public and parliamentary ridicule, was a decision that proved invaluable during the invasion.[64]

Fortunately for Wellington, the new administration survived the Walcheren inquiry and the spring session of Parliament. As a result, Liverpool found a new sense of confidence. He informed Wellington that "the greatest satisfaction and the fullest sense of confidence is placed in your discretion in the important and delicate service in which you are engaged."[65] However, the cabinet's survival was not as influential as the support from an unlikely source. In April, the king's military secretary had written Liverpool, "His Majesty gives a very high opinion of Lord Wellington's sense and of the resources of his mind as a soldier. His Majesty trusts that [the cabinet] would join [the king] and allow [Lord Wellington] to proceed according to his judgment and discretion . . . unhindered by instructions which might embarrass [Wellington] in the execution of his general plan."[66] The combination of external pressure and internal victory had a dramatic effect on Liverpool. He even visited Wellington's wife and two sons and reported that they "were all very well and growing stout."[67]

Appreciative of the newfound support but wary of the political intrigue at home, Wellington continued his defensive preparation of Portugal. In retrospect, Liverpool's caution throughout the fall of 1809 seems justified. The connection between political developments in England and the fortunes of military campaigns was a common theme during this period and each military reverse often led to a crisis in personal relations within the cabinet. Despite its rough beginning, Wellington's relationship with Liverpool grew over time. While it would never blossom into the personal friendship he had had with Castlereagh, Wellington's confidence in Liverpool was also reinforced by the minister's faith in Wellington's brothers Richard and Henry. Henry, who had replaced Richard as the minster plenipotentiary to Spain in December, was made a member of the Privy Council by the king to give him more power with the Spanish. Wellington was bolstered by the proximity and support of his family and the hard work of the Portuguese, who labored to turn their country into an impregnable fortress; he was resolved to ensure that no evacuation would be forced on him and was prepared for the hammer blow to come.

5

THE CRUCIBLE: MASSÉNA'S INVASION OF PORTUGAL, 1810–1811

> I tremble when I think I shall have to embark the Leopards in front of Bonaparte aided by such a man.
>
> Wellington to Wellesley-Pole, 26 January 1810

On 17 April 1810, Napoleon resolved to end the Peninsular War by invading Portugal and destroying Wellington's army. To carry out the task, he created the *armée du Portugal*.[1] Napoleon appointed as its commander his most competent and trusted subordinate, Marshal André Masséna, a veteran of nearly thirty-five years. Masséna, who was in poor health and had been inactive for several months, reluctantly agreed to lead the invasion. Napoleon promised him that his army would "lack nothing" and that the French invasion force would be supported with all the men, supplies, and materiel necessary to complete the task. In May, Masséna crossed the Pyrenees Mountains and took command of his army.[2]

To eliminate the mistakes of the two failed Portuguese invasions, Napoleon ordered a "methodical march into Portugal." Because the French had no knowledge of Wellington's fortification of Lisbon, Napoleon ordered Masséna to spend the summer besieging Ciudad Rodrigo and Almeida, which guarded the primary invasion route into the country.[3] In accordance with the Emperor's orders, the French invested the Spanish city of Ciudad Rodrigo on 28 June until it fell on 10 July. The French then resumed their advance into Portugal, and on 28 August, they successfully captured the Portuguese fortress of Almeida. With his invasion route secure, Masséna now prepared for the final task, the destruction of Wellington's army.[4]

During the outset of the French invasion, Wellington chose not to reinforce the garrison of Ciudad Rodrigo. Instead, his army, minus a division of light infantry, which deployed in support of Almeida, remained in the mountains north of Lisbon, where the terrain was more advantageous to the defense. It was a decision that proved both wise and unpopular as his actions drew criticism in London and Cadiz for abandoning the people of Ciudad Rodrigo to the French. A commissary officer who served on Wellington's staff wrote, "Our army is in full retreat, and I expect that I will be home before Christmas. Lord Wellington keeps to himself, which makes it difficult to discover his intentions; but judging from all appearances, everything to me indicates flight not fight."[5]

Wellington had good reason not to risk his army in the "open country," where it could be destroyed by the superior French cavalry.[6] Instead he concentrated on the peak of Serra de Bussaco, which dominated the surrounding terrain and barred the French invasion route. On 27 September, the Anglo-Portuguese army fought the French, for the first time since Talavera, in the battle of Bussaco.[7] It was a brutal battle, and Wellington's occupation of the high ground proved critical. Despite the valor of the French columns that attempted to penetrate his center by a series of frontal assaults, Wellington's infantry repulsed the two major attacks. Unable to break the allied line, Masséna attempted to outflank Wellington's position. Wary of being separated from his line of communication to Lisbon, Wellington withdrew his army south toward the protection of the completed Lines of Torres Vedras. Masséna pursued, only to be stopped short by the barrier. Masséna had become aware of the presence of the defensive fortifications only two days before discovering them and was completely surprised by the strength and depth of the lines. Masséna's *chef de battalion*, Col. Jean-Jacques Pelet, described the French reaction upon discovering the fortifications: "At last we clearly discerned the English system of operation and the goal of their movements, which we had scorned until then. . . . We had no indication of their plan." On 14 October, Masséna probed the lines with two divisions, only to encounter Wellington's positions and nearly thirty thousand defenders. Unable to penetrate the fortifications or break through the allied army deployed behind it, the French laid siege to the lines.[8]

For the next month, Masséna's army suffered immensely in the wasteland in front of the lines as Wellington's defensive preparations took their toll. With his men's strength and morale dwindling, Masséna decided to withdraw into a more secure location. In October, he moved his army thirty miles northeast to the city of Santarém. For the next four months, the Army of Portugal maintained its vigil at a cost of more than twenty-five thousand men. Of these, only two thousand were killed in action, and nearly eight thousand were captured or deserted, while the rest fell to disease and starvation. Meanwhile, the French received fewer than seven thousand reinforcements and virtually no supplies from France.[9]

By now, Wellington knew what to expect from London and encountered government opposition throughout his campaign of 1810–1811. Unlike Masséna, however, whose army was isolated, Wellington faced political opposition from the Horse Guards and Admiralty concerning existing policies, as well as continual pressure from Liverpool about his refusal to consider a more defensive posture, especially his failure to implement a withdrawal plan from Portugal. Furthermore, Wellington was continually plagued by Treasury scrutiny of the escalating cost of the war.

In nearly every dispatch sent from England to the peninsula for six months, the challenge for Wellington was to conserve money while not risking his army. Following his withdrawal from Almeida in August, Wellington had complained to Liverpool that the constant pessimism from London had been "irksome." Furthermore, Wellington refused to fight without reinforcements under the same "cautious system of warfare" that Liverpool advocated. If he was going to stand, then he would need more men.[10] He also told Liverpool: "Nothing could be more desirable that either the contest should be given up at once, or that it should be continued with a force so sufficient as to render all opposition hopeless. . . . It has appeared to me the Government themselves felt no confidence in the measures which they were adopting; and that [no officer from England has arrived] who has not told me that it was generally expected that he would, on his arrival find the army embarking; and even some have told me that this expectation was entertained by some of the King's ministers."[11]

Wellington was also angry that the government had not provided the number of reinforcements he needed, despite Liverpool's promises in the spring of 8,000 reinforcements. It was not a new problem. Despite the growth of the British army from 150,000 troops in 1804 to well over 200,000 in 1809, the government was desperately short of able-bodied men to serve away from Britain. While service in the militia increased in popularity during the threat of invasion in 1804 and 1805, desertion in regular army units and religious disenfranchisement in Ireland had prevented the cabinet from tapping into a reliable stream of reinforcements and recruits. Therefore, the cabinet looked to British "overseas garrisons," the Portuguese, and allied nations for help in supplying Wellington with troops. While the Portuguese troops and the King's German Legion fought bravely, the majority of allied units did not. A particular thorn in Wellington's side, the Duke of Brunswick-Oels Jäger, had a notorious reputation for poor discipline, brawling, and desertion.[12]

Due to these troubles, Wellington requested Liverpool's assistance in forcing the commanders to transfer the designated troops to the peninsula.[13] The commander of the Maltese garrison, Sir John Stuart, refused to send the 3,630 men as he was ordered by London. By 1 August 1810, Wellington had received only a battalion from Halifax, numbering seven hundred men. With no sign of additional troops, Wellington told Liverpool, "it was very probable that [he would] be disappointed in the arrival of the reinforcements from the Mediterranean and North America." He also asked permission to draw troops from Cadiz until the others arrived. Liverpool agreed, and Wellington detached two thousands men from Cadiz to supplement the reinforcements from England. Unfortunately, many of the troops from England were suffering from the effects of the Walcheren fever and were unable to participate in Wellington's stand at Bussaco.[14]

Wellington persisted again by asking Liverpool for assistance in sending "positive orders" to the commanders in Halifax, Malta, and Sicily to provide reinforcements.[15] An irate Wellington told Pole, "I have terrible disadvantages to contend with. The army was and indeed still is, the worst British Army ever sent from England. The General Officers are generally very bad and indeed some of them a disgrace to the service. I am positively in no scrape; and if the country can be saved, we shall save it. Government had behaved in their usual weakness and folly about reinforcements and I shall get none of those been promised to me, but the [Brunswick-Oels Jäger] infantry, the whole Corps of which will desert!"[16]

In the wake of Wellington's complaints, Liverpool acerbated the situation by continuing to issue duplicitous messages. During the fall of 1810, as Masséna's army pursued Wellington toward Lisbon, Liverpool told Wellington, "I am at a loss to conceive upon what grounds you have supposed that the King's Minister's had no Confidence in the Measures adopted for the defense of Portugal." However, he added, "I never knew a question on which there was less difference of opinion in Cabinet, than upon the Subject of Portugal either as to the expediency of preserving in the defense of it as long as could be consistent with the safety of the British Army or as to the belief that there existed a fair chance of success." Because army officers wrote despondent letters home, Liverpool told Wellington, "Not one officer as far as I recollect expressed on the occasion any confidence as to probable success, and not a mail arrived from Lisbon which did not bring letters from officers of rank in the Army (many of which were communicated to me) avowing their opinions as the probability and even necessity of a speedy evacuation of the country."[17]

In a clear example of the secretary for war's inconsistency throughout the period, Liverpool told Wellington that he would order the British commander in Sicily to ship four regiments immediately. In the same message, however, he cautioned Wellington, "We must [choose] between a steady and continued exertion upon a moderate scale, and a great and extraordinary effort for a limited time.... If that the latter would bring the contest to a speedy and successful conclusion, it would certainly be the wisest course; but unfortunately the experience of the last fifteen years is not encouraging in this respect."[18]

In December, when it appeared that Wellington and the army had withstood the worst, Liverpool bombarded him with requests to save money: "Masséna's Retreat has given great satisfaction here.... In the mean time, if you find yourself quite secure for the next six months, it would be very desirable to make as large a saving as possible during that period under the Head of Transports."[19]

Liverpool's incessant demands to save money combined with the government's expectation that Wellington defend Portugal with minimal soldiers drove the general to tell his brother, "I doubt whether this government have the power or the inclination, or the nerves to do all that ought to be done to carry the contest on as it [ought] to be." Wellington also questioned the government's confidence in him: "I think you are mistaken in your conjectures respecting the confidence reposed in me by the Cabinet and the desire to reinforce this Army. [Liverpool] has been dabbling in a game separate from that to be played in this country ever since he came to office and he has never acted with me upon any broad or liberal system of confidence."[20]

Pole reassured his brother and gave him some candid advice. He instructed Wellington to be more open and critical in his dispatches with Liverpool: "If anything has happened that you disapprove of would it not be wise to confide it fully to Lord Liverpool? If you think him too reserved in his communications would it not be advisable to tell him?" To remedy the growing discordance between Wellington and the cabinet ministers, Pole advised Wellington to become more assertive in his future correspondence and to ask bluntly for what he needed.[21]

Wellington would heed his brother's advice in the future, but he could not escape the continued pleas from Westminster to save money. Even before Masséna's withdrawal in February 1811, Liverpool complained that Wellington was spending too much money. Compared with the campaigns of 1808 and 1809, in which the government spent £2.6 and £2.7 million, the campaign of 1810 cost the government nearly £9.2 million, which included the maintenance of the transports in the Tagus River. An anxious Liverpool wrote, "It is absolutely impossible to continue our exertion upon the present scale in the Peninsula for any considerable time. If the present amount and condition of our army is likely to enable us to bring the contest in Portugal to a short and successful issue, we must meet the difficulties. However, we must otherwise look, at no very distant period, wither to a reduction of the scale of our exertion or to the necessity of withdrawing our army altogether."[22]

Wellington responded sharply by telling Liverpool that it was impossible to compare the campaign of 1810 to 1808 because of the scale of operations involved. Furthermore, the costs of keeping the transports in the Tagus were the result of government's insistence and had not been included in the figures for 1808 and 1809. Wellington also told Liverpool that it cost more to keep troops in England than abroad. Finally, Wellington declared, "I have no doubt that if the British army were for any reason to withdraw from the peninsula, and the French government were relieved from the pressure of military operations on the Continent, they would incur all risks to land an army in His Majesty's dominions. Then His Majesty's subjects would discover what are the miseries of war.... God forbid that I should be a witness, much less an actor in the scene."[23]

Although Wellington's complaints about not possessing the confidence of the ministers were overstated, his brother's advice was certainly sound. Liverpool's statements regarding peninsular strategy were duplicitous. Government opposition to Wellington's plans always reached its peak as the threat of Masséna's invading army drew near, and relief came when victory was secure. Wellington would accomplish his mission of defending Lisbon and expelling the French from Portugal, and his success can be attributed to many factors; but the most important was his ability to identify French shortcomings and devise a strategy that capitalized on the obstacles Masséna faced.[24]

Wellington's logistics problems paled in comparison to Masséna's, largely due to Wellington's personal and professional relationship with Admiral Berkeley.[25] The relationship began inauspiciously, and at the beginning of the campaign, a great deal of tension existed between the two men. In a letter to Pole, who served as an undersecretary to the Admiralty, Wellington stated, "You and Lord Mulgrave have a general knowledge of the character of [Admiral Berkeley], but you have no notion of the difficulty of dealing with him in matters of detail.... His activity is unbounded and interferes with everything.... I have never seen a man with such a good education whose understanding is so defective and who has such a passion for new invented modes of doing ordinary things and such a contempt for everything that is practicable."[26] To the autocratically minded Wellington, Berkeley's incessant tactical and operational suggestions were a nuisance. The combination of Liverpool's constant questions and Berkeley's unsolicited advice concerning the evacuation of the army drove Wellington to write, "I tremble when I think I shall have to embark the Leopards in front of Bonaparte aided by such a man. [Berkeley] has already invented twenty new methods of putting Leopards into boats. Ever since I came to Portugal, I have been teased to death ... with propositions for new modes and methods of doing everything [from] the [reorganizing of the] Commissariat to the Artillery. I cannot help but to treat [these suggestions] with the contempt which they deserve."[27]

Although Wellington used humor to relay his concern, he quickly lost his patience with Berkeley: "I am obliged to give [Berkeley] answers, and to reason, to temporize, to delay, and to get rid of his impracticable nonsense in the best and least offensive mode in my power. But how is it to be when our decisions must go hand in hand; when everything to be done is to be understood by those who are to execute it is their daily business and must be performed immediately or cannot be performed at all."[28] In April, Wellington suggested to Pole that they transfer Berkeley to another command: "I do not much care whether Berkeley goes or not, and I hope that he not go rather than he should be removed against his wishes. . . . I think I have managed him better lately and have explained to him more than once that I am responsible and not he for all military matters in this country. Yet he still bores me and the heads of the departments to death and more than one of them has expressed a wish that [Admiral Berkeley] was not so great a general. . . . Your Admiral who has nothing to do in his own department of the service is a terrible bore [to all others.]"[29]

After receiving his brother's repeated complaints, Pole took action:

> I received your letter concerning Admiral Berkeley, which I thought so serious that I carried it to Lord Mulgrave [The first lord of the Admiralty] and authorized him to confidentially speak to the cabinet. The consequences I believe are that Lord Mulgrave has offered Berkeley command at Plymouth which if he accepts I hope Admiral Pellew will be sent to you. I do not know what will be done if Berkeley declines Plymouth. It is a melancholy thing indeed that all too often the interests of the country are sacrificed to private considerations. Lord Mulgrave I know will do what he can on the subject.[30]

In April, Mulgrave offered Admiral Berkeley command of the channel fleet based at Plymouth. Berkeley declined because he was currently serving in the only place where the Royal Navy was making a difference. He wrote Wellington, "Undoubtedly in the situation I am now placed, in the only spot almost where any active and essential service can be performed, it could not be expected I should accept [the Plymouth command].[31] Berkeley's willingness to subordinate his personal ambition for the war effort solidified Wellington's trust, and from that point forward, the two men's relationship improved dramatically. Wellington was fortunate that Berkeley remained on station, because the admiral became an invaluable ally. Berkeley's mastery of joint operations and logistics provided Wellington with the resources necessary to defeat Masséna, and the admiral's growing resolve to extrapolate on his orders from the Admiralty concerning supplies and the transportation of prisoners of war also helped Wellington defeat the French.

The problem of the disposition of French prisoners of war began in August 1810 when an entire Swiss battalion surrendered to a British unit in Porto. Wellington sent these prisoners to England in September 1810. During the next several months, more than eight thousand prisoners surrendered or were taken, more than one thousand wounded French soldiers captured at a hospital in Coimbra. The sick and starving French prisoners surrendered at a rate of more than fifty a day and quickly overwhelmed Wellington's ability to care for them.[32] Initially, Wellington held the French prisoners in barges anchored in Lisbon Harbor. The prison barges soon proved unacceptable because dysentery and disease spread quickly in the miserable conditions. Wellington responded by transporting the prisoners to England, where they would be held on prison barges at Plymouth, Portsmouth, and Norman Cross. To minimize cost, the prisoners would be sent to England in navy transports, which were already scheduled to return. In a letter to Berkeley, Wellington outlined his plan: "The way in which the matter is managed here is that all French prisoners are transported to Lisbon where they are collected and application is then made by [you to] transport them to England when there are sufficient numbers of prisoners to render it worth while to send a ship home with them."[33] This was not a new practice, as Wellington had sent more than two thousand prisoners of war, captured in a French hospital in Porto, to England in May 1809. The government had not complained of the practice then, but as the number of French prisoners increased in 1810 and 1811, Wellington faced stiff opposition from the lords of the Admiralty.[34]

The Admiralty Board informed Berkeley that the number of French prisoners of war in England was too great, and that the prisoners should remain in Portugal. Berkeley relayed the Admiralty's orders, and on 4 November, Wellington responded: "I beg to acquaint you that it is impossible to keep the [French] prisoners of war in [Portugal] and I hope you will send them home according to the former arrangements by the earliest opportunity."[35] Wellington placed Berkeley in a difficult position. Faced with disobeying his government or his commander, Berkeley chose to pursue a compromise solution. Instead of shipping the prisoners to England, Berkeley inquired about transporting the prisoners to the Cape Verde Islands, where the transports could be used to return horses to the peninsula.[36] Wellington agreed with Berkeley's suggestion: "I do not know of any objection to sending some of the prisoners to the Cape de Verde Islands; and if the Government should state none, I have no objection to allow vessels to go with them, as the voyage will not be longer than to England."[37]

Above all else, Wellington was insistent that the French prisoners not remain in Lisbon: "All I want is to get rid of the prisoners from Lisbon ... notwithstanding the orders of the Admiralty. These orders after all, are not positive." The problem with the Cape Verde Islands was that Berkeley had not consulted the governor of the islands prior to sending the first shipment of prisoners. The governor thus refused to allow the prisoners' entrance, and the deal was rejected.[38]

As the number of French prisoners grew throughout the winter and spring of 1811, Wellington resumed shipment of prisoners to England. Berkeley notified the Admiralty Office that negotiations with the governor of the Cape Verde Islands required more than two months, and this was time that Wellington could not afford. After he received "Wellington's most pressing directions," Berkeley informed the Admiralty, "I have therefore ventured to infringe upon their Lordships said recommendation and have availed myself to send part of the French officers and men, aboard the ship, HMS *Dolphin* to England."[39] Berkeley's actions angered the Lords, who could not comprehend an admiral subjugating their instructions for a British general. The secretary of the Admiralty, Sir John Barrow, wrote Berkeley, "I am commanded to acquaint you that the Lords of the Admiralty are extremely sorry that you have found it necessary to send these prisoners to England. There are now about 50,000 French prisoners in [England] and the difficulty of disposing of them is very great." He repeated "in the strongest terms the [Admiralty's] expectation that nothing short of absolute necessity shall induce you to send home any other prisoners except officers, and they trust that some arrangement may be speedily made for disposing of them in the Cape Verde Islands, as proposed by the Portuguese Government or elsewhere."[40]

Another concern was the transmission of disease among detainees. The Admiralty informed Berkeley, "the number of sick prisoners already brought to this country from Portugal has not only filled our hospitals but also has spread contagion to a considerable degree among the prisoners who were in health." However, their greatest concern was the cost: "Any further increase of prisoners of this description must be attended with very great inconvenience and expense . . . the prisoners of war in Portugal to be kept there for the present, rather than to be sent to this country."[41]

The Admiralty had no command authority over Wellington, so it forwarded its concerns to Lord Liverpool for action. Lt. Col. Henry Bunbury, Liverpool's military secretary, presented the concerns to Liverpool on 3 December. Within a week, Liverpool responded by writing to Wellington "on the subject of the very serious inconvenience that is occasioned by the increasing number of French prisoners in this country." He informed Wellington that "in consequence of these representations, you will adopt such measures as may be practicable to dispose of the French prisoners (with the exception of the officers) who may fall into your hands in Portugal, in any other way than that of sending them to England."[42] Liverpool also forwarded a report from a British admiral, who complained "of the fatal effects which have resulted from sending home French Prisoners among whom a very dangerous fever presided aboard the Ship-of-War. The greatest care should be taken not to embark any who may bring with them the hazard of infectious or contagious diseases."[43] Liverpool insisted that the Portuguese government care for the prisoners.

Wellington responded to Liverpool's direct order with guarded compliance: "I have received your letter concerning the French prisoners, and the directions, which it contains, will of course be attended to." Yet, he disagreed with Liverpool's assessment of the Portuguese ability to care for the prisoners: "It is vain to expect any assistance, either in money or otherwise from the Portuguese Government to provide for the removal of these prisoners or for the care of them at Lisbon, or in any distant part of the world." Wellington concluded with a condemning appraisal of his government's conduct of the entire situation: The care of the French prisoners, "as well as everything else, must fall on me; and I must take the best care of them I can."[44]

Wellington was also unwilling to parole French officers and prisoners. Some French officers who had been paroled had returned to serve against him. Wellington warned Admiral Berkeley of this practice: "I am sorry to say that under the existing circumstances, no confidence can be placed in the parole of any French officer. I know many that have been allowed to leave England and who are now serving with the French armies in the Peninsula." His rationale was that the men served as intelligence: "At this moment, though my whole army are within a few miles of [the French], they do not know where we are; but if disabled prisoners are to be sent to them, they will get all the information they require.... I am therefore of the opinion that the disabled as well as other prisoners ought to be sent to England and thence France, if the Government is desirous of getting rid of them."[45]

After the freedom of Portugal was assured by Wellington's victory at Fuentes d'Oñoro, Liverpool reversed his policy concerning the shipment of French prisoners to England. On 25 June, Wellington informed Berkeley to resume the prisoner transfers. Berkeley was happy to do so, and over the course of the next several years, Wellington sent nearly twenty thousand French prisoners to England.[46] Nevertheless, during the crucial months of October 1810–March 1811, Berkeley supported Wellington by sending French prisoners to England despite his instructions from London. While the government claimed that holding French prisoners in England spread disease, it showed little reluctance to send thousands of British reinforcements to the peninsula who suffered from the Walcheren fever. Ultimately, the government's unwillingness to accept French prisoners was driven by finance, and not inconvenience.

Therefore, Wellington must be credited for his focus on strategic goals and his ability to prevent political interference from altering the course of victory in 1810–1811. Yet, his struggles for appointment authority with the Horse Guards and his struggle with the Royal Navy would continue throughout the remainder of the war, as would the problem of securing financial support and public approval to wage it. Nevertheless, the defense of Portugal in 1810–1811 was a pivotal point of Wellington's two-front war. Never again would he be forced to seek such desperate measures on the path to a peninsular victory.

William Grenville, 1st Baron Grenville, by John Hoppner. Leader of the opposition Whig Party. (Reproduced courtesy of the National Portrait Gallery, London.)

Richard Colley Wellesley, Marquess Wellesley, by J. P. Davis. Wellington's oldest brother and a source of political contention in 1812. (Reproduced courtesy of the National Portrait Gallery, London.)

George Canning, by Sir Thomas Lawrence. Foreign minister and great orator of his age. (Reproduced courtesy of the National Portrait Gallery, London.)

André Masséna, duc de Rivoli, prince d'Essling, marechal de l'Empire in 1804 (1756–1817), by Edme-Adolphe Fontaine. Wellington's worthy adversary in 1810–1811. (Reproduced courtesy of Réunion des Musées Nationaux / Art Resource, NY)

Henry Bathurst, 3rd Earl of Bathurst, by William Salter. As secretary of war, he delivered the required support and prioritization to Wellington's army. (Reproduced courtesy of the National Portrait Gallery, London.)

Robert Stewart, 2nd Marquess of Londonderry (Lord Castlereagh), by Sir Thomas Lawrence. Secretary for War and personal friend, Castlereagh was most responsible for dispatching Wellesley to Iberia in 1808 and for giving him a second chance in 1809. (Reproduced courtesy of the National Portrait Gallery, London.)

Robert Jenkinson, 2nd Earl of Liverpool, by Sir Thomas Lawrence. Secretary for War, prime minister, and frequent target of Wellington's tirades, Liverpool ultimately gave Wellington the required support for victory. (Reproduced courtesy of the National Portrait Gallery, London.)

Robert Dundas, 2nd Viscount Melville, by Charles Turner. First lord of the Admiralty. Leader of the most powerful navy in the world, he struggled to provide Wellington with required resources in 1813. (Reproduced courtesy of the National Portrait Gallery, London.)

Arthur Wellesley, 1st Duke of Wellington, study for a portrait by Francisco de Goya. The cumulative strain of a lengthy campaign on his face, Wellington sat for a portrait shortly after his liberation of Madrid in 1812. (© The Trustees of the British Museum.)

6

THE TIDE TURNS: THE PURSUIT OF MASSÉNA, 1811–1812

> If Boney had been there, we should have been beaten.
> Wellington to Wellesley-Pole, 2 July 1811

In the spring of 1811, following his failed invasion of Portugal, Marshal André Masséna retreated into Spain with Wellington in pursuit. Yet, despite his brilliant defense of Lisbon against determined French attacks, Wellington was still unable to fully exploit his success against Masséna's battle-weary army due to three major French-held fortresses—Badajoz, Almeida, and Ciudad Rodrigo—that guarded the approaches into the heart of Spain.

Situated on the Guadiana River opposite the Portuguese fortress of Elvas, Badajoz commanded the routes in southern and central Spain from Portugal south of the Tagus River. Compounding Wellington's problem, on 11 March the French captured Badajoz. In a letter to his brother Henry, British ambassador to Cadiz, Wellington termed the surrender of Badajoz as "the most significant event of the Peninsular War."[1] Wellington's statement was an exaggeration, but the French capture of Badajoz forced Wellington to spend the remainder of 1811 assembling a field army and siege train for breaching the walls of the fortress. The resulting delay cost the allies critical time and delayed the pursuit of Masséna's army.

In addition to Badajoz, which controlled the southern route into Spain, the fortresses of Almeida and Ciudad Rodrigo controlled access to the northern invasion route into Spain. Although neither Ciudad Rodrigo nor Badajoz would fall to the British until 1812, control of these key fortifications would bring about several important battles throughout the remainder of 1811.

As Wellington pursued Masséna toward the Spanish border, he resolved to recapture Almeida. In late April, Wellington besieged the fortress, and Masséna sought to relieve Almeida's French garrison. From 3–5 May, the two armies clashed for the last time as Wellington's army eventually repulsed the French attempt to relieve the siege at the village of Fuentes d'Oñoro. Although Wellington's victory at Fuentes d'Oñoro was a tactical success, lack of coordination and willful disobedience of his orders by several of his commanders allowed the French garrison of Almeida to escape.[2]

In a parallel action to the south, Marshal Nicholas Soult attempted to relieve the garrison of Badajoz. While Wellington led the allied army in the north, Marshal William Carr Beresford, acting in place of the convalescent Gen. Rowland Hill, commanded the allied army that besieged Badajoz. On 16 May, Soult forces attacked Beresford's troops at Albuera in one of the most disjointed and bloody fights of the war. During the battle, French cavalry outflanked Beresford's right flank and threatened his headquarters staff. Beresford was personally involved in hand-to-hand combat with a Polish lancer. In the close fighting, the marshal panicked and issued a series of contradictory orders that confused his subordinate commanders. Ultimately, Beresford's subordinates accurately assessed the situation and fought the battle to its conclusion. The results of the battle were mixed: Soult lost approximately eight thousand men and abandoned his relief attempt. Beresford claimed a hollow victory in the process, but he still lost about six thousand men. After Albuera, Marshal Soult withdrew, and Wellington moved south to relieve Beresford and resume the allied siege of Badajoz.[3]

Despite repulsing both French armies, the heavy casualties suffered in the battles of Fuentes d'Oñoro and Albuera characteristically caused many of Wellington's detractors in London to once again question his strategy. The opposition party attacked Wellington for not pursuing the French more rapidly, and after major battles, they blamed Wellington for high casualty rates. Wellington remained optimistic and was largely unperturbed by his critics. He kept his own counsel and was determined to build a broad base of communications and logistics before he ventured into the unforgiving and bare plains of Spain. He wrote his friend Charles Arbuthnot, who later served as Liverpool's patronage secretary, "I hope that we should get on [with the campaign in Portugal] prosperously. But people in England must not be in too great a hurry. They must give us time to do things by degrees and I hope I shall be able to perform them without great loss." Believing that war would break out in 1811 in central Europe, Wellington cautiously added, "If there is a war in the north, Boney's situation in Spain will not be a bed of roses this year . . . however, if there is not a war in the north, it is impossible that [Napoleon's] fraudulent and disgusting tyranny can be endured much longer." Wellington concluded by arguing for increased support in the peninsula: "If Great Britain can only hold out, I think we shall yet bring the affairs of the Peninsula to a satisfactory termination."[4]

Despite Wellington's pleas for support and patience, the opposition blamed him personally for the losses suffered at Albuera. In addition, they questioned Wellington's selection of Beresford as his second in command. Despite Marshal Beresford's personal bravery, he was viewed as foolhardy. Adding to the chorus of skeptics, Pole warned Wellington about the implications of allowing Beresford to remain in charge of such an important force. It appeared to some in London that Beresford's personal courage on the battlefield was more befitting an infantryman than a commanding general. Pole explained,

> Beresford's action is considered here as a proof of the astonishing bravery of the British troops, which appears to have saved him and his army—there are so many letters from the army detailing particulars that everybody knows the whole story, even to the General's loss of Head and ordering the retreat etc. . . . But the truth is Beresford has entirely lost all hope of being considered by us lookers on as general and I think it most fortunate that you did not leave him longer to himself. And also that you propose to give his command to Hill or rather let Hill take what is naturally his and leave General Beresford to arrange the Portuguese.[5]

Wellington understood only too well that his political masters were subject to public opinion; so any forthcoming financial and materiel support depended on the public's perception of victory. In the eyes of a fickle and skeptical Parliament, Wellington's failure to prevent the escape of the Almeida garrison tainted his subsequent defeat of Masséna at Fuentes d'Oñoro and his other successes in 1811. Pole attempted to relieve Wellington's concern by writing, "The whole of your proceeding of the siege of Fortress of Almeida and escape of the Garrison are perfectly understood here and I do not think you have ever gained any more achievement than by the battle of Fuentes d'Oñoro. The escape of the Garrison of Almeida is thoroughly well understood here and the blame falls where it ought on the *gallant officers* who certainly upon that occasion worthy of the character in which I have always given them."[6]

Despite his brother's reassurance, Wellington was not able to distance himself from the incompetence of his generals. Even the House of Commons withheld its accustomed praise for Wellington's campaign. While the escape of the garrison was not Wellington's fault, he realized that all operations were his responsibility, and therefore he understood Parliament's decision, as he explained to Pole: "Lord Liverpool was quite right not to move 'thanks' for the battle at Fuentes d'Oñoro; though it was the most difficult one I was ever concerned in, and against the greatest odds. If Boney had been there, we should have been beaten."[7]

Wellington was a fast learner who appreciated that printer's ink could be more deadly to his cause than the enemy's sword. Unwilling to allow the press to sway public opinion once again against him, Wellington resolved to alter his dispatches and strictly manage all casualty reporting, even when those figures were misleading or wrong. Therefore, after Albuera, Wellington took measures to ensure the battle was viewed as a victory at home. After reading Beresford's preliminary dispatch of 17 May, Wellington a instructed his military secretary to rewrite the "whining report."[8] To Pole, he boasted, "The battle of Albuera was a strange concern. [The Allies] were never determined to fight it; they did not occupy the ground as they ought; they were ready to run away at every moment from the time it commenced till the French retired; and if it had not been for me, who am now suffering from the loss and disorganization occasioned by the battle, [Beresford] would have written a whining report on it, which would have driven the people in England mad. However, I prevented that."[9]

In Beresford's original dispatch, the general had downplayed the size of Marshal Soult's force and despondently claimed, "I need not say how adverse I have been to and how much I dislike the situation my army is at present placed. . . . I consented to oppose Soult. . . . we have by beating him escaped total destruction which must have been the consequence and I am very far from feeling happy after our triumph."[10] Concerned about Beresford's losses and disposition after the battle, Wellington traveled to meet him at Albuera on 21 May. In the meantime, Wellington's military secretary, Fitzroy Somerset, revised the original dispatch to reflect a more optimistic tone before it was sent home to London. Several lines were added to reinforce the appearance of victory and the presence of adequate command and control: "Thou we faced the enemy's principal attack . . . we acted in a most noble manner, leading on the [attack] in admirable order."[11] In a subsequent dispatch to Beresford, Wellington reassured his general, "Your loss by all accounts has been very large, but I hope that it will not prove so large as was first supposed. You could not be successful in such an action without a large loss; and we must make up our minds to affairs of this kind sometimes, or give up the game."[12] Wellington was completely unapologetic and never regretted his actions to change the public and political perception of the battle. Many years later at a dinner party in 1836, his friend, Lord Stanhope, recorded Wellington's reaction to a question concerning his amendment of the Albuera dispatch for the English papers. Wellington claimed, "Beresford's letter was quite in a desponding tone. It was brought to me the next day . . . and I said directly 'this won't do, write me down a victory.' The dispatch was altered accordingly."[13]

To assist Wellington in his administration, the government provided a small military press corps to accompany his headquarters. The role of this press contingent was nothing like the modern sense; they printed general orders and other documents intended for circulation. Closely supervised by Wellington's adjutant, the press was better controlled to influence opinion at home.[14]

The success of the British advance through Portugal and the victory at Fuentes d'Oñoro had further enhanced Wellington's prestige in England. The opposition's hostility toward the war in Portugal had waned, and the ministers reveled in the glory of the moment. When Wellington's amended dispatch of 7 May reached London, it found the government in discussion over several important decisions that would affect British long-term strategy in the peninsula. Accordingly, Liverpool notified Wellington that the government would not reduce the size of his army and instead had agreed to reinforce him with more than six thousand infantry, a fresh regiment of light cavalry, and a shipment of horses. Furthermore, they granted him the authority to withdraw troops from Cadiz if he deemed necessary. Most important, they finally granted him complete operational discretion to carry out offensive operations in Portugal and in Spain.[15] In his letter to Wellington, Liverpool stated, "His Royal Highness is sensible to the great advantage which may arise from investing in you with full discretion to undertake such operation as may be best calculated at the time to bring the war to a successful termination; and you will consider yourself therefore at liberty to employ the means necessary . . . to attain that important object."[16]

This decision marked a significant shift in the government's policy. For the first time since the government had been formed in 1809, Wellington was granted the ability not only to defend Portugal, but also to undertake any offensive action to protect the peninsula as a whole. While the fruits of their decision would not be realized until 1813, when Wellington moved his combined allied army into France, the reaction to the ministry's renewed pledge of support in London was mixed. Although the opposition party remained unconvinced that Albuera was a victory, it could not effectively challenge the ministry in Parliament. Masséna's withdrawal and Wellington's victory in the spring of 1811 facilitated the opposition's decline in power and led to a dramatic change in the Whig Party's stance toward the war. No issue provides more clarity on this shift than does the debate over increasing the Portuguese subsidy in the spring of 1811.

In late January 1811, Wellington advocated an increase in the 1809 subsidy of £1 million annually. The subsidy did not adequately cover the thirty thousand troops it was designed for, and Wellington did not think the Portuguese Regency Council was doing enough to raise its own money. Furthermore, corruption existed at every level of the Portuguese government, and loan payments were not guaranteed to reach the troops. All these problems coincided with an antiquated and grossly inefficient Portuguese commissariat. In January, Wellington told his brother Richard that, as a consequence of the abuses within the Portuguese system, twelve thousand to fourteen thousand Portuguese troops "are literally starving."[17] By March, the situation was worse. Wellington told Stuart, "matters cannot go on as they are; there must be a radical change in the whole system of Government, in respect for carrying on the war, or I shall recommend to His Majesty's government to withdraw his army."[18] Unlike loan payments, Wellington had control of the subsidy payments, and he saw them as a tool with which he could manipulate Forjaz and the various ministers to reform the Portuguese commissariat.[19] He also wanted to ensure that the kingdom's provincial governors reformed their administration and transport systems.[20]

Despite the need for an increased subsidy, Wellington's proposal had to first successfully navigate the corridors of Westminster, where pessimism was common and the ability of the Portuguese to contribute to the war was continually questioned. In March 1811, the Whigs had attacked the government's proposal to double the Portuguese subsidy from £1 million to £2 million. William Ponsonby, the Whig leader in the House of Commons, remarked that "our success consists in having lost almost all of Portugal, and that our army is now confined or hemmed in between Lisbon and Cartaxo." Furthermore, he asked, "How long can this country support this expense?"[21] Gen. Banastre Tarleton, a persistent critic of the government's handling of the Peninsular War, echoed this sentiment. Tarleton believed that "ruin alone could be the result" of increasing the subsidy.[22] However, there was less debate in the House of Lords. In a private letter Grenville, the Whig leader, Lord Auckland, wrote "that three campaigns had shown the government's incompetence and impolicy."[23]

In response to the parliamentary criticism, Liverpool notified Wellington that England could no longer support an offensive war at the current level of expenditure, but with the caveat that England could support a defensive war. His justification was based purely on mathematics. The expenditures of 1810 were in excess of £6 million, far exceeding those of 1808, which Liverpool estimated at £2.7 million, and more than £3 million over the limits established at the conclusion of the 1809 campaign. Liverpool feared that offensive operations in 1811 would quickly exceed England's ability to pay for the war. He told Wellington, "It is the unanimous opinion of every member of the government and of every person associated with finances that it is absolutely impossible to continue our exertion under the present scale . . . for any considerable time."[24]

Wellington viewed the government's inability to defend the expenditure of his operations as a weakness. Furthermore, he resented that Liverpool's comparison of the expenditures of 1810 with 1809. In his mind, the two were not the same. Liverpool failed to consider the increased cost of maintaining transports in the region throughout Masséna's invasion to extricate the army, which was certainly not Wellington's intention or directive, and failed to recognize the increased cost of procuring specie. He told his brother, "The British Army in Portugal did not cost more than a million or a million and a half more [in 1810] and this is the mighty sum which Great Britain cannot afford?" An exasperated Wellington concluded, "I can only assure the Government that if it does not give Boney employment here . . . he will give them employment at home; and they will not find it so easy to husband our resources as imagined."[25]

The first reports of Masséna's withdrawal into Spain reached London on 26 March 1811, immensely affecting Liverpool's assessment of Wellington's operations and the subsidy arrangement.[26] Although Wellington's official dispatches did not arrive until 6 April, a Whig observer noted, "I must tell you that people as usual begin to give Lord Wellington great credit for the campaign; those who were before abusing his delay are now applauding his foresight and wisdom. . . . Every prediction on the part of the Opposition with respect to the issue of the campaign—that we should lose our whole army, be obliged to embark in six weeks, etc, etc. was said too heedlessly, and too frequently, has been successively refuted by the event, and given the people a poor opinion of [the opposition's] sagacity. Meanwhile [the Ministry] triumph over them and with some good reason."[27] Following Wellington's victory, the government increased the subsidy from £1 million to £2 million.[28] Liverpool thanked Wellington for the news and promised more aid: "You know our means both military and financial are limited, but such as they are, we are determined not to be diverted from the Peninsula to other objects. If we can strike a blow we will strike it there. . . . The good news you have sent us [concerning Masséna's withdrawal] has greatly assisted us. Perceval's character is completely established in the House of Commons—He has acquired an authority there beyond any Minister within my recollection except William Pitt."[29]

The opposition also reluctantly seconded Liverpool's recommendation for a vote of thanks for Wellington and his campaign. Even the venerable Whig leader, Lord Grey, admitted that this marked a complete reversal of his previous stance, and now he anticipated a favorable result to the campaign. In a rare moment of praise for Wellington, Grey stated, "By the most patient perseverance under unfavorable circumstances, and at the moment of action by the most skilful combination of force and the most determined courage, a great success has been achieved by Lord Wellington." Along with praise, Grey averred that the war was far from over and that the Spanish would have to assume a greater role.[30]

Both houses of Parliament issued their thanks for the successful defense of Portugal and repulsion of Masséna. However, by the time the measure had passed, the battle of Albuera had occurred. Because Wellington altered the dispatch, Albuera was viewed as victory, but he had not been present on the field and therefore was not included in Parliament's "thanks." In a letter to Wellington, Pole explained the peculiar circumstances of Parliament's decision to not include him:

> Lord Liverpool told me that he had written to you respecting the conversation that took place in the House of Lords when the thanks were moved to Beresford—I told him that I was sure you would feel the Ministers were right in not thanking you on that occasion as you had already been thanked for the campaign, it would have appeared as if the Ministers had determined not to thank other officers without giving you a share of it. And I am sure they proposed properly a vote of thanks more or less to you is of no consequence to your reputation—and Beresford had a fair right after his more bloody battle to a vote of thanks—I need not tell you how highly you now stand with all ranks and parties. You must already know it from the Public Prints and private correspondence I think you are now above any intrigue that can be served against you.[31]

Despite Pole's confidence and praise, and the Whig's reversal concerning the war, the opposition remained privately pessimistic about Wellington's chances for victory. In a private letter to Grenville, Grey wrote, "The French are on the point of making a great effort in Portugal . . . which Lord Wellington will find himself unable to resist. But even if such an effort could not take place or should not succeed, I am convinced the period when we shall be obliged to give up the contest from an absolute inability to support the expense is fast approaching." Grenville replied, "I hope to presume whether you are as strongly impressed as myself with the desperate and hopeless character of waging war on the continent."[32]

The opposition leaders were prophetic—Wellington and the allied army still occupied a precarious position in the peninsula. While the allies controlled the approaches into Spain and had begun to formally besiege Badajoz and Ciudad Rodrigo in the summer of 1811, the French still outnumbered Wellington's forces by five to one in the peninsula. Furthermore, despite Spanish resistance in the provinces of Valencia and Cadiz, the French still controlled most of the major cities in Spain.

With their apparent advantage, it did not take the French long to regroup. In June 1811, in response to Wellington's operations against Badajoz, Marshal Soult and Marshal Auguste Marmont, who had replaced Masséna as the commander of the *armée du Portugal*, massed their forces in southern Spain and marched in support of the besieged French garrison. Wellington lifted his siege of Badajoz, withdrew into Portugal, and occupied a position between the fortresses of Elvas and Campo Maior. The French, relieved that Wellington withdrew, chose not to attack, and Soult withdrew to the south. Marmont occupied a defensive position near the Portuguese border for nearly a month; however, running short on supplies, he retired to Old Castille on 15 July. Wellington pursued him to Fuente Guinaldo.[33]

In the fall, Wellington established a strong defensive position in the north at Fuente Guinaldo, awaiting an opportunity to attack Ciudad Rodrigo. His chance came in January 1812, as Marmont transferred troops east from Ciudad Rodrigo to aid Marshal Louis Gabriel Suchet in Valencia. Wellington's troops stormed the fortress on 19 January 1812.[34] In his report, Wellington remarked that the French had made a serious mistake leaving the border fortress unprotected by a covering force and complained about the deplorable condition of his army due to supply shortages. He mused that the French "were convinced that we were too sickly to undertake anything."[35]

Capitalizing on his advantage, Wellington quickly used surprise and marched his army south to again capture Badajoz. Despite severe hardship and delay to move an adequate siege train into position, Wellington's troops took the fortress after a particularly bloody assault on 6 April.[36]

The assaults on Ciudad Rodrigo and Badajoz brought out the worst in Wellington's army, as his men sacked and looted both towns. The most severe breach of discipline occurred after the storming of Badajoz, as thousands of British soldiers unleashed a torrent of rape and destruction on the city's population. According to a British officer who observed the scene, "The place was completely sacked by our troops; every atom of furniture broke; beds ripped open in search of treasure; and one street literally strewed with articles, knee deep. A convent was in flames, the poor nuns in dishabille, striving in vain to burrow themselves into some place of security. Officers who tried to restrain their men were murdered."[37] One soldier witnessed, "Women [being] dragged from hiding and raped, even in the churches where they had fled for their safety." Order was finally restored forty-eight hours later when Wellington's provost marshal erected gallows in the city center.[38]

In his dispatches following the sacking of Badajoz, Wellington never mentioned the total loss of control of his army. Instead, his report included the comment, "It is impossible that any expressions of mine can convey the sense which I entertain of the gallantry of our officers and troops on this occasion."[39] Furthermore, no mention of the breach of discipline was reported in the London papers. Not surprisingly, in reaction to the news of the occupation of Badajoz, Parliament voted Wellington its "thanks."[40] In the wake of a bloody siege, the actions of his men and the relentless pursuit of destruction were overlooked. Therefore, the most serious issue of restoring discipline in Wellington's army went unresolved until Vitoria in 1813.

Following his victory at Badajoz, Wellington again moved into Spain. He preceded his advance by encouraging guerilla activity in Asturias, Andalucia, and several other Spanish provinces.[41] Liverpool, sensing success, supported Wellington's advance by ordering a series of diversionary operations against French coastal targets. The first units involved were troops under Sir William Bentinck, commander of British forces in Sicily. He was ordered to launch a diversionary attack against Marshal Suchet on the east coast of Spain. Liverpool also approved joint operations against the French positions along the Bay of Biscay in northern Spain. Although these diversions were not decisive, they were an example of the War Department coordinating operations in support of Wellington's primary objective: the destruction of Marshal Marmont's force, which held Old Castille.[42]

Wellington finally marched against Marmont on 13 June. Three days later, he entered the city of Salamanca. Marmont's army was dispersed and required time to organize and consolidate. On 22 July, after nearly a month of maneuvering and repositioning, the French and allied armies met again at the battle of Salamanca. It was a bloody yet glorious day for Wellington—his army inflicted over fourteen thousand French casualties, including the capture of over seven thousand prisoners. Even Wellington, although not seriously hurt, did not escape the fighting; a ricocheted musket ball at the close of the day's fighting hit him in the leg. The French army retired, and after an ineffectual pursuit, Wellington moved into central Spain.[43]

Despite the heavy casualties on both sides, Salamanca proved that Wellington and his Anglo-Portuguese army could maneuver and attack as effectively as they could mount a stubborn defense. Except for the defense of Lisbon in 1810, Wellington usually opted for offensive operations. Up until Salamanca, defensive operations were more popular with cautious politicians in London, who consistently feared the excessive casualty list that large battles always brought. The spectacular victory at Salamanca changed London's appraisal of the contest and expectations rose accordingly. After the battle, politicians consistently favored offensive action and questioned Wellington's inability to pursue and destroy French armies.

The ministers also failed to realize the hazards of operating in central Spain, which meant that Wellington was surrounded by French forces and was forced to requisition supplies in desolate conditions. While poor roads and barren country plagued both armies, Wellington was also hampered by ineffectual coordination with the Spanish. After Talavera in 1809, Wellington vowed never to rely on Spanish generals again. However, to exploit the hard-fought gains of Salamanca and to prevent Marmont's escape required the support and compliance of the Spanish army. Despite their efforts to help Wellington, the Spanish failed to block a key river crossing at Alba de Tormes, allowing Marmont and his shattered army to escape.[44] The magnitude of the victory could not be undone by the error, and Wellington's popularity with the Spanish legislative body in Cadiz, the Cortes, swelled to unprecedented levels with the victory. Henry, in Cadiz, wrote,

> I heartily wish you joy of your glorious victory, and I wish you could have witnessed the effect it produced here. It is the only

time I have witnessed in this town anything like the feelings of patriotism and enthusiasm which I believe to exist in other parts of Spain. . . . The Cortes at the recommendation of the Regency has conferred upon you the order of the Golden Fleece. . . . In short, ample justice is done to your exertions. . . . I am sure there is not a man in Cadiz (with the exception of those who are Frenchmen at heart) who does not feel that it is to our exertions that there is still a probability of his being delivered from the French.[45]

Despite the victory and adulation of the Spanish Cortes, some in London viewed the 1812 campaign as the ruination of the British economy and a prelude to military disaster. Silenced by the victory in Parliament, private opposition was abundant. The Whig leader Lord Auckland claimed, "Marmont's unaccountable folly has given a fortunate brilliancy to Wellington's campaign which was leading to a lame and impotent conclusion." Auckland further suggested that future peninsular operations combined with the ongoing support to Russia would drain England of its resources: "More battles must be risked, more blood must be spilt, the boundless and distressing expenditure must be greater than ever, and further campaigns must be prepared. Add all of this the new incalculable drains from Russia and from America. . . . On the whole I see our home predicament with entire disgust and indignation, and our foreign speculations with dismay and despair."[46] Auckland's complaints were valid: England's global war against Napoleon caused a severe financial crisis that threatened Wellington's 1812 campaign.

By the summer of 1812, Britain's Iberian operations were in deep financial trouble because the Iberian Peninsula was but one of three major global endeavors against France. In addition to the peninsula, the British subsidized the Russian armies and were waging war on the high seas off North America. Wellington's financial problems, while important, were but one of many principal demands on the crown's coffers.

The government had only two immediate sources of money to fund Wellington's army. The first of these was for the Bank of England to issue interest-bearing bonds and give the proceeds to the Treasury for distribution—Wellington was one of several recipients. The other, and more immediate, was for Wellington to order his commissariat to sequester (in exchange for promissory notes drawn upon the Bank of England) money from the major trading centers of Gibraltar, Cadiz, and Lisbon. Not surprising, a tremendous amount of friction in London resulted from the existence of these two separate sources of funding. On one hand, the Treasury and the commissary in chief, who supervised the local commissariat officers in the peninsula, felt that their subordinate peninsular commissariat departments had failed to adopt the best methods to raise cash locally and therefore reduce expenditure. On the other hand, Wellington and his staff of commissariat officers felt that the Treasury in London and the commissary in chief failed to aggressively procure specie abroad and deliberately withheld the money in English banks, thereby forcing Wellington to make do with the funds given.[47]

Procuring enough money in 1812 from local trade was not a new problem. When Wellington returned to the peninsula in April 1809, the most important local source of cash was the sale of bills of exchange (or Treasury bills) by a private citizen, Sir James Duff, at Cadiz.[48] In late 1809, the British minister in Portugal, Charles Villiers, proposed a similar arrangement in Lisbon, and thereafter, the sale of Treasury bills in the Lisbon market became the principal money source for Wellington's army. In 1810, the Treasury investigated the activity of these private citizens to procure money, but it never stopped the practice. Wellington felt men with knowledge of local commerce presented him with an advantage, and so he defended the employment of Duff and Enrique Sampaio, the Portuguese citizen who purchased the majority of Treasury Bills in Lisbon.[49]

Despite his confidence in and defense of these private financiers, Wellington did not favor having his primary means of obtaining money rest on the unpredictable peninsular markets. He worried that sale of bills, dependent on an expensive rate of exchange, was often influenced by the current operational situation in the peninsula.[50] Furthermore, he felt that selling Treasury bills, assisted by occasional shipments of surplus money from the garrisons of Cadiz and Gibraltar to serve as the primary means of supply, was unreliable and in the long run would prove insufficient to support large combat operations. In Wellington's mind, the government should designate his army as the most important recipient of monetary shipments.

The underlying problem was twofold. First, the cost of the war had outpaced England's ability to fund it. By 1811, the cost of the war had jumped to nearly £11 million, of which 75 percent had been paid for in Treasury bills. The discount on these notes was nearly 25 percent, while the exchange rate dropped so low that 1 pound sterling would buy only 3.5 Spanish dollars, not 5. Second, from 1811 to 1812, there existed a worldwide shortage of gold and silver, primarily because of a large revolt in the Spanish American gold and silver mines. While the supply of gold was curtailed by events in the Spanish colonies, the demand for gold increased. To further restrict supply, the French captured the silver mines of southern Spain in the spring of 1810. The disruption of Britain's trade by Napoleon's Continental System also added to the general shortage. Furthermore, Britain's war against the United States in 1812 and Napoleon's invasion of Russia increased the demands on British gold worldwide. As a result of these factors, from 1811 to mid-1812, the price of gold on worldwide markets increased by nearly 25 percent.[51]

The effect of these price increases exacerbated the government's ability to supply Wellington with the gold he required. The commissary in chief, which from 1811 to 1816 was the young, well-respected financier John Herries, felt that Wellington underestimated the amount of money that could be produced locally and failed to appreciate the difficulty that the government had procuring gold and silver abroad. Furthermore, because of the fragmented command and control structure of the British army, Herries supervised Wellington's commissary officers in the peninsula through his own chain of command. The dual-headed command relationship led to problems because Herries and his band of bureaucrats in London often superseded Wellington's instructions to the men charged with providing money and supplies and the growing need for convoys for his army. Wellington could not even promote deserving commissary officers without London's approval. The problem affected Wellington's operations for the remainder of the war and was not resolved until the office of commissary in chief was abolished in 1816.[52]

By April 1811, Wellington was uncertain if Liverpool and the government had solved his financial problems. He informed Marshal Beresford, "I have not now the money to answer the demands of the British Army. . . . Let Government provide only decently for the British Army and I will be satisfied; or let them take the whole concern out of my hands, and I shall be happy to resign it."[53] By August, Wellington was unable to pay for local supplies, and his troops survived almost entirely on supplies transported from the coast by the navy at great inconvenience and expense. Furthermore, his Portuguese mule drivers went unpaid for six months. Fearing that the British might evacuate the peninsula and therefore not pay their expenses, the local mule drivers refused Treasury bills or credit payments. Wellington's troops were two months in arrears, with no relief in sight. Wellington complained bitterly for help. Aware of the danger of unpaid and ill-disciplined troops, an outraged Wellington felt that the government failed to consider his difficulty.[54]

In London, Liverpool tried to help. Temporary relief came at the end of August—$2 million dollars, worth approximately £500,000, from Cadiz merchants. The government promptly allocated $400,000 of this sum for Wellington's army. The ministry raised an additional $400,000 from foreign trade and shipped it to Wellington.[55] Wellington gave the Treasury rare praise and informed Liverpool that his distress had been relieved.[56] The relief was short lived, however, and by November, the army was once more in financial difficulty. Liverpool attempted to reassure his general that imminent relief would come from recent trade with the East Indies. Nevertheless, by the end of the year, this had produced minimal gain, and Liverpool informed Wellington that he could not send any more money for the remainder of the year. Wellington was also concerned that the government's inability to finance his soldiers would affect the Portuguese, in particular the commissariat that had performed so poorly.[57]

Despite Wellington's incessant pleas for relief, the gold shipments from England stopped. Liverpool defended the government's actions and assured Wellington that everything possible was being done to remedy the shortage. He also informed Wellington that during the last year, over 10 million Spanish dollars had been anticipated from South American trade, though only 1 million had been received. Despite this shortfall, the government managed to earn another 6.3 million dollars from trade with Portugal, the Cadiz merchants, and other areas around the Mediterranean. Furthermore, due to added demands on its gold reserves caused by increased subsidies to Russia, the government could only allocate another £400,000 to Wellington. Liverpool explained that demands for internal circulation and trade considerations had also hampered his supply of coinage. All sources of supply available within England had been considered and used, and the government remained unable to help. Liverpool solicited ideas from Wellington to relieve the burden.⁵⁸ Wellington suggested the remedy he had contemplated since 1809: issuing the commissary general interest-bearing Treasury bills to be sold to merchants in Portugal and Cadiz periodically to generate a source of independent revenue for his army.⁵⁹

The Treasury Board disagreed with Wellington's proposal on several points. First, Herries and the prime minister favored a cautionary fiscal policy. Above all else, the prime minister worried about allocating England's credit to the peninsula when victory there, despite Masséna's withdrawal and Wellington's resumption of the offensive, was still not assured. After all, in early 1812, Wellington was still vastly outnumbered in the peninsula, and the prospect of victory in Spain, despite Napoleon's plans to invade Russia, was still unknown. Also, Perceval and Herries feared that the mass dissemination of Exchequer bills in the peninsula would lead to forgery. As a result, issuing the bills not only could devalue Portuguese paper currency, but could also jeopardize the markets in Cadiz and London where these bills could be redeemed for stock. Liverpool relayed the government's concerns to Wellington and explained that if the bills were issued in accordance with his plan, the security of bills could not be guaranteed.⁶⁰

As Wellington planned the spring offensive of 1812, he answered Liverpool's caution by expressing his concern that the war could not continue under existing financial arrangements and that future operations could not be planned or conducted unless the British government could supply more money. To this end, Wellington told Liverpool, "we cannot expect to subsist exclusively on our magazines if we are to move the war into Spain. We shall get nothing from the Spanish people excepting from payment of money." Wellington also attempted to defuse the government's fears of forgery by claiming that his headquarters would issue small numbers of Exchequer bills and that because circulation would be kept at a minimum, forgery would be unlikely. He assured Liverpool that a minimal circulation of bills would not adversely affect Portuguese currency and added, "I may be mistaken in my expectations of getting anything for these bills, but I think the experiment is worth a trial. It can do no harm."⁶¹

Liverpool remained unconvinced that Wellington could provide security for the notes. In his response, he used the example of a recent mail shipment received from northern Europe where notes, circulated by Jewish merchants, had been forged. In London, Herries decided that too much "inconvenience" would result from Wellington's initial plan and that the Treasury would issue certificates worth 1,000 Spanish dollars to remedy the shortage. Herries's proposal was to offer interest-bearing certificates in return for dollars. He recommended an open-ended exchange rate, which, valued at five shillings, would be considerably lower than its issue price. Furthermore, the entire operation could be financed by government investment in the English stock market. It was hoped that Spanish investors would view the notes as a long-term investment, particularly because the notes drew semiannual interest, but also because the investor could redeem the certificates in either dollars or pounds sterling and therefore reduce the risk of losing money. The notes accumulated a semiannual rate of 5 percent interest and were redeemable in Cadiz, Lisbon, or England every three years.[62]

Very soon thereafter, Liverpool sent Wellington the first of the certificates. Although Wellington did not object to them, he felt they were inadequate and only a temporary measure to solve what he viewed as a temporary specie shortage in England. Wellington favored setting a two-year redemption period. In his mind, as long as the government repaid the notes after the exchange decreased, it would be impossible for the government to lose money. It was hoped through this arrangement that Wellington would issue the notes from his headquarters and, therefore, better control the actions of local merchants and mule drivers.[63]

The Treasury again disagreed with Wellington's plan. In a letter to Liverpool, Herries advised Perceval against setting a fixed expiration date on the notes, pointing out that the failure to pay in the peninsula was inevitable if a large number of holders presented their paper at the earliest redeemable date; thus the ensuing loss of credit would be too damaging to the English market to risk.[64] The prime minister compromised between the two-year maturities that Wellington wanted and open-ended maturity recommended by Herries with the three-year redemption stipulation. Wellington was angered that the government failed to act on his specific recommendation, fearful that the scheme would cause more harm than good. Consequently, he refused to issue the three-year certificates, and his money problems continued.[65]

Wellington viewed the true problem to be the government's systemic inability to solve the hard currency shortage. Until the government could find a solution, his operations would be jeopardized. To make matters worse, the bureaucrats in the Treasury from time to time exercised their long-distance control over the local commissary officials with written reprimands. One such reprimand was delivered to the acting commissary general, John Bissett, by Herries for obtaining $400,000 from Gibraltar at a price of 5 shillings 8 pence when the price in London was 4 pence less. Herries concern was that specie supplies for the army might be influenced by the higher Lisbon price, thereby making it much more expensive to purchase gold in the London market.[66]

Wellington viewed the charge as outrageous and intrusive and felt that the government did not understand the exigencies of a wartime environment. Wellington complained to Liverpool directly about Herries and the bureaucrats, who interfered with the commissary officers "on the spot" who attempted to raise money:

> I am only concerned that the Lords of the Treasury, who have invariably been made acquainted with these contracts did not make known their disapprobation of them at an earlier period, as if they had, I should not have sanctioned those offered. I can justify the measure adopted . . . upon no other ground than necessity. I also thought that it was the wish of the Lords of the Treasury, and of Government in general that I should authorize the adoption of every measure that was practicable, in order to procure specie for the army; but it appears that I have been mistaken, and I hope that Government will take measures to supply the deficiency which must exist in our funds from my refusal to sanction contracts of this description in the future.[67]

Smarting from Bissett's reprimand, and from what he felt was unwarranted interference from London, Wellington refused to accept the gold and silver that was exchanged in Gibraltar. In all, Wellington, despite his difficulties over money, refused several shipments that totaled nearly 500,000 Spanish dollars. Until he felt that the government had implemented a permanent solution and quit the absurd practice of reprimanding his commissary officers for trying to raise his money, he refused temporary solutions. He informed Liverpool, "I should have been in Andalucia, at the head of 40,000 men [raising the siege of Cadiz] . . . if it not for the want of money." He added:

I can scarcely believe that the Treasury is aware of the distresses of this army. We owe not less than 5 million dollars; the troops are two months in arrears and I have been able to allot only 100,000 dollars to the payment of the Portuguese subsidy in this month. The Commissary General is very apprehensive that he shall not be able to make good his engagements for the payment of meat for the troops. . . . It will be quite impossible to carry up salt meat as well as bread to the troops from the seacoast. The Treasury cannot expect that I shall take upon myself to sanction the measures of which they have expressed their positive disapprobation; and I hope that they will recall that disapprobation; or that they will adopt some efficient measures to serve this army with specie. . . . Your Lordship will observe that it is not improbable that we may not be able to take advantage of the enemy's comparative weakness in this campaign for the want of money.[68]

To make matters worse, in early 1812 political opposition surfaced yet again in Westminster concerning the cost of the war. In the House of Lords, the opposition party leadership questioned the commitment of England's gold reserves in what they considered a losing venture. In a private letter to Grenville, Grey reflected the opposition party's lack of resolve in continuing the war. As an example of the speculation in London that a peaceful solution could be negotiated in the peninsula, Grey referenced a peace treaty that Napoleon reportedly offered Britain prior to his invasion of Russia. In the House of Commons, the peace offer had been debated but never considered credible.[69] Privately, the prevailing defeatist attitude of the opposition leadership was clearly evident. Grey wrote that the government should accept the French peace proposal to end the war under the following conditions: "I know from undoubted authority what was brought by the flag of truce, but you must not repeat it to anybody. It was a proposal for peace; the terms offered England to keep all the colonies in her possession . . . Portugal to be restored to the House of Braganza. Spain to be confirmed to the King of Spain, Naples to the King of Naples; Sicily to the King of Sicily. The answer I have not heard; I should be very much inclined to say 'Done.'" Grey concluded his letter with a blanket condemnation of the government's willingness to support Wellington's strategy at the expense of the nation:

"The news from Portugal you will see in the papers is just enough to show that all this immense expense of blood and treasure is fruitless."[70] While Grey's assertions were shortsighted, they reflected the extent of worry about financial constraints in both England and the peninsula.

The financial hardship became so contentious that in May, Wellington asked Charles Stuart, in Lisbon, to no longer route any complaints from the Portuguese Regency Council about money to him. Instead, Wellington informed Stuart to relay the council's complaints directly to the Treasury officials in London: "I am not the Minister of Finance, nor is the Commissary General. It is the duty of the King's Ministers to provide supplies for the service, and not to undertake a service for which they cannot provide adequate supplies of money and every other requisite. They have thrown upon me a very unpleasant task in leaving me to decide what proportion of the money shall be applied to the service of the British Army, and what shall be paid to the King's Minister . . . and left me to find money to carry on the war as I could, they have, by their orders, cut off some of the resources which I had."[71]

Fortunately for Wellington, monetary relief came in a most unlikely and brutal manner. On 10 May 1812, Lord Perceval was assassinated in the lobby of Parliament. Liverpool was appointed the new prime minister; he immediately named Lord Henry Bathurst to succeed him in the War Department. While the politics did not change, the policies did, and Wellington was the beneficiary.

A long-standing, well-respected politician, Bathurst had served in cabinet positions in several administrations, including lord of the Admiralty and lord of the Treasury. Since 1804, Bathurst had served as the master of the mint and president of the Board of Trade. This experience and insight gained by his long service in financial matters greatly aided Wellington throughout the remainder of the Peninsular War.[72]

Bathurst viewed his first priority as maintaining Wellington's momentum by providing him with the country's full fiscal support. In doing so, Bathurst approached the monetary problem with speed and energy. He recognized that the government could not supply Wellington through purchases of gold on the open market because this would simply drive the price and demand for gold higher. Therefore, he sought an alternative. Bathurst demanded that the Bank of England immediately release the majority of its gold and silver reserves. By August, he raised £76,424, and two weeks later, he produced an additional £100,000 in gold for Wellington. With support of Liverpool and the chancellor of the Exchequer, Nicholas Vansittart, Bathurst demanded a further £100,000, and by mid-October, the Bank of England reluctantly agreed to supply Wellington's army with £100,000 for an additional four months.[73]

These sums far exceeded the bank's gold coin reserve, and the Bank of England, a powerful political entity, resisted government interference. In response, Bathurst exploited a legal loophole that permitted the emergency exportation of gold to pay British troops serving abroad. Herries objected to the measure and in his memoir dubbed them "above the law" because Bathurst did not stipulate how the money should be spent.[74] Nevertheless, Bathurst forced the bank to increase the supply of gold to Wellington, placing no restriction on how he was to spend the money. Bathurst's initiative afforded Wellington a temporary surge of money to plan offensive operations, and it also assured him that the new ministry had found a way to give him the fiscal support required to win the war.[75]

Bathurst's plan was not without economic and political risk. Challenging the powerful Bank of England and establishing no restriction on the use of the money could lead to his removal. This was not lost on Bathurst, who mentioned his concern in a letter to his friend Charles Harrowby: "For this I shall have my head off, if we should not succeed." Harrowby, a former foreign secretary and diplomat, reassured Bathurst: "I hope you will not lose your head for your dealings with the Bank. You and all of us should deserve to lose it if we refrained from using a vigor beyond the law to enable Lord Wellington to pursue his successes and it is fortunate that you have a decent legal cloak for so good a deed."[76]

Luckily for Wellington and Bathurst, the opposition was unaware of this arrangement, and the directors of the Bank of England shipped £400,000 in return for a promise that the demand would not be repeated. Despite Bathurst's assurances, the directors were induced to release a further £300,000 in the spring of 1813. Bathurst notified Wellington of the impending gold shipments in October 1812; he assured him that despite the bank's resistance, monetary shipments should arrive regularly for four months. True to his word, the first shipment of gold reached the peninsula in November. The money reached Wellington at a crucial period, when the British army was forced to withdraw from it disastrous siege of Burgos.[77]

Although Wellington was relieved, he offered Bathurst and the government his typical minimal praise for its actions. However, being able to pay his soldiers and indigenous mule drivers undoubtedly kept most of his army intact during one of its most arduous times. Shipping England's foreign gold reserve to the peninsula caused great strain on the already fragile British economy, but despite the global gold shortage and the demand of supporting the continental coalition arrayed against Napoleon, Bathurst viewed it as a political and economic gamble necessary to preserve the gains of Wellington's hard-fought victories of 1812.

In addition to forcing the Bank of England to deplete its vaults, Bathurst ultimately solved the currency problem with the help of one of the most powerful speculators in Europe, Nathan Rothschild. Bathurst and Rothschild established an elaborate and clandestine system of purchasing Treasury bills cheaply and then cashing them for gold bullion at the Treasury. This gold was then sent to Rothschild's brother in Paris, who through a series of banks and business firms exchanged the gold for Spanish dollars. Wellington preferred to pay his local debts in dollars, and therefore without Rothschild's help, he would have been forced to spend valuable time and money converting the gold at market.[78]

By 1813, Herries had settled his differences with Wellington and aided the Rothschilds by conducting most of the correspondence between Rothschild and the British banks. The scheme was immensely successful for the shipments between 19 November 1812 and 15 July 1813, totaling about £1.15 million in gold. Nevertheless, even in times of prosperity, the main support of the Peninsular War was maintained by British credit and the sale of Treasury bills. As they had been in 1809, Wellington and the commissariat were plagued until the end of the war by the lack of ready money, and the issue continued as a long running sore.[79]

Another major disagreement between Wellington and his political masters throughout the campaign of 1811–1812 involved the operations of the Royal Navy in light of the outbreak of hostilities with the fledgling United States. Joint operations had been a great operational advantage throughout the war. In early 1811, the Royal Navy had supplied vast amounts of food and materiel to the army and the

Portuguese population and had almost singlehandedly assured that Wellington's army behind the Lines of Torres Vedras during Masséna's invasion did not starve. By late 1811, this relationship was threatened by competing requirements for the Royal Navy in America. Wellington had become dependent on the supplies delivered by the navy because much of the grain supplied by Wellington to the Portuguese came from America.[80]

In early 1812, the immediate problem for Wellington centered on the disposition of his friend and the great practitioner of joint operations Adm. George Berkeley. In May, Berkeley was chosen to command the channel fleet, the command he had turned down in April 1810.[81] Berkeley's reassignment concerned Wellington, and though he was powerless to prevent Berkeley's departure, he displayed his political influence by nominating Berkeley's replacement in the Tagus. In February 1812, Wellington asked Liverpool to recommend that the Admiralty appoint Vice Adm. George Martin as Berkeley's successor in Portugal. Wellington wanted an admiral capable of embarking and evacuating the British army from the peninsula if necessary, but most important, he wanted an admiral with a "conciliating disposition." The Admiralty replaced Berkeley with Martin on 27 June 1812.[82]

Despite his influence in naming Berkeley's replacement, Wellington encountered increased resistance from the Admiralty throughout the remainder of the campaign. The first issue involved the threat of American and French privateers operating in the Bay of Biscay and therefore threatening Wellington's lines of communication and supply. Although the Americans could not openly challenge the Royal Navy on the high seas, their presence forced an already stretched Royal Navy to add protection of transports and supply convoys to the routine task of blockade duty all along the French and northern Spanish coasts. Wellington asked Bathurst to request naval reinforcements from the Admiralty to secure his communications. Wellington was also concerned that the privateers might commandeer one of the ships carrying needed money and therefore asked the Admiralty to augment the Lisbon squadron with additional frigates and sloops that could deter the smaller and faster American ships.[83]

Bathurst relayed Wellington's request to the Admiralty, but Lord Melville, the first lord of the Admiralty, declined. In his response, he stated that the security of Wellington's communication ships were the responsibility of the postmaster general and not the Royal Navy!

Furthermore, he declined to reposition naval vessels under the apprehension of American privateers in the mouth of the channel or off the coast of Portugal. Melville also informed Bathurst that Admiral Martin would not receive additional ships because protection of British trade was more vital in other quarters of the world where American privateers could strike, such as off the American coast.[84]

Wellington, obsessed by his own difficulties, was furious at the Admiralty's disregard of his request and viewed the redeployment of ships to chase American privateers around the oceans of the world as a wasteful allocation of naval resources. In his mind, given the increased difficulty in procuring specie, the navy's ships would be far better used in the Bay of Biscay, where they could effectively guard his supply lines and monetary shipments to the peninsula. In his response to Bathurst, Wellington regretfully stated, "This is what a gentlemen gets by interfering in the business of others."[85]

Adding to his difficulties, political issues in London forced Wellington to make key decisions that not only undermined his political position, but affected his family as well. It all began before Perceval's assassination, when in February 1812 Wellington's brother Richard resigned as foreign secretary due to differences on two primary issues: he did not feel that the cabinet had supported Wellington and Spain with needed men, money, and supplies during the financial crisis of the past year, and in a peripheral matter to Iberia, he differed from his peers concerning one of the most contentious domestic issues of the day—granting political freedom to Catholics in Great Britain.[86]

While Wellesley's resignation came as a surprise to Perceval and the cabinet, it was by no means unwelcome. Since 1810, Wellesley's disdain for Perceval and Liverpool had been common knowledge in London. The opposition party leader, Lord Holland, noted,

> Lord Wellesley treated Mr. Perceval and the other [Cabinet] Ministers with scorn and contempt. . . . Wellesley was a most uncertain speaker. . . . When he did rise to [speak in the House of Lords] it was often doubtful which side he would espouse, what topics he would select, and whether he would treat them with ability and eloquence or lapse into frothy, trite, and unmeaning declamation, or entitle himself in some metaphysical disquisition which he was quite unequal to unravel or expound. . . . Yet there was a smack of greatness in all he did

and although his speeches, his manners, and his actions were very open to ridicule, those who smiled and even laughed could not despise him.[87]

Even Pole candidly remarked about Richard's political conduct:

> I am afraid to show your letter to Lord Wellesley for I do not know of what terms he is with his colleagues and indeed his life is so strange that it is difficult for him to be considered among Ministers as he might be if he gave his talents fairly. He is very seldom at his office and he lives entirely out of office. Between his friends and his family affairs—the best of whom complain that they cannot get him to do anything—his colleagues complain they never see him in the House of Lords and he seldom takes any part by which he has lost much ground. . . . I shall feel very unhappy if you are unable to persuade ministers to keep your force to the fullest extent possible. For I am reminded that if they leave you with so small an army as will prevent you from attaining the advantages you have gained—that it will be difficult to prevent you from being blamed where the fault would be conclusively of your sympathizers and all hope you shall not suffer them to convince you to undertake operations with a force that you may consider inadequate to its object—or to what is expected from it—Things here continue on an uncomfortable, discreditable and unpleasant state.[88]

In addition to Wellesley's public conduct, his private life was also a topic of general discussion between the brothers. Richard was a notorious philanderer, and in 1810, Wellington told Pole, "I firmly believe that Wellesley should be castrated."[89]

Despite distaste for his brother's personal conduct, Wellington was surprised by Richard's resignation, which could not have come at a worse time because he was forced to decide his loyalty between his brother and the government. Wellesley's resignation and attempts to form a new ministry also fueled a struggle in Parliament that threatened the government's unity and forced the newly formed Liverpool administration to fight for its political survival.[90]

In response, Perceval and Liverpool attempted to maintain Wellington's support. Throughout the political turmoil in London, both men wrote private letters to Wellington and Henry about Richard's erratic behavior. In their letters, they reassured both men that despite their disagreements with Richard, the government remained loyal to the cause of defeating Napoleon in the peninsula and pledged to support the war with renewed vigor.[91]

As a sign of their public commitment to Wellington and Henry, the cabinet recommended both men for honors.[92] The prime minister informed Wellington that he had been elevated to an earldom, which carried with it an increased pension of £2,000 a year for life. Two weeks later, for his efforts to pacify the Cortes and garner support in Cadiz, Henry was made a Knight of the Bath. Wellington appreciated the honors bestowed on him and Henry, and although he wrote sympathetically to Richard, he knew that support of the administration was much more important for his operations to proceed. Ultimately, when forced to decide his loyalty, Wellington refrained from coming to Richard's defense.[93]

The entire political landscape changed on 11 May when Spencer Perceval was assassinated in the lobby of Parliament. Like others, Wellington was shocked by the news of Perceval's death, but he did not privately mourn the politician, whom he viewed as a shrewd opponent to Britain's distant war in the Iberian Peninsula. In a letter to Pole, Wellington eulogized the prime minister who had caused him so much trouble: "Mr. Perceval was a very honest man, whose views were rather limited by professional habits and those acquired by long practice in the [House of Commons.] I think he did not take a sufficiently enlarged view of our situation here; nor does Lord Liverpool."[94]

Perceval's assassination reinvigorated Richard Wellesley's attempts to form a new ministry. First, Richard attempted to combine forces with George Canning to form a new Tory government, even proposing that Liverpool join him.[95] Lord Bathurst noted, "The basis of [Wellesley's Administration] was to be taking the Catholic claims into serious consideration and attention, and to prosecute the war in the Peninsula with the best means of the country. . . . Each of these principles are lax in the expression. . . . [And] the answer we gave was that all of us were bound to decline."[96] When Liverpool refused to join him, Wellesley approached the opposition Whig Party to form a ministry. The Whigs, once united against the Tory Party, could not reach a unified platform on the future course of the war and also declined Richard's invitation. Left alone, Richard's attempt fell short.[97]

To a lesser extent, Wellington was also distracted by his brother Pole. Prior to Richard's resignation, Perceval had planned to bring Pole into the cabinet as the treasurer of the navy. Unsurprisingly, Pole's letters to Wellington during that period reflected the government's praise, even though he was upset that he was not being offered a higher position in the cabinet.[98] A confidential source of political intrigue at home, Pole, who had remained chief secretary for Ireland since 1810, lost his position in Ireland when Perceval died and Liverpool formed a new government. Liverpool responded by suggesting Pole take the important position of secretary at war.[99] However, this move was blocked by the prince regent, who rightfully joined Pole with Richard's camp. Whether Pole would have accepted the invitation to lead the largely administrative War Office is debatable. He could not escape that he had erroneously viewed Perceval's assassination as a catalyst to push for increased political influence and had chosen to join Richard and fight for control of Parliament by using the emotive issue of Catholic emancipation to win support. It was the wrong issue at the wrong time. While Richard lobbied extensively in the House of Lords, Pole hoped the momentum would carry over into the House of Commons.[100] In his mind, it was an all-or-nothing gamble, which if successful would show Richard his loyalty and hopefully garner an even higher position in Richard's cabinet. Unfortunately, the vote was defeated in the Lords and the measure was never brought before the House of Commons.[101]

Wellington felt that Pole would have served admirably in the new government, but he refused to ask Liverpool to reconsider his position and told Pole that although he was grateful for his help in the past, "it [was] impossible . . . to do more." Furthermore, because Liverpool had already filled the other positions in his cabinet, Wellington was reluctant to ask Liverpool to remove any person that currently served. Wellington had not approved of Pole's stand on the Catholic emancipation issue and felt that his brother had fallen victim to a shortsighted role in Richard's attempt to form a new government. He told Pole that he was not willing to take part in "domestic politics and that he fully understood the minister's objections" to Lord Wellesley.[102]

While serving on the periphery of the political intrigue at home, Wellington's role in the affair was detached and pragmatic. Although Richard's actions placed him in a difficult position and cost Pole his seat in the government, and despite his reservations about Liverpool and his ability to win control of Parliament, Wellington understood that if he backed his brother and was unsuccessful, he would assuredly face political reprisals that would develop into increased operational scrutiny, lack of support, or even outright dismissal. Instead, Wellington chose to support Liverpool against Richard. In a letter to the new prime minister, Wellington congratulated Liverpool: "I am much obliged to you and I sincerely congratulate you upon the favorable prospect which you have before you."[103]

Much more dangerous to Wellington's cause in the peninsula, Henry, who had resented Liverpool's treatment of his eldest brother, threatened to resign from his post in Cadiz: "I cannot think the Ministers justifiable in their conduct to Lord Wellesley, nor should anything induce me to remain here after the treatment he has met with at their hands, were I not apprehensive that my sudden resignation might be attended with inconvenience both to the public service and to Lord Wellington personally."[104] Wellington's victory at Salamanca relieved both the French siege of Cadiz and Henry's concern. Henry's decision to remain in Spain was important for Wellington because the tactical and political situation between the two countries entered a delicate phase in the summer and fall of 1812. The government had increased the subsidy to the Spanish by £400,000, and Wellington relied on his brother to administer the aid but also to provide stability to the Spanish. Had Henry resigned his post in Cadiz, Wellington's relations with the intransigent members of the Spanish Cortes would have surely suffered, since no British diplomat possessed Henry's knowledge and influence.[105]

By the summer of 1812, it was clear that Wellington's political star was rising as fast as his military career. On the other hand, despite his long-standing record of public service, Richard Wellesley's political career was on the decline. Furthermore, Liverpool's ministry survived the tumultuous sequence of events that followed Perceval's assassination. The additions of Lord Castlereagh, who joined as the foreign secretary, and Bathurst, brought experience and confidence to the War Department, and the government seemed to be primed for success. In this view, Wellington's diversions into domestic politics were both justified and pragmatic.

Despite the financial and political crises that diverted Wellington's energy from the war, the extended campaigns of 1811–1812 were decisive. Through long, hot marches and the sieges of Ciudad Rodrigo and Badajoz, Wellington secured Portugal and opened Spain for invasion. In addition, he consolidated these victories with a decisive victory over Marshal Marmont at Salamanca, opening the path to Madrid. Yet despite his success on the battlefield, in terms of public and political pressure, Wellington remained on the defensive.

Military success also turned out to be ruinously expensive. Wellington's operations drained England of it precious gold and silver reserves and sparked a renewed rivalry with the Admiralty over the limitations of their power. This contest for resources would resurface in the decisive campaigns of late 1812 and 1813. His Iberian operations also drained England of its most precious commodity—men. For the remainder of the war, the issue of reinforcements would loom over Wellington, as would the continuing struggle to obtain money for the Spanish and Portuguese. The uncertainty in London and hostility directed at Wellington was also demonstrated in private opposition letters. Auckland told Grenville, "The war in the Peninsula continues in all the activity of a corroding cancer, the mischief of which will never be acknowledged until it is too late to be remedied."[106] While Britain's attention was focused on Portugal and Spain, these events paled in comparison to what transpired in Russia, where, throughout the fall of 1812, the Russians gave ground to Napoleon's *grande armée*.

7

EXPLOITATION: THE BURGOS CAMPAIGN, 1812–1813

> I have nothing to do with the choice of general officers sent out here or with their numbers, or with the army with which they serve; and when they do come, I must employ them as I am ordered.
>
> Wellington to General John Vandeleur, 26 April 1813

Despite his victory at Salamanca, Wellington faced an operational dilemma. Although the battle had eliminated Marshal Marmont's force, three more French armies in Spain threatened his operational base: Gen. Marie-François Caffarelli's *armée du Nord*, which occupied the fortresses along the Bay of Biscay; Marshal Suchet's force in the eastern province of Valencia; and Marshal Soult, whose army besieged the fortress of Cadiz in the south. In aggregate, these forces numbered nearly 260,000 men. Although each of the French armies was widely dispersed, if allowed to consolidate, they could easily outnumber the British. Wellington also had the problem of exposing his flank if he chose to attack either French army. Faced with these difficult choices, Wellington chose to move toward Madrid and force Napoleon's brother Joseph Bonaparte to abandon the capital. Wellington entered Madrid on 12 August 1812. Although the Spanish capital yielded substantial quantities of arms and ammunition, liberating Madrid had little military significance. Nevertheless, the liberation gave the Spanish people an emotional lift, and, under considerable pressure, a group of liberal Spanish politicians responded by making Wellington *generalissimo* of their armies—which is covered later in this chapter. More significant than Spanish praise, however, Wellington's occupation of Madrid blocked Marshal Soult's lines of communication in the south, forcing him to lift his siege of Cadiz. Soult marched north to join King Joseph and Suchet in Valencia.[1]

Soult's departure presented Wellington with an operational dilemma. He could remain in Madrid surrounded by several French armies that could converge against him, or he could leave Madrid and march with a portion of his army northward in pursuit of the defeated *armée du Portugal*. Wellington chose the latter. On 1 September 1812, he moved north with some thirty thousand troops, but he had made two critical mistakes that would greatly hinder subsequent operations. First, he had left his most experienced troops in Madrid, under the command of General Hill, and second, he had failed to order an adequate siege train to follow his army.[2]

Wellington's operations in 1812–1813 also forced him to improvise his logistics system. Leaving his operational base in Portugal—and the predictability of shipments of supplies there from the Royal Navy—he would depend almost exclusively on contracted civilian vessels for his logistics requirements. Throughout the previous year's campaign, Wellington had received mixed support from the navy. Adm. George Berkeley endeavored to transport supplies up the Douro River to the allied army during its siege of Badajoz; yet Wellington gave little praise because the navy had not increased the number of Berkeley's transports and supply ships operating between England and the peninsula. Wellington felt that the navy was under strength to accomplish the two primary tasks that he required. Concerned about the security of sea lines of communication from the threat of American privateers, Wellington recommended that the navy station a warship off Cape Finisterre to guard against the fast-moving pirates. He was also concerned about maintaining communications along the perimeter of his area of operations, which extended from Coruña in the north to Gibraltar in the south. To support this objective, Wellington wanted the navy to send more frigates and transports to Admiral Martin's squadron in Lisbon.[3]

While pleading for increased support, Wellington was aided by a series of small amphibious raids conducted by the Royal Navy along the northern coast of Spain.[4] The raids had previously been proposed and unsuccessfully executed by British commodore Sir Home Popham in 1810; however, by early 1812, the conditions for these operations proved more favorable.[5] In May 1812, Popham, a veteran of several amphibious campaigns, received orders from the Admiralty to again lead a series of diversionary attacks along the Bay of Biscay in support of Wellington's invasion of Spain.[6]

Thus, throughout the summer and fall of 1812, Popham ushered in a new series of successful joint operations, preventing French reinforcement of Marmont during the Salamanca campaign. Elsewhere, events in the Spanish interior, particularly the ill-fated siege of Burgos from September through October, prevented Wellington from taking advantage of Popham's operations. Furthermore, in what was becoming a pattern of ingratitude, Wellington failed to acknowledge the extent of naval cooperation he received. His reservations about the navy not only decreased his effectiveness in 1812, but also would have grave implications for his offensive operations in 1813.

To understand the implications of this strained relationship with the navy, it is necessary to understand the operational significance of the Bay of Biscay coastline. Due to the lack of a suitable road network throughout northern and central Spain, the French relied on the complicated and interdependent system of Spanish fortresses along the Biscay coastline to transport supplies from Bayonne to the Spanish interior. The fortresses were also the focus for future operations. To oust the French from the peninsula, Wellington must first deny the use of these fortifications to the enemy.[7]

The disposition of the thirty-five-thousand-man French *armée du Nord*, situated along the Bay of Biscay, was also vital to Wellington's operations. Under the command of General Caffarelli, the troops were the operational reserve for Marmont's *armée du Portugal* as well as the occupation force for the northern Spanish provinces of Navarre, Santander, and Burgos. Not only had these northern Spanish provinces provided a haven for Spanish guerillas, but they were also key strategic and operational locations because they protected the ports of Santander and Pasajes. Furthermore, the disposition of the *armée du Nord* was a problem for Wellington. While more than half of Caffarelli's men were fixed in garrison duty, the remainder was free to support Marmont in Old Castille or threaten Wellington's line of communications. Furthermore, several large cities and two harbors along the coastline served as important trade and commerce centers for both the French and Spanish. Not surprisingly, the British viewed these cities and harbors as objectives for British marine and Spanish guerilla attacks.[8]

As he had attempted in 1810, Popham planned to mount attacks along the Biscay coastline, but due to the extensive commitment of naval forces to blockade duty, only a very limited number of ships and men could be committed to the amphibious operations. As a result, Popham devised a plan to take advantage of the summer months of 1812 and favorable weather to renew the attacks on the French-held coastline. Popham wrote to his commanding officer, commander of the channel fleet Adm. Lord George Keith, that "the interception of the enemy's supplies coastwise and the establishment of a position to hold frequent and uninterrupted [supply] intercourse with guerillas" were his objectives. As Wellington planned his incursion into central Spain, he recognized the value of Admiral Popham's diversionary plan and requested that the War Department support the operations.[9]

In addition to direct naval attacks, Popham encouraged Spanish guerillas to disrupt French logistics while he used his Royal Marines to raid Spanish ports. It was hoped that these diversionary attacks would force Caffarelli to chase Popham and therefore free Wellington in the south.[10] In London, the Admiralty agreed to support Wellington's offensive by using Popham's forces. In a letter to Bathurst, first lord of the Admiralty Melville stated, "the most satisfactory state of affairs would be that [Popham] with his own force only should harass the enemy as much as possible, and prevent their moving or detaching from the coast, either to reinforce Marmont or check the guerillas, and that the latter should thus be enabled with less interruption and hazard to annoy the rear of the French Army."[11] They also dispatched more ships. In July, Melville reinforced Popham's squadron, which consisted of six ships of the line and several smaller vessels, with a battalion of marines and an artillery battery to disrupt and in some instances bombard French garrison towns along the Biscay coast.[12]

Popham launched his first attack in June 1812 and continued offensive operations into August. In all, his operations were extremely effective. To Wellington's pleasure, Popham's occupation of the port of Santander ensured that Caffarelli could not reinforce Marmont prior to the battle of Salamanca. Moreover, the capture of the port also allowed Popham to move needed supplies and material to Wellington's army for use in the fall, when his operations shifted north. Popham's economy of force operations forced the French *armée du Nord* to retain its garrisons along the Bay of Biscay coastline so it could not move against Wellington for nearly four months.[13] In a letter to Popham, an atypical Wellington stated, "I beg leave to congratulate you upon the success of your operations. They have been great use to me, as I know Caffarelli was prevented from detailing more than cavalry to Marmont's assistance [at Salamanca] and that he even recalled a division of [infantry].... I trust you will not discontinue the raids."[14] In late September 1812, when Wellington was running short on ammunition and gunpowder, he appealed to Popham for forty barrels of gunpowder. Popham promptly landed the supplies and sent them along very poor roads over a distance of some seventy miles through the mountains to Wellington's army, which was besieging Burgos. Wellington received the supplies a week later.[15]

In addition to gunpowder, Popham offered to supply Wellington with naval guns to breach the heavily fortified walls of Burgos. The guns Wellington had brought from Madrid were too small in caliber for the task. The idea of transporting the naval guns overland to support Wellington originated with Popham's personal aide, Sir Howard Douglas. Douglas, who occupied no official position in the army or navy, traveled to Burgos on September 20, the first day of the siege, to personally offer his assistance. He observed that the French guns in the fortress were 24-pounders and therefore outgunned Wellington's three 18-pounders and five 24-pound howitzers. Douglas feared that without the heavy artillery, a successful breach could not be made.[16]

Wellington declined Douglas's offer because of the time and men required to bring guns from the coast. In his reply to Popham, Wellington bluntly stated that despite the advantages gained by the heavy guns, his lack of mule transport prohibited his action: "It is unfortunate that you should have plenty of cannon and ammunition, but that you want good soldiers, and I now want of the latter, but very little of the former. The means of transport, however required to move a train from the coast or Madrid, where we have plenty of artillery... would be impracticable."[17] In addition to logistics, Wellington and his chief engineer, John Burgoyne, felt that since Douglas did not hold an official position in the army, his opinions were uninformed and not worthy of action. Burgoyne, who referred to Douglas as one of those "unauthorized persons" who volunteers useless advice, favored a quick siege by mining under the walls and assaulting the fortress walls with infantry. Wellington agreed with his engineer.[18]

On October 2, after two failed infantry assaults and nearly four hundred casualties against an able French defense, Wellington reconsidered his original position and accepted Douglas's plan to transport Popham's guns from the coast.[19] Popham offered the guns from his flagship, the *Venerable* (74). Similar to the gunpowder, the guns would be transported ashore and hauled overland to Wellington's army by mule and ox carts. In a letter to Melville, Popham informed his superior of the great service he hoped to provide the army: "I hope that tomorrow the *Venerable*'s guns will be playing on the castle of Burgos, and I do not think that when you sent me on this service did you ever expect that our ship guns would ever have got so far inland."[20] A week later, Popham transported the guns ashore, and by 18 October, the guns had been transported to Reynosa, only fifty miles from Burgos. Meanwhile, an impatient Wellington ordered another infantry assault on the fortress. Wellington's third and equally fruitless attack yielded another four hundred British casualties and no positive results.[21]

Despite his losses and ineffective siege operations, Wellington worried most about losing the naval support. Above all else, he feared that if Popham's squadron were recalled or left its station, Caffarelli would be free to move south against him. Wellington told Popham, "the enemy, as well as the Spaniards, will be convinced that nothing is intended to be done, even though the Marines remain, if you should go away in the *Venerable*; and I apprehend that shall I have upon my hands in Castille more of the enemy than I can manage."[22] Therefore, despite the threat of stormy weather in the Bay of Biscay, he requested that Popham maintain his operations off the northern Spanish coast:

> The possession of Santoña is very important in every point of view, particularly if the possession should facilitate your remaining on the coast. You know best whether you can obtain the possession with means in your power. If you cannot and if you think that the attempt will draw you towards the enemy's operations, and that you may be obliged to withdraw

from Santander, it is much better that the attempt should not be made. What I want is, that your squadron and marines should remain on the coast during the winter by which they will render me the important service of preventing the enemy from taking the whole army of the North across the Ebro River. If they should lose Santander, it is very obvious that they must go to Coruña or home; and either would be a misfortune under present circumstances.[23]

Wellington's fears that the Admiralty would recall the squadron were justified. As early as September, Lord Keith had mentioned the possibility. Keith feared the upcoming fall and winter weather and the increased activity of American privateers would threaten Popham's squadron. Nevertheless, Keith reluctantly permitted Popham to remain on station until December 21. In a letter to Popham, he relayed the Admiralty's cautious support: "It is extremely important that the naval force under your orders should remain on the north coast of Spain so long as it can [support] the operations of Lord Wellington, but you are never to forget that if [Wellington] retires, or suddenly withdraws, the enemy will rapidly advance and that if the wind should be westerly or northerly, the ships in the Santander harbor would be in danger; and while you continue to use that harbor, you may protect yourself from such a calamity, [by] soliciting [from Wellington] the most speedy notice of [his departure]."[24] Despite obvious risk to Popham's ships, the Admiralty acquiesced to Wellington's request, and Popham's squadron remained in the Bay of Biscay until late November, well after Wellington began his retreat from Burgos.[25]

By late October, the French had rallied and moved to support the beleaguered fortress. Caffarelli, who deduced that Popham's forces were a diversion, left twenty thousand men to occupy the garrisons and moved the remainder of his troops, approximately ten thousand infantry and sixteen hundred cavalry, south toward Burgos. Joining him were another thirty-five thousand men under Gen. Joseph Souham.[26] In all, an estimated fifty thousand French troops marched against Wellington's army, which numbered around twenty-four thousand men.

In the south, the situation was worse. Marshal Soult joined the forces under King Joseph Bonaparte. Together, they had nearly sixty thousand men. Resolved to recapture Madrid, the two French armies marched on the capital. Wellington had left Madrid defended by only thirty-eight thousand men under General Hill, and since early October, he had received reports from Hill that Soult and Joseph's force were marching toward Madrid.[27] In response to these renewed threats, Wellington ordered both armies to withdraw toward the Portuguese border. In the north, Wellington ordered Popham's guns returned to Santander and a full withdrawal of his forces from Burgos. He also ordered General Hill to abandon his defense of the Spanish capital. This was completed on 31 October, when Hill left Madrid, less than four months after it had been liberated.[28]

The orderly withdrawal turned into a full-scale retreat. Fortunately for Wellington and Hill, the autumn rains that had bedeviled Wellington outside the fortress during the siege turned the usually poor roads into quagmires, which slowed the French pursuit. In the end, Wellington's attempts to capture Burgos without proper artillery cost the allies more than two thousand casualties. The delay to request proper artillery support from Popham also provided the surrounding French armies time to consolidate their forces and march to the fortress's relief.[29]

Although Popham's squadron supported Wellington's operations for more than six months and kept thousands of French soldiers far from Wellington's battlefields, the mercurial Wellington claimed that the naval operations failed to divert forces away from him, not only in the north but also in eastern Spain, where a naval expedition, under the command of Lt. Gen. Frederick Maitland, failed to divert Soult and Joseph's force. He also blamed Popham for not delaying Caffarelli's force longer.[30]

In a clumsy effort to disguise his own shortcomings during the siege of Burgos, Wellington wrote Liverpool, "The fault of which I was guilty in the expedition to Burgos was, not that I undertook the operation with inadequate means, but that I took there the most inexperienced troops instead of the best." Furthermore, Wellington gave the prime minister his rationale for not moving the much-needed siege artillery from Madrid or the coast sooner:

> In regard to means, there were ample means, both at Madrid and at Santander, for the siege of the strongest fortress. That which was wanting at both places was the means of trans-

porting ordnance and military stores. The people of England, so happy as they are in every respect, so rich in resources of every description, having the use of such excellent roads, etc., will not readily believe that important results here frequently depend upon 50 or 60 mules more or less or a few bundles of straw to feed them; but the fact is so, notwithstanding their incredulity. I could not find means of moving a single gun from Madrid.[31]

In the end, Wellington blamed logistics for his delay in requesting Popham's artillery and further asserted that Popham did not understand the difficulties of his transport limitations: "Sir Home Popham is a gentleman who piques himself on overcoming all difficulties. He knows the time it took to find transport even for about 100 barrels of powder and few hundred thousand rounds of musket ammunition that he sent me. As for the two guns that he endeavored to send me, I was obliged to send my own cattle to draw them, and felt the great inconvenience from the want of those cattle in subsequent movements of the army."[32]

Wellington's reluctance to give Popham or the Admiralty due credit for aiding his operations is puzzling. After all, the navy's well-planned and executed diversionary raids along the coast drew significant French forces away from Wellington's campaign, and Popham's ability to arm and supply guerillas forced General Caffarelli not only to leave twenty thousand men to guard the coast, but also to return in 1813 to protect the French lines of communication. Popham's seizure and retention of the port of Santander, though of limited value in 1812, had residual effects during the decisive campaign of 1813, when Wellington returned to the region to besiege the fortress of San Sebastián. Without use of the deep-water port, French lines of supply were severely hindered and required extensive rerouting to relieve the siege.[33]

On a strategic level, Wellington had little choice but to retreat from Burgos. However, on a tactical level, his poor management of the siege and subsequent retreat were one of his lowest points in the Peninsular War. Even to the lowest-ranking officer in his army, Wellington's underestimation of the French defenses and fortress strength were apparent. Lt. William Swabey, of the Royal Horse Artillery, wrote in his diary, "At the head of the immediate causes that obliged our retreat I must place the failure before Burgos, and in justice to my profession I must censure, though unwillingly, the conduct of Lord Wellington. Though frequently warned that the means were totally inadequate for success, and while confessing that the fate of the place was not of importance, he would not, after once sitting down before it, raise the siege till Soult was encouraged to advance and General Souham had arrived in superior force in his front."[34]

At home, the political opposition, which had been muted since the victories in the summer, attacked Wellington. In a letter to Grenville, Grey remarked, "In Spain the prospect does not appear encouraging. Nothing but the division of the French armies and the jealousies prevailing between the commanders could have afforded us the successes which we have had, and if any one efficient commander had the sole direction of the force even now in the Peninsula, I cannot doubt that according to all reasonable grounds of calculation we should very speedily be compelled to abandon the country."[35]

Although Wellington deserved much of the blame for the outcome of the Burgos campaign, the lack of competent and aggressive general officers in his army also contributed. He was further burdened by his inability to gain control of personnel assignments in his army. In December 1809 he had written Liverpool to complain about the quality of his general officers: "I wish to draw your attention to the list of general officers in this army, and I believe you will admit, with some exceptions, there never was an army so ill provided for."[36] Liverpool responded that he had considered the problem, but he was unable to find suitable general officers, cavalrymen in particular, available for service. He did not have the power to appoint officers who were stationed in Britain: "I wish I knew how to propose to you a satisfactory arrangement with respect to the cavalry [officers], however no private consideration would prevent it. But if you look at the Army List and advert to the rules of our service, you will see all the difficulties of which I allude."[37]

No example demonstrates the ramifications of the system that produced general officers for Wellington's army better than the actions of Maj. Gen. Sir William Erskine.[38] After the escape of Almeida's garrison in May 1811, Wellington wrote Liverpool to explain the situation. Despite being surrounded, 1,400 French troops, marching under the cover of darkness, eluded capture. Because Erskine delayed issuing orders to an infantry regiment to block a road junction, Wellington's plan to prevent the garrison's escape was unsuccessful. In his letter to Liverpool, Wellington was furious, calling it the "most disgraceful military event that has occurred to us" and asserting that he might have prevented the garrison's escape if he had been there in person. He also vented his frustration about the quality of general officers serving in his peninsular army: "I certainly feel every day, more and more the difficulty of the situation in which I am placed. I am obliged to be everywhere, and if absent from any operation, something goes wrong." He hoped that "the general officers of the army will at last acquire that experience which will teach them that success can be attained only by attention to the most minute details."[39] In a letter to his brother, Wellington was much more critical: "They had about 13,000 men to watch 1,400 . . . and to infinite surprise of the enemy, they allowed the garrison to slip through their fingers and to escape after blowing up some of the works of the place! There they were all sleeping in their spurs even but the French got off."[40]

Wellington's anger toward Erskine's incompetence seems perfectly justified. A commander must have faith that his orders will be obeyed and that his subordinate commanders possess the ability to execute them correctly. Almost a year before Almeida, Wellington had questioned Erskine's appointment, rightfully complaining to the military secretary at the Horse Guards, Col. Henry Torrens, and referencing General Erskine's questionable mental state: "I have received your letter announcing the appointment of General Erskine to this army, who I generally understood to be a madman."[41] In a spirited reply, Torrens acknowledged Wellington's concern but made no attempt to change the officer's assignment: "No doubt General Erskine is sometimes a little mad, but in his lucid intervals he is an uncommonly clever fellow; and I trust he will have no fit during the campaign, though he looked a little wild as he embarked . . . Erskine is brave as a lion, though I only hope that he will be tame for your campaign!"[42] In his reply to Torrens, Wellington complained, "When I reflect upon [the character and attainment] of the general officers of this army, and consider that these are persons on whom I am to rely to lead columns against the French generals, and who are to carry my instructions into execution, I tremble." He added, "I only hope that when the enemy reads the list of their names, he trembles as I do."[43]

Wellington's fear of facing the French with his generals was justified; many of his generals should never have been sent to the peninsula. The Horse Guards promoted solely on the basis of seniority and amended the regulations only in special circumstances, such as Wellington's promotion over several higher-ranking general officers in 1808 to assume the temporary command of an expeditionary force. Therefore, the army was filled with senior, often incompetent officers who had gained rank after succeeding as politicians. While this was certainly not the case throughout Wellington's army—several of his commanders, including Sir Rowland Hill and Sir John Hope were effective professional soldiers—most of his senior officers had not served in continental Europe in over a decade. In addition to their lack of recent field service, most of these men had not prepared themselves in the intervening periods for intense combat operations. Wellington was different. While he owed his promotion to his family's political connections, he was a new breed of British professional officer who served in a seniority-based system that did not always reward the traits he possessed and coveted.[44]

Nevertheless, the Horse Guards were also under considerable political pressure to appoint part-time soldier-politicians when they volunteered for service. Torrens reminded Wellington that despite having over six hundred officers of the rank of major general or higher available for service, not all were competent or, more important, willing: "You will recollect my dear general that we have not the choicest set to select your General Officers from!"[45]

Another source of contention between Wellington and the Horse Guards was the selection of Wellington's second in command. The autocratic Wellington had always opposed the position, openly remarking that it was useless. After the war he declared, "When the Horse Guards were obliged to employ a fellow like me in whom they have no confidence, they give him what is called a second-in-command—one whom they have confidence—a kind of dry nurse."[46] Although seniority dictated who would be second in command, the Horse Guards found a way to bend the rules when politics was concerned. In May 1810, Lt. Gen. Sir Brent Spencer, a close friend of the royal family, was appointed Wellington's second in command, although he was outranked by several officers on Wellington's staff. Overlooking his own appointment in 1808, Wellington wasted little time in informing him, "I did not know what the words second-in-command mean, any more than third or fourth in command mean, and that I alone command the army." As far as succession was concerned, Wellington told

Spencer, "General officers command divisions and if anything should happen to [me], the senior survivor would take command of the army, not Spencer." Wellington added that he "would have no officer to serve as second-in-command in the sense of having anything like a joint command or superintending control.... [he] would not only take but insist upon the whole and undivided responsibility of all that should happen while the army was under his control."[47]

Wellington told his brother: "[Spencer] was sent here as second in command and is very unfit for his situation. He is a good executive officer, but he has no mind and is incapable of forming an opinion of his own and he is the center of all vulgar and foolish opinions of the day.... I cannot depend on him for anything. He gives his opinion on every subject, and then changes it with the wind." Wellington did not trust Spencer's political inclinations; he was often drawn into indiscretions at the royal dinner parties he attended on leave. Wellington told his brother, "If any misfortune occurs or his recommendations are disapproved, he no longer offers his support. On the contrary, the Royal Family at their dinners and card parties [can] make him say what they please, [which] he always swears [were his opinions] afterwards."[48]

In the end, Wellington was forced to accept Spencer's appointment; however, he never subordinated any of his command authority to him. Wellington viewed the appointment of his second in command as a personal choice. In a letter to Marshal Beresford, Wellington noted, "It is certain that the Government have always thought it necessary to have an officer here, selected by them to succeed my command. And there are some in the Government so partial to old practice and precedent that they do not like a departure from either. It might look good in a newspaper to see that there is a general officer who is second in command. But there is no duty for the second in command to perform, and the office is useless."[49] Several senior lieutenants general in the peninsula, including Sir Thomas Graham, Sir Rowland Hill, and Sir Stapleton Cotton, were available for the position. All of them outranked Wellington's personal choice for the job, William Carr Beresford. The Duke of York contended that Beresford, despite his rank (marshal in the Portuguese army), could not command senior British generals because of his lower date of rank and seniority in the British army. In a letter to the secretary for war, the Duke of York expressed his insistence on holding firm to the seniority-based system: "It appears that there remains but one of two alternatives [to solving the problem], each of which are injurious to the service; One, recall Marshal Beresford from the Peninsula in case he should persevere in his claim [to outrank the other Generals] and the other in case [Lord Wellington] insists that [Beresford] be the second-in-command to recall all the British Lieutenant Generals who are senior to him in our own army."[50]

In the end Beresford was appointed second in command, but not before several of the officers senior to him, including Spencer, returned to England for "personal reasons" or removed themselves from contention for the position of Wellington's possible successor. Although the issue conveniently settled itself for Wellington, it was yet another example of interference from the Horse Guards and of the smothering influence of seniority dates on command appointments.[51]

Wellington was not alone in his criticism of the lack of quality general officers in his army. Many in London, including the master general of the ordnance, agreed. In a letter to Bathurst, Lord Mulgrave admitted,

> There is no part of Wellington's character more admirable or more rare than his temper and fortitude under great disappointment arising from the weakness or neglect of others. General Hill is I fear the only officer he has who can be safely trusted with a separate corps. Paget is an excellent officer but, with a better claim to self-confidence than any of his family. Lord Wellington is the active conductor of all enterprises where a serious operation is to be carried on. He is playing a very deep game . . . for the very circumstance which risks his exposure proves that the war in the Peninsula would be desperate, if he were lost.[52]

Mulgrave also noted that Wellington was at a disadvantage when compared with Napoleon because the French generals were promoted on merit.

To increase Wellington's capability and area of responsibility, Mulgrave suggested to his peer that competent officers such as General Maitland, serving under Sir William Bentinck's Anglo-Sicilian command, be transferred to Wellington's command. Mulgrave further suggested that if measures were not taken to strengthen Wellington's forces, the cause in the peninsula would be lost: "Bonaparte has conquered the greatest part of Europe by doing but one thing at a time, and doing it with all his heart, with all his soul, and with all his strength. If you succeed in the Peninsula, nothing of yours will go on ill elsewhere; if you fail, nothing will go on at all anywhere else!"[53]

Desperately short of brigade commanders as early as 1810, Wellington sought to fill his command positions able, proficient senior officers. Because the Horse Guards could not recall officers from overseas posts without Parliament's approval, Wellington was forced to request from the secretary for war a transfer of officers from either Sicily or the Americas. In 1810, Wellington wrote, "I beg to inform you that I have now three brigades in this army without officers of the rank of colonel to even command them and I have not a general officer to spare for any service."[54] By 1812, the situation had reversed itself, at least as far as actual numbers of senior officers. Again complaining of having too many poor generals, Wellington wrote to the Horse Guards after the retreat from Burgos: "In lieu of Generals [Stewart, Chowne, Bernewitz, and Robinson], I wish none be sent at all."[55]

Wellington also struggled with the Horse Guards to keep his better general officers in the peninsula. The problem again stemmed directly from the Horse Guards's supervisory role of the army list. Although Wellington was commander of all forces, the Horse Guards never relinquished their supervisory role of all infantry and cavalry officers who composed the army's regiments. Therefore, while Wellington controlled the officers who served on his staff, the Horse Guards refused to relinquish its approval authority to honor leave requests of officers who served in the line regiments. In fact, Wellington was often informed by the Horse Guards after the fact of the officers who applied for and were granted a leave of absence. This infuriated Wellington, who felt as commander that he was responsible for maintaining the composition of his regiments, and therefore he alone should approve leaves of absence.[56]

During the summer of 1811, when shortages of officers affected offensive operations, Wellington turned his full attention to the matter. He complained on several occasions about general officers who asked to return to England for various reasons. Although the most common reason given was convalescence, several officers actually returned for "personal reasons" or to attend to business matters.[57] Furthermore, these officers often stayed in England for several months. Wellington instituted several measures to curb excessive leave requests. First, he denied officers the authority to leave until a replacement was found. In this sense, Wellington used the Horse Guards approval authority against itself. He reasoned that if the Horse Guards could approve a leave request, it could immediately send a replacement.[58] In most instances this worked, though in some cases, when a regiment was critically short of officers, Wellington was forced to find a replacement from within the field army. In one such instance, Wellington informed the commander of an officer who Wellington denied leave, "I beg to show you the letter from the Horse Guards, upon the numerous applications from the officers of the army for leave of absence, and also point out to you the inconvenience which results from absences at present. . . . I have felt the inconvenience so strongly that I have sent my own aide de camp to do duty with the regiment."[59]

In addition to denying requests until a replacement could be found, Wellington also instituted a plan that stopped the pay of officers who returned to England for more than two months for any reason other than wounds received in action. Because he could only enforce this measure with officers who served on his staff, Wellington requested that the Horse Guards enforce the same measure throughout the army: "I do not conceive that I have authority to extend the operation of this rule to the regimental staffs. It would be desirable, however, that some general rule should be made upon this subject, and that it should be clearly understood how long an officer on the staff of a regiment may be absent, and continue to receive his staff pay."[60] The Horse Guards refused to stop the pay of officers who returned to England for extended visits, so Wellington struggled with the problem of unauthorized officer absence for the remainder of the war. Nevertheless, he continued to try to remedy the problem the only way he could and that was to lead by example. Throughout the war, the only general officer to never return to England for a leave of absence was Wellington himself.

No time throughout the Peninsular War offers a greater glimpse of Wellington's struggle with officer quality and Horse Guards' interference with his staff as does the period surrounding the army's retreat from Burgos. The British suffered from poor tactical leadership and subsequent desertion. According to Lieutenant Swabey, the lack of tactical discipline as a result of drunkenness and disorderly conduct was rampant:

> 2 November—The retreat was continued at night through Valdemoro, and here a scene of the most disgraceful character ensued. It was at the time of the year when the new wine was in open vats and there were many vats at this place. Numbers of men fell out of the ranks and surrounded them and I saw with my own eyes many actually drowned in the vats! They were baling out the liquor with their caps to their comrades, till overcome, as much by the fumes of the wine and by what they drank, that they just sank down and expired in their glory. What a death for a reasonable being.... It is certain that the army lost 300 men in this manner![61]

To rectify the disgraceful situation, Wellington issued a general order on 16 November, stating, "The number of soldiers straggling from their regiments for no reason except to plunder is a disgrace to the army."[62] Unfortunately, the worst was yet to come.

On the night of 17 November, three of Wellington's division commanders committed acts of blatant insubordination. In a letter to the Horse Guards after the retreat, Wellington recalled how the three generals, General Stewart and two "newcomers" acting in concert with one another had met to disregard a direct order concerning the route on which they should withdraw: "Several of the Division Commanders held a council of war to decide whether they would obey my orders to march by a particular road. [Stewart] at the head, decided he would not. They marched by a road leading they did not know where, and when I found them in the morning they were in the utmost confusion, not knowing where to go or what to do." The problems associated with General Stewart were not new. Wellington told Torrens, "With the utmost zeal and good intentions, he cannot obey an order."[63] Fortunately for Wellington, the pursuing French forces were unable to capitalize on his generals' willful disobedience, so they were able to regroup and rejoin the remainder of the British force. Nevertheless, their actions drew their commander's wrath. No army in retreat can tolerate insubordination, and within weeks, two of the three were recommended for immediate recall to England.[64]

The retreat from Burgos could have badly shaken a lesser man's confidence and resolve, but on Wellington it had the opposite effect. Although his army had performed badly outside Burgos and in the subsequent retreat to Portugal, many aspects of the 1812 campaign were commendable. Nevertheless, he sent his army a clear message of his dissatisfaction. On 28 November, Wellington told his division and brigade commanders, The discipline of this army "is the worst I have ever seen or read.... Irregularities and outrages were committed with impunity, and losses have been sustained which ought never to have occurred.... I have no hesitation in attributing these evils to the habitual inattention of the Officers of the regiments as prescribed by the standing regulations of the service."[65] Targeted at the inability of his general and field grade officers to control their men, the order was deeply resented in the ranks. Copies of the order were also sent home, where they were published in the papers to once again discredit Wellington and the government.[66]

Wellington immediately attempted to reorganize his staff by calling for outright dismissal of five out of the seven cavalry generals and ten infantry divisional and brigade commanders.[67] Because Wellington did not have the power to appoint officers to command, he felt that he should not be the one to relieve the men. He complained about the responsibility that the Horse Guards placed on him for removing general officers that he had not recommended for command: "I request that general officers should not be sent out; and when those are sent out whom I conceive not to be fit for their situation and I request that they be removed, I am then to bear the responsibility or odium of their removal. What a situation is mine! It is impossible for me to prevent incapable men from being sent to the army; and when I complain that they are sent, I am to be responsible [for their removal]." Wellington's reluctance to accept this responsibility stemmed primarily from an awareness of the political and social stigma of their dismissal and the financial consequences that would fall upon them if they were removed from command. In a letter to the Horse Guards, Wellington uncharacteristically withdrew his aggressive stance and offered a suggestion for their future service: "I have protested against anything harsh being done to the officers who I wished to be removed.... I wish they should not be removed unless they can be otherwise provided for. I beg it that it may be understood that I am ready to bear all the responsibility or odium, which can attach to the person who causes their removal. I am responsible for the appointment of [General Erskine to the army].... In regard to the others; I have nothing to do with it. They were sent to this country from England."[68]

In London, even the opposition party sensed Wellington's frustration with the quality of his officers. After Napoleon's defeat in Russia, the opposition predicted that Napoleon would return to the peninsula to crush Wellington once and for all. In a letter to Grenville, Auckland remarked, "Bonaparte will undoubtedly raise another army, or employ increased exertions in the Peninsula. He may draw encouragement from the terms in which Lord Wellington proclaims that the British Army (our great and last hope) has disgraced itself by the inefficiency of the officers, the outrageous excesses of the men and unexampled want of discipline beyond anything that Wellington has seen or read of."[69] The predictions of the opposition would not come to fruition because Napoleon found himself in a far greater struggle in Russia and could not spare more troops to fight in the peninsula.

In December 1812, free of the pursuing French armies, Wellington turned his attention to another pressing matter—command of the Spanish armies. Gaining greater control of the Spanish forces was not a new problem for Wellington as he had been unhappy with the role the Spanish armies had played in his campaigns for some time. In 1811, Wellington had remarked, "The Spanish armies are neither disciplined nor provided nor equipped in such a manner as that they can perform any operation even of the most trifling nature if there should be any opposition on the part of the enemy."[70] The Spanish had done very little throughout the next year, to include suffering a miserable defeat at Castalla on 12 July, to change his opinion. Furthermore, because of the Spanish commissariat's inability to consistently supply and feed the troops garrisoned within Ciudad Rodrigo, the Spanish were in danger of losing the fortress.[71]

In Wellington's mind, the solution was simple: in order to turn the Spanish army into a reliable ally, he should be given command of the country's armies and should also be given the power to pay, equip, and supply its forces. Despite the merit of his logic, many issues—including unreasonable demands by the Spanish for financial support for greater control of their troops—had derailed all previous attempts toward a lasting arrangement. Throughout the previous year, Henry had lobbied for a more sympathetic voting audience in Cadiz and had parlayed British support to arm, feed, and equip 100,000 soldiers in exchange for Wellington's control of Spanish troops. The sticking point was control of the money, and Henry's proposal was denied by the British government until conditions could be placed on the aid. Wellington agreed. He knew that Britain lacked the financial resources to assume paying, training, and equipping the Spanish in 1811. He also understood that until the financial arrangements of subsidy payments could be met, there would be no incentive for Spanish forces to adhere to any of his orders. He was also wary of the Spanish political entanglements that command of the Spanish armies would bring. Instead, he favored direct control of subsidy payments, which he could distribute directly to Spanish commanders in exchange for their support. Henry rejected this proposal; such an arrangement would strip him of needed influence at Cadiz.[72]

Another millstone for Wellington and Henry was obtaining the support of the liberal minority at Cadiz. The *liberales*, in the wake of the sack of Ciduad Rodrigo and Badajoz, were wary of submitting control of their armies to the British. Authors of the liberal Constitution of 1812, the *liberales* feared the Cortes, which had grown increasingly conservative, and therefore would not vote for Wellington until their power base was secure. Wellington had long been suspicious of the *liberales* and the Constitution of 1812, which he saw as meaningless until lasting reform of the Spanish political system could be undertaken. In his eyes, a balance between the conservatives and *liberales* had to be struck before any lasting agreement could be met. Despite the political challenges associated with securing the command for Wellington, Henry continued to lobby the Cortes in Cadiz for support of his brother.[73]

Wellington's opportunity to gain increased control over the Spanish came after the battle of Salamanca and the liberation of Madrid in August. The victories marked a dramatic shift in Anglo-Spanish relations, as Wellington was heralded throughout Spain. Wellington entered Madrid and received a hero's welcome. Flanked by the Spanish General España and the guerilla Sánchez, he publicly proclaimed his support of the Constitution of 1812. The effect of this display of solidarity was immediately felt in Cadiz, and the Cortes replied with honors and titles. However, nothing could conceal that it was Wellington's Anglo-Portuguese army, not the Spanish, that liberated the capital. In Cadiz, Henry used Wellington's popularity to once again pose the question of his command of the Spanish armies. The Cortes could no longer deny that cooperation with Wellington's army presented the best possible course of action to rid Spain of the French.

With the help of a newly elected pro-British president of the Cortes, Andrés de la Vega, Henry was able to assure the *liberales* that Wellington's command would not be accompanied by economic arrangements that would threaten Spanish markets. On September 22, the Cortes passed a decree appointing Wellington command of the Spanish field armies. Henry was ecstatic. Wellington was rightfully cautious. The language of the decree gave Wellington operational control of the field armies but was unclear on Wellington's political power to control the pay, discipline, and logistics within the army. Unwilling to take responsibility of a force he did not bear the responsibility of equipping and supplying, Wellington referred the Spanish offer to the British government for approval. The government gave its approval on the principle that Wellington be granted the powers he requested, and on 22 November Wellington formally accepted control of the Spanish forces.[74]

In Wellington's acceptance letter, he made his demands on the Spanish government. He insisted on complete control over all personnel appointments and disciplinary actions in the Spanish army: "It is impossible for me to perform the duties [as commander in chief] as they ought to be performed unless I possess sufficient powers," he wrote. ". . . . First, officers should be promoted and should be appointed to commands solely at my recommendation. Neither promotion nor appointment of any description should be made to any command, whether in chief or division, or to any other description, excepting at my recommendation."[75] The Cortes agreed to relinquish control to Wellington; however, as he feared, insufficient funds and disagreement from Spanish generals over appointments within the Spanish army plagued him until the end of the war. While Wellington was better able to coordinate their efforts, Spanish generals were adamantly opposed to centralized control of their armies. In the end, Wellington's control over the Spanish armies did not assuage any of his or the British government's burdens as Anglo-Spanish relations would continue to deteriorate throughout the remainder of the war. On one hand, his command of the Spanish armies aided the allied cause, but Wellington suffered under the political responsibility while his soldiers and their Spanish allies struggled to liberate Spain over the next two years.[76]

The appropriate number of troops and reinforcements, cavalry regiments in particular, was yet another issue for Wellington during the campaign. The problems stemmed from Parliament's restrictions governing the size and employment of the home army to the British Isles and the domestic turmoil that broke out in Britain during the war. The cavalry regiments Wellington requested were also urgently needed at home to restore order. In 1812 Parliament regulated the size of the home army at fifty-three thousand men.[77] During the campaign of 1811, Wellington requested and received three cavalry regiments, but after these were sent to the peninsula, only sixteen cavalry regiments remained in England and Ireland. During the fall of 1812, three additional cavalry regiments sailed for the peninsula. However, they did not arrive until after major combat actions had ceased, so they were counted in the totals for 1813.[78]

Parliament kept forty-five infantry regiments at home that Wellington could have used. He received only seven battalions of reinforcements in 1812, but three arrived in time to fight. In addition to these units, the government dispatched nearly ten thousand individual replacements; however, only seven thousand of these troops saw action in 1812.[79]

To combat this shortage, the government recruited allied units and shipped them to the peninsula. While some of these units, including the King's German Legion, served with distinction, the majority of allied units did not.[80]

Wellington needed cavalry regiments desperately to counter the numerous French cavalry units, which were larger and of better quality than his own. In a letter to Bathurst, Wellington complained, "The enemy's superiority now consists in his cavalry alone. . . . I think it would be desirable to keep in this country only three squadrons, or six troops of each regiment, and two squadrons, or four troops at home; the home squadrons could then supply the casualties, as well as of men and horses of those abroad and we should have at all times an equally efficient cavalry at a smaller expense."[81]

The government came under public and political scrutiny for withholding crucial manpower and resources from Wellington. A *Times* editorial read: "The decisive assaults of Ciudad Rodrigo and Badajoz overwhelmed the enemy with astonishment and overwhelmed his plans, but this great benefit was not purchased at a trifling expense. The army lost from 7,000 to 8,000 men in those two sieges. A war minister should have had his eye on those bold measures and have been ready to improve them to the utmost. There were 53,000 regulars in England. Shall we be told that they were wanted here? For what? To keep down the Irish Catholics, and Yorkshire weavers! Oh Shame, where is thy blush?"[82] Not surprising, the main political opposition came from Wellington's brother Richard, who, seeking to detach himself to form a new government, accused Liverpool of withholding troops from Wellington. In his criticism, Richard declared that at least fifteen thousand men could have been spared from service at home and shipped to the peninsula. The arrival of these troops, Richard argued, would have enabled Wellington to pursue and destroy Marmont's army after Salamanca.[83]

While the government defended its policies in providing support for Wellington, the Horse Guards assured Wellington that it was doing all it could to send needed cavalry regiments to the peninsula. Torrens insisted, "I wish you had still more cavalry. The Hussars brigade was reviewed at Hounslow a few days ago, and I could not help wishing it had been sent to you."[84] Nevertheless, due to the intertwined bureaucracy of British army, the Horse Guards was not willing to send more. Parliament's decision to withhold troops was due to the lack of a mounted constabulary force in England and Ireland. Because cavalry regiments, particularly light cavalry, or dragoons, were requested by local governments to preserve the peace, they could not be freed for duty abroad. This reduced the available number of cavalry; a more contentious domestic issue prevented the remaining horsemen from being deployed to the peninsula. Due to several mass subsidies provided to Russia in 1812, mounted regiments were frequently called upon to suppress worker riots with all force necessary. This was a result of the rise in food prices. In Lancashire and Yorkshire, inflation and the introduction of factory machinery caused unemployment and mass unrest among the local populace.[85] In addition to civil unrest, the growing number of French prisoners sent to England by Wellington required more troops to guard them, and thus fewer were available for Wellington's campaign. In some instances, these same troops were also called on to track down parole violators, further straining the military resources needed to win the war. Finally, due to the excessive number of troops who suffered from disease during the summer and fall of 1812 in the peninsula, Wellington asked the government to refrain from sending reinforcements to the area except in the early months of the year. This practice reduced his numbers because reinforcements arriving after the summer were unlikely to affect the campaign season. In a letter to Liverpool on this matter, he wrote, "It is very desirable that you should send us any reinforcements, that you may intend for us at an early period in the season. If they should be late, they will arrive in the unhealthy season [and] they will be too late to be of use."[86]

In addition to managing a reserve cavalry force at home, the War Department also struggled with requisitioning soldiers serving abroad to augment Wellington's army. By the fall of 1812, the government requisitioned all available troops serving abroad that could be sent to the peninsula. The most readily available troops were assigned to Sicily under the command of Sir William Bentinck.[87]

In October, Bentinck submitted a proposal to launch an offensive against Venice to seize the banking and commerce centers. Bentinck's proposal was denied because the government could not afford to subsidize more Sicilian troops for his command. More important, Bathurst was unwilling to subsidize more foreign troops, whose value remained questionable.[88] Bathurst also believed the prospect of success was far less than the cost of reallocating those forces to the peninsula. His military secretary, Col. Henry Bunbury, recommended that the troops be sent to the peninsula instead: "I cannot help to think that it would be more satisfactory for Wellington as well as more useful toward the success of the war to direct him to carry every man that could be spared from Sicily and Malta and to unite them with Maitland's Corps in eastern Spain under the command of Wellington." Bunbury knew that Bentinck would resist the measure. He commented, "Of course Bentinck would rather employ 12,000 men in Spain for six months, than be paralyzed by the absence of 6,000 men for twelve months." Bunbury further recommended the reduction of operations in Malta in favor of reinforcing Wellington. Bunbury's candid criticism of the prospects of supporting operations was refreshing and rare. Nevertheless, Bathurst did not reallocate troops to Wellington from Sicily and Malta.[89]

One reason Bathurst hesitated was the situation in Russia. By October, the French had begun their arduous retreat from Moscow, and it seemed that the Russians had withstood the brunt of Napoleon's invasion. Furthermore, repositioning army assets would curtail the navy's ability to prosecute the war against America. Nevertheless, the fact that the government even briefly considered curtailing other external operations to support the Peninsular War was positive for Wellington.

Despite the government's inability to augment Wellington with men from Bentinck's little-used Sicilian force, the War Department had reinforced Wellington with nearly 20,000 troops from England since December 1811. In addition to the troops from England, 4,700 more men under the command of Gen. John Skerrett were detached to Wellington's force from Cadiz.[90]

Unfortunately, after Wellington's yearlong struggle and hard fighting at Badajoz, Salamanca, and Burgos in 1812, the reinforcements sent from England did not significantly alter his available troop strength. According to the records maintained by the Horse Guards, 10,207 British soldiers died during 1812; another 1,720 were discharged; and 1,092 deserted. In all, throughout 1812, more than 13,000 British soldiers were lost. In addition to these losses, sickness further reduced the strength of Wellington's army. The number of invalided soldiers had reached 13,000 by January 1812. By August, that number had risen to over 20,000, nearly 40 percent of Wellington's total force. As a result, Wellington's effective combat strength never rose above 40,000 troops, despite the arrival of nearly 20,000 reinforcements from England.[91]

By September 1812, Wellington claimed that the number of sick had decreased and the "army in general is more healthy than it was at this season last year." He attributed the positive statistics not to any act of the government, but to measures taken by his medical staff and to the training and exposure of seasoned units in the peninsula. In a letter to Bathurst, Wellington noted that the sickness rate in veteran peninsular units was negligible compared with those who had recently arrived from Britain or elsewhere: "I am afraid that our soldiers are not sufficiently exercised in marching, when at home or in foreign garrisons; and they become sickly as soon as they are obliged to make a march."[92]

In his letter, Wellington named Dr. McGregor as the person responsible for curbing the overall sickness rate in the army and requested that "something be done for him." Because the Medical Board in London supervised the doctors on his staff and supervised appointments and promotions for all the army's physicians, Wellington was powerless to promote deserving medical officers such as McGregor.

The general's request for McGregor's promotion was indicative of a much greater problem for Wellington, because he viewed the board's appointment and promotion procedures as a burden. Consequently, he complained that the "medical board waited until the last moment to send officers to the Peninsula." To reinforce his point, Wellington stated that "medical returns go to them regularly, but because they choose to promote officers based on availability and seniority, they waste three to four months to actually fill the request." In addition to the delay of receiving doctors, Wellington claimed, "all who do arrive are sick in the first instance." Instead, Wellington urged Bathurst to allow the Medical Board to promote his medical officers in the field and send junior replacements from England or elsewhere. Furthermore, he felt that if the board promoted deserving officers already serving the peninsula, the army would benefit from their experience and acclimation. In the end, the board did not stop promoting based on "vacancy," and Wellington's doctors continued to operate undermanned. Nevertheless, their efforts to mend the sick and wounded after the siege and retreat from Burgos prepared Wellington's army for victory in 1813.[93]

Despite the setback at Burgos, the campaign of 1812 had been a tremendous victory for the Spanish cause. The Spanish Cortes responded by bestowing Wellington with the command of their field armies. Furthermore, the British army proved that it could fight and win offensive operations against the French, an important facet for upcoming operations.

The campaign also marked an improving situation between Wellington and the government. After Perceval's assassination in May, the Liverpool administration survived several attempts by politicians, Richard Wellesley among them, to form a new government. Furthermore, the additions of Bathurst to the War Office and the return of Castlereagh to the Foreign Office stabilized the government and provided Liverpool with competent and experienced men who would manage the two offices for the remainder of the war. As Wellington planned decisive offensive operations for 1813, both Bathurst and Castlereagh gave him the support he required on the home front. In turn, Wellington never faced public and political scrutiny as he had in the past. Furthermore, he parlayed the government's support to gain a level of political influence unrivaled by any previous British general.

Despite the vote of confidence from the cabinet, Wellington feared that the war with the United States would continue to drain his army of the vital naval support he required and would also draw the public's and therefore Parliament's attention away from the peninsula. Like the failed Walcheren Expedition of 1809, the United States diverted much needed resources and manpower away from what Wellington deemed Britain's most dangerous adversary—Napoleon. For the Admiralty, the war with America demonstrated its inability to balance the strategic expectations of supporting Wellington's army in Iberia and defeating America on the high seas with the operational reality of a finite number of resources to do both. As Wellington prepared to liberate the Iberian Peninsula in 1813, the burden of those demands would be shouldered most by Wellington and his men.

8

OPPORTUNITY ARRESTED: THE CAMPAIGN OF 1813

[The Royal Navy] must not be dazzled by these splendid victories of Lord Wellington . . . so as to lose sight of the truly British axiom: Britain's best bulwarks are her wooden walls.

Naval Chronicle, 6 August 1813

As Wellington withdrew from Burgos during the winter of 1812, over two thousand miles to the east in Russia, Napoleon's *grande armée* was involved in an even more disastrous retreat. Napoleon's defeat in the east ushered in a new phase of the Peninsular War and presented the British with several promising courses of action. As the French emperor issued his famous 29th Bulletin, declaring that the Russian invasion had failed, Liverpool solicited Wellington's advice for the upcoming campaign:

> There has been no example within the last twenty years, among all the extraordinary events of the French Revolution, of such a change of fortune as Bonaparte has experienced during the last five months. The most formidable army every collected has been substantially destroyed. . . . By best accounts the Russians have taken no less than 100,000 prisoners. The French cavalry is now never mentioned in any of the French Bulletins and must in fact ceased to exist. . . . The greater part of the artillery has either been taken or aban-

doned.... Under these circumstances the question naturally occurs whether he will leave the French army in Spain?[1]

Liverpool speculated on three probable courses of action. First, Napoleon could abandon Spain altogether in favor of having the majority of his army available for action in Germany. Second, the emperor could choose to reduce the number of forces in Spain, send those troops to Germany, and order the remainder to conduct defensive operations. Or third, he might proceed with his original concept and leave the French forces in Spain, waging war the best he could with the remaining troops in central Europe.[2]

As Wellington planned his next move, Liverpool resolved to send Wellington the money he needed. Accordingly, Bathurst and the chancellor of the Exchequer, Herries, forced the Bank of England to empty its coffers and send Wellington all its available gold and silver. A very precarious legal loophole justified Bathurst and Herries's policies, but nonetheless, the Bank of England's reserves were shipped in unspecified sums. Although these shipments provided temporary relief, Wellington preferred predictable monthly shipments to meet his long-term requirements.[3]

Above all, Napoleon's defeat in Russia benefited Wellington immeasurably. The emperor's retreat from Russia was followed by a general French withdrawal from central Europe. The massive French withdrawal precipitated the collapse of the Continental System, which allowed England to gain access to powerful European bankers and profitable markets. Herries and Bathurst parlayed these events with the aggressive pursuit of gold and silver specie for Wellington's army. Herries himself directed operations in Europe. With the help of powerful bankers, including Nathan Rothschild, Herries raised funds sufficient to meet British subsidy obligations to its allies and promised an additional £100,000 per month to Wellington's army. This was not nearly sufficient to meet all of Wellington's demands, but it was a great deal more than had been delivered up to that point. From November 1812 to 15 July 1813, over £1,150,000 in gold was shipped to Wellington's army.[4]

Not surprising, the majority of Wellington's letters throughout the campaign of 1813 praised Bathurst and Herries's efforts to send money. In March, Wellington joked, "Your Lordship's monthly £100,000 has been of such use to us, that not only has the produce of our bills been greater since we have received this supply regularly, but what is still more extraordinary, I do not believe you have received any complaints [for want] of money [from me] in many months."[5] The regular shipments of money also affected morale. In August, Wellington told Bathurst, "Our having so much money has enabled me to adopt a plan for paying every non-commissioned officer and soldier a day's pay every day, which I think will produce a great reform in their conduct. Many of their outrages are certainly attributed to want of money."[6]

Napoleon reduced the number of troops in the Iberian Peninsula in 1812, but he had no plans to cede control of the peninsula. With two hundred thousand men south of the Pyrenees, the French still outnumbered the allied armies. However, French power was fragile. Spread thin due to their limited ability to forage the countryside, the French could not concentrate their forces for an extended period and therefore held only a tenuous position in Spain, controlling only the area occupied by their troops.

The Royal Navy added to Napoleon's strategic problems in the peninsula with its ability to supply guerillas and land troops anywhere along the coastline. Prior to launching his offensive in the spring of 1813, Wellington ordered Sir John Murray to conduct a diversionary operation in the eastern province of Valencia. He was to land, join forces with Spanish troops, seize the city of Tarragona, and ultimately drive the French forces under Marshal Louis Gabriel Suchet from the lower Ebro.[7] Murray landed his troops in June 1813; however, they were quickly contained by Marshal Suchet and forced to withdraw.[8]

Despite Murray's diversionary operations in the east, the most precarious situation for the French in the spring of 1813 was along the Biscay coast in northern Spain. The Royal Navy continued its operations to supply guerilla forces during the winter, which forced General Marie-François Caffarelli and his French army to return to the province.[9]

The situation in the south of Spain also changed as several thousand veteran troops under Marshal Soult were recalled from Andalucia in 1811 to serve with Napoleon in Russia. Wellington's victory at Salamanca forced the remainder of Soult's Army of the South to withdraw into Valencia, where it reconstituted its strength. In November, the combined armies of Joseph and Soult re-took Madrid and forced Hill to retreat to a defensible line near Salamanca. After moving north, Marshal Soult was replaced by General Theodore Gazan. Overall command of all French forces was placed under Joseph while Marshal Jean-Baptiste Jourdan served as his chief of staff. The veteran marshal, with three French armies numbering approximately ninety-five thousand men under his command, inherited the difficult tasks of coordinating the French armies against Wellington and subduing the growing Spanish resistance.[10]

The emperor also ordered Joseph to move his capital from Madrid to Valladolid, a more central and defensible position in the center of the country. Despite removing substantial numbers of men, Napoleon also instructed his elder brother to use his remaining forces to suppress the Spanish uprising in the north, subdue the contentious province of Navarre, and recapture the port of Santander from the British. He also ordered Joseph to attack Wellington in the south. Napoleon's multiple orders contained two fatal flaws. First, he underestimated the strength of Wellington's army, and second, he once again overestimated the capabilities of King Joseph and Marshal Jourdan.[11]

Wellington was unable to determine Napoleon's intentions until the spring. On 10 March he detected the first major movements of French troops northward and wrote Bathurst to inform him of the departure from Spain of Marshal Soult and General Caffarelli.[12] Unlike the deteriorating French situation, by the spring of 1813, Wellington's strategic situation in the peninsula had improved. Having spent the winter of 1812–13 behind the protection of the Portuguese border fortress, Ciudad Rodrigo, Wellington's army was rejuvenated and prepared for action. His objective for the upcoming campaign was to drive the French from Spain; his plan also aimed to prevent the recurrence of his previous year's failures. Thus, he proposed an imaginative use of sea power to solve the problem of long supply lines and the difficulty of transporting heavy siege guns in a fast-moving, offensive campaign. To accomplish the task, Wellington made arrangements for the Royal Navy to move his primary supply point of embarkation from Lisbon to Santander. Because the inadequate road network would not facilitate large movements of material from Portugal northward, it was hoped that transporting supplies by sea and river would save valuable time and money. Though having resisted the idea in the past, Wellington recognized that any offensive in the mountainous north of Spain would be most easily supplied from ships delivering goods to coastal ports along the Biscay coast. Therefore, he transferred the responsibility of maintaining his vital lines of supply and communication to the Royal Navy.[13]

To deny the French the same maritime advantage, Wellington planned a coastal offensive toward the Pyrenees. But the immediate problem was that the French held the key fortifications of San Sebastián and Pamplona. Designed to block the major coastal and interior roads that led to the Pyrenees, these forts, Wellington understood, would have to be seized before any drive toward France could be mounted. Accordingly, Wellington planned to move quickly to prevent the French from concentrating their forces in the north-central portions of the country.[14]

While planning his offensive, Wellington once again turned his attention to the question of political support for the war back in London. He thanked his government and assured it that victory was attainable. In a letter to the prince regent, Wellington wrote, "I hope you will permit me to avail my warmest thanks for the numerous favors your Royal Highness has conferred upon me. Not only have all the means which the resources at the disposal of your Royal Highness could command, been given to support the efforts making in this country with my direction, but I have been encouraged in every manner to act with confidence in the support of your Royal Highness; and I have been favored and rewarded to a degree not only far beyond my deserving, but far beyond what any subject has yet been by his Sovereign."[15]

He recognized that support from Westminster was vital. The failed siege of Burgos had tested the public's patience with Liverpool's government. In December 1812, a *Times* editorial proclaimed that Liverpool "had shown himself a shallow speculator, unfit for the desk of a common insurance office." The article added that Liverpool had "disregarded the first lesson of vulgar arithmetic.... [He] had forfeited all claims to common humanity, every life [Liverpool] destroyed in this now, fruitless contest, cries aloud for vengeance; every dollar wasted is a debt on which we shall levy execution .... The British army starves, is unpaid and defeated. The people starve, and are disappointed, and disgraced. England is ruined, [Liverpool] is ruined."[16] While the press savaged Liverpool and his administration, the opposition party questioned renewal of the British East India Company's charter in Parliament. It was a welcome reprieve for the ministry as Liverpool told Wellington, "Our Parliamentary business is going on well. . . . At present there is little union between the different branches of opposition. The old opposition are evidently disheartened [by your success], and our friends are in good spirits."[17]

Notwithstanding Liverpool's optimism, the opposition still privately questioned Wellington's ability to win the war. A Whig leader wrote, "I am no detractor from Lord Wellington, but it is quite ridiculous to state him as driving the French out of Spain, when in truth they are making no efforts in it. They have withdrawn all the elite forces in their army [from Spain] to carry it to Saxony. It is when the French are in force and are in earnest in the Spanish War that we must see whether Wellington can keep them out of it."[18]

Opposition from yet another source surfaced in London. In December 1812, the army's commander in chief, the Duke of York, questioned Wellington on the matter of troop rotation and reinforcements. The catalyst for the duke's actions were the exceptionally high casualty lists from the storming of Ciudad Rodrigo in January, Badajoz in April, the battle of Salamanca in July, and the retreat from Burgos in November. Their cumulative effect lowered the combat strength of many infantry and cavalry units to well below 50 percent. Of the fifty-five infantry battalions in Wellington's army, twelve battalions could field only three hundred bayonets out of their prewar strength of one thousand men. An additional thirteen more battalions had more sick men in the ranks than healthy.[19]

The common practice of the day determined that when British infantry battalions and cavalry squadrons fell below 40 percent of their strength, the entire battalion was redeployed for reconstitution. The practice was effective because each regiment usually consisted of two battalions; one served abroad while the second was trained, recruited, and prepared to send reinforcements. However, due to the scale of Britain's military effort against France and its efforts to maintain the empire, by 1812 the majority of British infantry regiments either consisted of one battalion (seven of which were in the peninsula) or had each of their two battalions deployed abroad. With only one depot to supply each regiment, there was often no reserve or replacement apparatus in place to reconstitute or resupply these veteran units with fresh replacements.[20] Concerned about the relative weakness of the twelve battalions in Wellington's army, which numbered fewer than four hundred men, and without the capability of sending reinforcements to bring these units up to marginal strength of five hundred men, the Duke of York insisted that Wellington redeploy depleted veteran units to recruit and reconstitute their losses. In exchange, the Duke of York informed Wellington, he would dispatch an equal number of fresh, yet inexperienced, battalions to replace the troops he sent home. The Duke of York proposed the same plan for the cavalry, which, like the infantry, listed several regiments below their effective strength of 250 men.[21]

Wellington strongly objected to the idea of exchanging veteran troops for inexperienced recruits. Instead, he instituted a plan to combine several of his depleted, yet veteran, units into provisional battalions. Instead of withdrawing to reconstitute their strength, these provisional battalions would remain in the peninsula. They would comprise a mixture of officers and noncommissioned officers of four depleted infantry battalions with the privates of four additional depleted battalions. The remaining officers, noncommissioned officers, and privates of the eight depleted battalions would be sent home to reconstitute and recruit. In defense of his position, Wellington informed the Duke of York, "Experience has shown that [veteran and acclimatized troops] could not be replaced by three times their numbers brought from England or any other part of the world."[22] On 6 December Wellington issued his orders to constitute three provisional battalions and made plans to carry out the same arrangement for several others. For the cavalry, Wellington intended to do the same by reducing four regiments to two squadrons, sending the remaining officers, minus their horses, home to be returned at the Horse Guards' discretion.[23]

The Duke of York disagreed with the concept of provisional units. He informed Wellington that when a depleted battalion was returned to England, the corps of veteran soldiers was required to return to England to help train and recruit replacements.

> Experience has shown that in every instance wherein a battalion has brought home a skeleton, composed of its officers, NCOs, and certain foundation of the old and experienced soldiers, the greatest success has attended its reformation for any service with a short period. . . . But if a corps reduced in numbers be broken up by the division of its establishment, it is quite impossible but that such an interruption must be

occasioned in its interior economy and *esprit de corps* as a regiment as would effectually prevent that speedy completion of numbers and reorganization which I look to as the only means of providing for the demands for foreign service.

The Duke of York added, "I am aware that it has been and is justly urged, that men who are seasoned to the climate and experienced in the field are more valuable than a greater number of fresh troops from England. . . . I think it would be inexpedient and improvident, for the sake of a present and comparatively trifling advantage, to sacrifice the only foundation upon which can look to the eventual efficiency of the army."[24]

Although Wellington commanded the largest British Expeditionary Force, it was not the only expeditionary force deployed abroad, and therefore it was the Duke of York's responsibility to take the broader picture into perspective. Despite Wellington's proposal to form provisional units, the Duke of York wanted the depleted units to be sent home at once. As a sign of his understanding, however, the commander in chief reassured Wellington that he had no intention of withdrawing any troops without sending reinforcements to take their place.[25]

Wellington implemented the Duke of York's instructions at his discretion. By not recalling specific infantry units by name, Wellington inferred that the Duke of York's instructions were advisory and not binding. Instead, Wellington responded to the Duke of York's military secretary, Henry Torrens, by stating, "I take a very different view of these questions." He acknowledged that the Duke of York had the entire army to be concerned about, including troops in Sicily and North America; however, it was Wellington's responsibility to offer suggestions that best suited his situation. In this case, Wellington argued, "I am of the opinion that it is better to have one or two soldiers who have served on a campaign than three or four who have not. Not only do new soldiers perform no service, but by filling the hospital they are a burden to us." Refusing to redeploy the provisional units he had recently formed, Wellington told Torrens, "I am so unwilling to part with the men whom I have formed into the provisional battalions and I never will part with them as long as it is left to my discretion." In addressing the cavalry, Wellington stated that he had four depleted cavalry regiments without the appropriate number of horses. Instead of sending them home with their mounts, he preferred to keep their horses in the peninsula and issue their mounts to his other cavalry regiments.[26]

The Duke of York sought a compromise. He told Wellington, "I am the last person in the world to wish to diminish your force or cripple your exertions, but necessity knows no law . . . and I am obliged to consider the many other services which I am called upon to supply." He did not specifically name the infantry regiments to be recalled and therefore allowed Wellington to use his discretion on which infantry battalions to send home. However, the Duke of York was less forthcoming with the cavalry. He ordered five depleted cavalry regiments to return to England. He did, however, accede to Wellington on the horses. He wrote, "Horses in general are becoming very difficult to procure; but horses of sufficient age to be fit for immediate active service [are] impossible to purchase." Furthermore, the cost of transporting fresh horses from England to the peninsula far outweighed the cost of keeping them in country. Therefore, he allowed Wellington to keep all his cavalry horses in the country.[27]

Wellington complied with the Duke of York's instructions concerning the cavalry and issued instructions for the Fourth Dragoon Guards, Ninth and Eleventh Light Dragoons, and Second Hussars of the King's German Legion to embark for Lisbon for transport home.[28] However, a paragraph in the general order reflected his reluctance to do so: "The measure of drafting their horses has been adopted as one of utility to the whole of the cavalry and the Commander of Forces regrets exceedingly that it has been found necessary to adopt it and that he should be deprived of the assistance of any of these brave troops, but he trusts that they will soon be remounted and reequipped, and that if necessary, they will join the army again in increased strength."[29]

As for the infantry, Wellington used the Duke of York's imprecise order to his advantage. He agreed to send home two of his weakest battalions, but he kept the remaining six of the original eight battalions the Duke of York had requested be sent home from the peninsula. To justify his decision Wellington spent the months of March and April reconstituting four of the six battalions with returned convalescents and replacements to an average strength of over four hundred men. He also proceeded with his original plan and formed three provisional battalions out of the remaining six battalions.[30]

Although Wellington's actions were a clear violation of the Duke of York's orders, no one in government questioned him. Noticeably absent from the discussion was Bathurst, whose power was limited by the fragmented command and control relationship of the British army. Nevertheless, Bathurst's silence in the matter boosted Wellington's confidence to pursue his course of action. The secretary of war and colonies' instructions to Wellington during the period never mentioned the subject of provisional battalions and instead centered on the operational disposition of Wellington's army and events in central Europe.[31]

The net result of the compromise between the Duke of York and Wellington increased Wellington's strength. He lost about 2,000 veteran infantry and cavalrymen but in return received four new cavalry regiments and six new infantry battalions, approximately 4,500 men. Although two new soldiers were not as effective as one veteran, nonetheless, his aggregate strength grew by forming provisional units and gaining replacements under the Duke of York's policy. In the end, Wellington felt that the reward of keeping his provisional battalions in the country at the expense of sending them home to reconstitute and recruit was worth the risk.[32]

While Wellington husbanded his veteran troops from the Duke of York, the government pestered Wellington throughout the campaign of 1813 with opinions about where his force should next be deployed. Whitehall preserved the hope of demonstrating its true continental commitment to its allies by landing forces in northern Europe, even though all its attempts to do so had failed. Nevertheless, in October 1812, Liverpool solicited Wellington's advice on where his army should go after Spain and Portugal were liberated. At the time, Liverpool told Wellington that "although he had no fixed or settled opinion, he favored a [continuation of the present] operation in southern France over any other."[33] Wellington agreed with Liverpool. First, it would take at least six months to transfer the army to any of the other locations. Besides the valuable time lost transferring the troops, such an army would be a "small force and it had no guarantee that it could [link up] with any other." Last, the British would not immediately gain the support of the local population in either Italy or northern Europe; he reminded Liverpool of his continuing struggle to gain local support from the Spanish and Portuguese governments and of the enormous cost of subsidizing both nations. The commander of any

British force that landed in Italy or northern Europe would incur great time and expense to gain the support of the people, which had already been purchased with blood and gold in Iberia. To reinforce his point, Wellington stated, "the Powers of the North would willingly avail themselves of the bravery of our troops; they would share in our riches, partake of the plenty of our camps, which our good arrangements and money should procure for us, but they would share nothing with us, but their distress."[34]

Despite Wellington's opinion on the subject, Napoleon's defeat in Russia produced new options for continental commitments and inspired "armchair strategists" in Parliament to make even wilder suggestions of where Wellington's army should be employed after Spain was liberated. The first of these options was stirred by revolts against French rule in Germany. Inspired by a March insurrection in Hamburg against the French, some of these strategists called for deploying the King's German Legion to northern Europe, possibly in Germany or Holland, to conduct an offensive in the Low Countries.[35] Concerned that the Germans under Wellington's command would rather fight for their homeland instead of serving in the peninsula, Bathurst stated, "I am afraid what is going in Germany will slacken the zeal of the officers of the German Legion serving under you.... The officers will not like fighting in the Peninsula when they might be engaged in a contest which is so much more interesting to them."[36] Although Wellington certainly understood the government's concern, he rebuked any course of action that took troops away from the peninsula. The King's German Legion included the finest troops in his army, and he could ill afford to lose their three cavalry regiments, five large infantry battalions, and one artillery battery. Nevertheless, he consulted the most respected German officer on his staff, Gen. Charles von Alten, about the feasibility of such an enterprise. Alten echoed Wellington's sentiment: "The best thing for England, Germany, and the world is to make the greatest possible effort [in the peninsula]." With regard to deploying a portion of the legion to Germany, even the German general felt that "its services would be very useful in the approaching campaign [in the peninsula] and would be entirely thrown away [if it was re-deployed to Germany.]"[37] Like Wellington, Alten felt that the addition of four thousand men would not alter events in central Europe, where hundreds of thousands of German, Austrian, and Russian troops were already massed against Napoleon.

However, the loss of only a thousand men could significantly alter the scope and effectiveness of the upcoming Iberian campaign of 1813. Bathurst relented. The government supported the Hanoverian uprising by sending five hundred German officers and men from a garrison in England to train and lead the German conscripts. In the end, Wellington lost no units.[38]

Nevertheless, Wellington would have to again defend his army from the politicians at home, or other generals serving abroad, who were convinced that his troops could be better used elsewhere. The second attempt to reposition his troops stemmed from a proposal to transfer units of his army from Spain to Italy.[39]

The irritant was General Bentinck. He was no stranger to the ire of his government or Wellington. Due to Wellington's success and a shortage of troops serving abroad, Bentinck had been forced to serve in a secondary capacity to Wellington. It was a role he did not like.[40] Despite receiving instructions from the Bathurst in March 1812 to prevent French forces in eastern Spain from joining Marmont's force, Bentinck waited until June to dispatch General Maitland with several thousand British troops to the peninsula. Because Maitland landed late and without proper transport, the operation failed. In a letter to Wellington concerning the conduct of General Bentinck, Liverpool gave no justification for Bentinck's delays: "The change of plans disappointed us most grievously. I cannot understand what his objections can have been. His instructions in March were as positive as any which can be given to a commander so circumstanced."[41] Despite failing to support Wellington, Bentinck retained his command. Nevertheless, neither he nor Wellington forgot the incident.

In the spring of 1813, Bentinck countered Wellington's proposal to invade southern France by requesting that a large portion of Wellington's army be moved to join his force in Sicily. He felt that the timing of Napoleon's defeat in Russia made Italy, not southern France, the most logical place for Britain to prosecute the war against the French in 1813–14.[42] By this time, Sicily had become a sideshow to major events in central Europe and Spain. As Napoleon was defending his empire from a coalition bent on his destruction, the French forces in Italy were essentially neutralized by geography and events. Drawing comparisons to the events that led Britain to the Iberian Peninsula in 1808, Bentinck assured the government that like the Spanish, the Sicilians, followed by the mainland Italians, would rise up and join

British arms against the French. Ambitious and shortsighted, Bentinck even held secret negotiations with the French marshal Joachim Murat, named king of Naples by Napoleon, to discuss his proposal for the division of the Italian peninsula. While Bentinck favored unifying Italy under one flag, Murat demurred, instead desiring to keep his throne in Naples. Although nothing came of the negotiations, Bentinck still lobbied London for support of his plan.[43]

Fortunately for Wellington, Bentinck's audience was not very large, and his most influential supporter was the undersecretary for war, Henry Bunbury. Bunbury, a minor political figure, agreed with Bentinck and felt that "the emancipation of Italy must be a point of vital importance to the British." Furthermore, Bunbury proposed that once Spain was freed, Wellington's army should be moved to Italy or northern Germany. There was a strategic advantage to keeping French forces occupied in guarding Napoleon's interests in Italy. However, it is doubtful that, given the seriousness of Napoleon's situation in Europe, he could have afforded to deploy more troops to Italy.[44]

Wellington was aware of the government's dilemma, and he understood Bentinck's rationale for suggesting the redeployment of a large portion of his army to Italy. Nevertheless, he was determined to prevent the government from making a colossal mistake by abandoning Spain at the moment of decision. Wellington wrote Bathurst, "The south of Italy is for many reasons, probably the best scene of operations for a British Army, except the Spanish Peninsula." Wellington also highlighted the difficulty and, more important, the expense of such an undertaking. In his view, the operation would succeed only if the British government raised and equipped Italian troops. Drawing on the difficulty and expense that his enterprise had been in the peninsula, Wellington deliberately reopened his old fights with the London establishment that had grudgingly supported his campaigns. His rationale was simple but effective. If the government found it difficult to support the Spanish and Portuguese war effort, how could it find the funds necessary to pacify a local population and equip local Italian troops from scratch? Wellington argued, "If the British did not agree to supporting the operation on the full scale it required . . . the plan would fail, and our troops would be forced to embark with loss and disgrace."[45] As Liverpool and Bathurst contemplated the two proposals, Wellington wasted no time and moved his army against the French. Once committed, it would be impossible to disengage troops in contact and deploy them elsewhere. The issue became moot.

From his protected position along the Portuguese border in May, Wellington moved his army against King Joseph's force in two unequal wings. Wellington personally led the thirty thousand troops of the southern wing of his army, and he appointed Sir Thomas Graham to command the northern wing, which numbered nearly sixty thousand.[46]

Graham's force moved undetected through the mountains of central Spain and outflanked the French army. Fooled by a brilliant deception operation conducted by Wellington's quartermaster general Sir George Murray, the French were unable to ascertain the direction of the main allied advance.[47] They were also uncertain of where Wellington would strike. Deceived by the personal presence of Wellington in the south, King Joseph and Marshal Jourdan never expected Graham to command the larger force. It worked to perfection as Graham's force outflanked the French and forced them to withdraw. For the next three weeks, Wellington pursued the French and forced them to abandon central Spain. In turn, this forced the French to blow up the castle at Burgos, the site of Wellington's frustrations six months before, and withdraw to hastily prepared positions in north-central Spain.[48] Wellington pursued the French army, and on 21 June the allies routed King Joseph's army at the battle of Vitoria. Not only were the French defeated, but Marshal Jourdan suffered a particular ignominious disgrace: his marshal's baton was taken from his abandoned luggage.[49]

Ever mindful of London politics, a delighted Wellington sent the captured baton for presentation to the prince regent. The trophy had its intended effect. On 3 July, the prince regent promoted Wellington to the rank of field marshal, which brought with it great fame and personal praise. He told Wellington, "Your glorious conduct is beyond all human praise, and far above my reward. I know of no language the world affords worthy to express it. . . . You have sent me, among the trophies of your unrivalled fame, the staff of a French Marshal, and I send you in return that of England."[50]

The victory at Vitoria also ended speculation about the fate of Wellington's army. After the battle, Bathurst notified his general, "I have considered it proper to acquaint you that His Majesty's government will entertain no objection to your pursuing the great objects of the war by whatever course your Lordship shall deem the most effectual; and I have the same time to convey to your full authority to levy with the territory of France such contributions, whether of provision, forage, military equipment, means of transport, or specie, as you may consider expedient to your command."[51] Wellington's army would remain under his control and would invade France. Once again success on the battlefield decisively swayed the pendulum of political support in his favor.

Wellington had gained an unprecedented level of government support for his plans after the campaign, but the difficult task of expelling the French from Spain still loomed ahead. To make matters more difficult, in the wake of his victory at Vitoria, he was forced to take desperate measures to restore discipline in his army. After the battle, instead of pursuing the fleeing French troops, thousands of British soldiers looted the French baggage trains. For nearly six hours, the soldiers refused orders to pursue the French and instead pillaged. Wellington was furious at his men for allowing the French to escape. In a letter to Bathurst he claimed, "We started with the army in the highest order and up to the day of the battle nothing could get on better; but that event has, as usual, totally annihilated all order and discipline. The soldiers of the army have got among them about a million sterling in [plundered] money with exception of about 100,000 dollars [which was recovered] in the French military chest."[52]

In an attack that reflected years of frustration, Wellington condemned the discipline of his army, but also took the opportunity to address what he considered the root cause of the problem—the quality of the replacements he had received from London: "This is the consequence of the state of discipline of the British army. We may gain the greatest victories; but we shall do no good until we alter our system, as to force all ranks to perform their duty. The new regiments [sent recently from London] are the worst of all."[53] Wellington concluded his vitriolic attack: "It is quite impossible for me or any other man to command a British army under the existing system. We have in the service the scum of the earth as common soldiers; and as of late, we have been doing everything in our power to relax the discipline by which alone such men can be kept in order." To reinforce the desperate situation, Wellington reported that since the battle of Vitoria, he had lost nearly 2,800 men to straggling and plundering.[54]

The government's inability to provide quality units and replacements had affected the British army since the start of the war. Similar breaches of discipline had occurred during Sir John Moore's retreat in 1809 and during Wellington's withdrawal from Burgos six months prior. His army suffered great hardship during this period. Victory also carried a price tag and in some instances led to more flagrant abuses of discipline.

Unlike the siege of Badajoz, where order was restored within two days, at Vitoria, the loss of discipline in the army had operational consequences. Nearly three weeks after the battle, Wellington was still unable to reestablish discipline in several units. On 9 July, he wrote Bathurst, "I do not know what measures to take about our vagabond soldiers. Yesterday, we had 12,500 men less under arms than we had on the day before the battle [of Vitoria.] They are not in hospitals, nor are they killed, nor have they fallen into the hands of the enemy. I have sent officers with parties of cavalry in all directions after them, but I have not yet heard of any of them. I believe they are concealed in the villages in the mountains." Unable to pursue Joseph's army, Wellington asked Bathurst for assistance.[55]

Reflective of changing times and its renewed confidence in Wellington, the government responded with speed and decision. Bathurst stated, "It is essentially necessary that the discipline of the army should be restored, the fate of your campaign may depend on it." To facilitate his general's task, Bathurst forwarded a copy of the amended Mutiny Act, which increased Wellington's ability to punish offenders and restore discipline in the ranks.[56] The Horse Guards also answered Wellington's call for assistance. As the overseer of regulations and discipline within the British army, the Duke of York informed Wellington, "The stigma of [irregularity and insubordination] does not attach itself to the private alone: on the contrary, much of the blame must lie with the officers, to whose want of exertion and attention to the discipline and conduct of their men, the irregularity of the troops must be wholly attributed." The commander in chief urged Wellington to "make examples among the higher ranks of the officers whose indolence and want of attention upon whom the principal blame must be attributed. You may depend upon receiving my cordial support in the dismissal of any officer, from the senior general to the lowest ensign."[57] Wellington responded by reorganizing several of his units under new leadership, and in the case of one cavalry regiment, he requisitioned all of their horses. After contemplating sending them back to England, he ordered the regiment to walk for the remainder of the campaign.[58]

Wellington's rapid victory at Vitoria forced him to transfer his primary supply depot from Coruña to Santander. He realized the poor roads in northern Spain were inadequate to support a quick offensive. Therefore, he decided to rely again upon the navy for the bulk of logistics support. The port of Santander was recognized as the only deep-water harbor close enough to allow the navy to land the amount of supplies Wellington's army required. Despite the increased risk of moving his supply depot closer to France, Wellington assumed that the Royal Navy could control the waters off northern Spain and provide the logistics support and protection he needed.[59]

In response to their defeat, the French repositioned their defense. After Vitoria, Joseph Bonaparte withdrew the main body of French troops from northern Spain. Ceding control of most of the region to Wellington and the Spanish, the French withdrew from all of their garrisons along the Biscay coastline with the exception of the city of Santoña and the formidable fortress of San Sebastián. Because of its position along the coastal road network, the fortress of San Sebastián would stunt any British advance. Furthermore, because the fortresses had access to the sea, the French could maintain their garrisons with supplies transported from France. Unable to completely cut off and attack both fortifications, Wellington bypassed Santoña, which ultimately fell in March 1814, and instead moved his army against San Sebastián. Because it created the greatest threat to the allied logistics routes, Wellington planned for an extensive siege operation to occupy the fortress. For the next several months, San Sebastián became the primary target for Wellington's force. The resulting operations along the coast caused a great point of contention between Wellington and the Royal Navy.[60]

San Sebastián was a daunting obstacle for the British advance. Located on a small peninsula that extended into the Bay of Biscay, the fortress was protected by extensive fortifications along its windward side. A single wall protected the western defenses, which faced the bay, and a single wall with several towers protected the eastern side. At the tip of the peninsula, the fortress was overlooked by Mount Urgul, which rose to nearly 400 feet.[61]

The problem for Wellington was that in the wake of his failure at Burgos, he could ill afford another lengthy, unsuccessful siege. To succeed, Wellington knew he would have to rely on the navy to perform critical functions: first, the navy had to blockade San Sebastián; and second, due to his flank exposure, he had to rely on the navy to secure his lines of supply and communication. The greatest threat to both was the increased presence of American and French privateers operating in the area. Although privateers posed little threat to warships, they posed a significant risk to troop transports and monetary shipments not protected by armed escort. Wellington's fears of privateers were justified; the Americans had commissioned over five hundred privateers at home and abroad to attack British shipping.[62] In December 1812, American privateers captured and ransomed HMS *Canada*, a horse transport that carried forty men and horses of the Eighteenth Hussars. The men and horses were ransomed for £3,000 and arrived safely in Lisbon Harbor in February 1813. The unit was rearmed and fought at the battle of Vitoria in June.[63] Prior to launching his campaign, Wellington outlined his fears to Bathurst: "I am sorry to say that we have had some privateers on the coast, which have taken and destroyed some ships off Porto. Others are missing and it is supposed have met a similar fate. I cannot express how much we shall be distressed if the navigation of the coast should not be secure from Coruña to Cadiz. We have money, provisions, clothing, military stores and equipment on all parts of the coast almost every day in the year, and the loss of one vessel only may create a delay and inconvenience, which may be of the utmost importance."[64]

Adding to Wellington's frustration was the realization that as American privateers preyed on his shipping along the Biscay coast, American food transports brought vital wheat shipments to feed his army.[65] Since Napoleon's invasion of Russia had severed the most important source of grain to Wellington's army, the British government turned to the American markets to supply his troops. Unfortunately for Wellington, American merchants in the peninsula had to be paid in gold or silver. Therefore, as Wellington's men went unpaid for months, American ships left the peninsula loaded with bouillon, which in turn the same shipping companies used to outfit more privateers. An exasperated Wellington told Bathurst, "I am certain . . . that since Great Britain has been a naval power, a British army has never been left in such a situation. . . . I hope it will not be deemed unreasonable to request to have the navigation of the coast of Spain and Portugal secured for me, without which you must not expect success [from my operations]."[66]

At its peak strength, the Royal Navy could have managed the privateer threat, secured the lines of communication, and isolated the fortress of San Sebastián. However, Britain's navy was overextended in 1813. It was unable to respond to the upstart American navy on the high seas, blockade French naval ports, control the ubiquitous privateers who ranged the Biscay coastline, and blockade San Sebastián. Prior to his offensive, Wellington sensed the navy's inability to perform all the required missions.

The causes for the navy's failure during the campaign were many. The first problem involved readiness. Ever since the Continental System had been implemented by Napoleon in 1806, six years of blockade duty off the coasts of European ports had left most British naval squadrons badly in need of repair. The Royal Navy also lost a great deal of its popular appeal. Since 1808, the English press had concentrated on Wellington's operations in the peninsula, at the expense of attention to the navy. All these factors left the navy devoid of its most scarce commodity, sailors. As a result of the lack of seamen and increased responsibilities, the Royal Navy impressed American sailors on the high seas, thereby igniting tensions with the United States.

To add to the navy's problems, the outbreak of war with the United States exposed the navy's pre-Napoleonic emphasis on building large ships-of-the-line. To counter the larger, more heavily armed French and Spanish fleets, the British had invested heavily in equally armed vessels. Although these fleets won victories at Aboukir Bay, Copenhagen, and Trafalgar, the emergence of the privateer threat and the United States Navy, with its large 44-gun frigates such as the *Constitution*, changed the paradigm at sea.[67] Between August and October 1812, the *Constitution* alone sank or captured three British frigates. Wellington, who had always maintained that the war with the United States was an unnecessary distraction, proclaimed, "I have been very uneasy about the American naval success. I think we should have peace with America . . . if we could take one or two of these damned frigates."[68] While the war with America was being fought at sea, Wellington's operations were not given strategic priority by the Admiralty. Nevertheless, Wellington believed the Admiralty's first responsibility was support of his army and protection of his communications.[69]

While the Admiralty assured Wellington that they could support both the blockade of San Sebastián and protect his supply lines, privately they communicated their fears about their ability to do both. In a letter to his commanding officer, Lord Keith, Adm. George Collier, commander of the naval squadron off the Biscay Coast, expressed doubts about the feasibility of guarding the coast against privateers: "I find Lord Wellington so anxious about the blockade of San Sebastián and so fearful that if there is not the appearance of many cruisers off it that the enemy will take advantage of it and [evacuate its force].... I know the enemy are exerting every nerve to attempt to relieve the garrison and send them ammunition.... My opinion is that half the Americans bound for France will make this coast. As it affords protection from the many small ports and the ease with which they may coast along it."[70]

Experienced in the waters off the peninsula, Collier was in a difficult position.[71] He was responsible for coordinating naval operations with not only Wellington but also Admiral Martin, who commanded the Tagus squadron off the coast of Lisbon. He was also expected to blockade all the French-held towns from Bayonne to Cape Finisterre, a distance of over four hundred miles, and ensure the security of Wellington's supply and transport ships.[72] The main problem for Collier was the lack of available ships. Since 1812, the Admiralty had gradually decreased the force structure of the two fleets that supported Wellington in the peninsula from over twenty ships to fewer than twelve. By 1813, Collier had only seven warships at his disposal.[73]

Wellington realized the difficulty of Collier's task, but he gave the admiral little sympathy. To ensure that Collier understood his intentions for the upcoming campaign, he devoted significant time in the spring detailing his instructions. Above all else, Wellington wanted the admiral's assurance that he could guard his supply lines and limit French communications along the coast.[74] In May, before launching his advance on Vitoria against Joseph and Jourdan, in anticipation of a victory and subsequent coastal drive toward France, Wellington informed Collier to move his forward logistics base from Coruña to Santander.[75]

Wellington feared that one or more of his objectives for the navy would not be accomplished because of the ship shortage. Wellington asked Collier for help: "Admiral Martin [off the coast of Lisbon] is very little able to give the protection to the communications which is so necessary to us. . . . It may be impossible for you even to do so much, but I shall be very much obliged if you can secure our communications."[76] In his reply, Collier pledged his support, but warned Wellington: "I find the Channel fleet and cruisers are becoming more and more reduced every day; consequently there is no chance of the squadron destined to act here in the summer months being increased."[77] Wellington understood Collier's limitations in terms of ships. But Collier's failure to pre-position supplies at Santander, despite instructions to do so, drew Wellington's wrath.

Collier procrastinated; he received his instructions from Wellington in May, but he did not make preparations to establish a base of operations at Santander until late June.[78] As a result, when Wellington's army arrived at Santander to draw supplies and pick up the needed siege artillery for San Sebastián, none were available. In a blistering tirade, Wellington told Bathurst, "Ammunition required for the army has lately been delayed at Lisbon for want of a convoy; and it has not arrived at Santander. I am obliged to use the French ammunition, of a smaller caliber than ours. . . . The army cannot remain in this part of the country without magazines. . . . These magazines must be brought by sea. . . . For the first time I believe it has happened to any British army, that its communication by sea is insecure."[79]

Two more weeks passed, and still no supplies arrived. Wellington wrote to Bathurst for assistance: "The ships which were ready in Lisbon on the 12th of May had not sailed on the 19th of June and our magazines which I expected to find at Santander had not yet arrived. . . . Surely the British Navy cannot be so hard run as not to be able to keep up the communication with Lisbon for his army."[80] In a joking tone, which did little to downplay the seriousness of the situation, Wellington warned Bathurst, "A British Army has never been left in such a situation. . . . if [the privateers] only take the ship with our shoes, we must halt for six weeks!"[81]

In July, Wellington was forced to begin siege operations against San Sebastián without a forward logistics base and without adequate siege artillery. To support the siege, Wellington also wanted an adequate number of ships available to blockade the fortress. The Admiralty reacted by dispatching several smaller vessels; by 21 July,

Collier's force grew from six to fourteen ships, but they were still anchored in Lisbon harbor.[82]

To make matters worse, the waters off San Sebastián did not provide adequate anchorage for the ships on station. Subject to the hazardous seas of Biscay, the threat of enterprising privateers, and miserable conditions, the navy's ships were frequently blown off station. By day, the British posted at most one frigate off the coast; however, by night, French ships sailed from St. Jean de Luz bringing needed men and supplies to the fortress. Collier remarked on the difficulty of his task: "I know the enemy is exerting every nerve to relieve the garrison and send them ammunition."[83]

Wellington learned of the condition of the French garrison and nightly supply runs by reading a French newspaper. He told Bathurst, "The blockade of the coast is merely nominal. The enemy has reinforced *by sea* the only two posts they have on the north coast of Spain."[84] In a letter to Gen. Sir Thomas Graham, who commanded the left wing of his army, Wellington stated, "I hear that besides supplies, the French have sent into San Sebastián, artillery, men, *sapeurs*, and officers of the medical staff. . . . In fact they may send who they please."[85] In response to his general's concern, Bathurst requested the Admiralty to send "a few ships-of-the-line" to assist in the siege.[86]

Wellington was angered that the Admiralty, despite promising their full support, had failed to reinforce Collier's squadron with more ships. He was also angry at Collier's ineffectiveness. He told Collier, "It will be quite impossible for me to interfere in any manner in the naval arrangements of this coast. The Admiralty is responsible for them; and I hope they will adopt some measures to give us a secure and easy communication along the coast, and the means of using its harbors with convenience. If they do not, they will [be] responsible for any failure that may occur."[87] This failure of the navy to isolate San Sebastián adequately had a dramatic effect on Wellington's first attempt to storm the fortress. On 25 July, the French garrison defeated the first major attempt. After Wellington suffered "considerable loss," the Admiralty became the convenient and frequent target of his wrath.[88]

In August, Wellington opened a new bureaucratic battle. He complained to Bathurst that the Admiralty's inability to provide Admiral Collier with men and boats had weakened his logistics capability. Without an adequate number of sailors and boats to transport supplies ashore, Wellington was forced to employ women to navigate light and weakly constructed harbor boats to the ships anchored offshore. Wellington felt that women were "unequal to the labor" of unloading the ships. In desperation, he asked Bathurst to request more resources from the Admiralty: "I have never been in the habit of troubling the Government with requisitions for force, but have always carried on the service to the best of my ability with that which has been placed at my disposal. If the Navy of Great Britain can not afford more than one frigate and a few brigs and cutters, fit and used only to carry dispatches, to co-operate with this army in the siege of a maritime place, the possession of which is as important to the army as well as the navy, I must be satisfied and do the best I can."[89]

Admiral Collier forwarded Wellington's complaints to Lord Keith. Powerless in the struggle between Wellington and the Admiralty, Lord Keith abstained from either defending or attacking Wellington. Instead, the senior admiral forwarded messages from Wellington to the Admiralty. Keith's inaction was not atypical, since he had a longstanding record of remaining on the periphery of major decision. He told Collier, however, "I have constantly given [the army] preference, and left other stations [such as the Loire, Gironde, and L'Orient] fewer vessels than [the Admiralty's] orders or even prudence demanded."[90] Keith understood Wellington's frustration. He told the Admiralty, "I fear that if the privateers fall in with any of the convoys laden with supplies for Lord Wellington's army, they may do considerable mischief, as I have not the means of increasing the force off the coast."[91]

Bathurst relayed Wellington's complaints to the first lord of the Admiralty, Lord Melville. Since June, Melville had received reports of Wellington's dissatisfaction with his naval support.[92] In a personal defense of the admirals on station, he responded to Wellington's criticism: "I am quite content to be abused in Parliament or the papers for events for which I never had, or never could have had any control of . . . but with the exception of yourself, for which I feel that some explanation is due, I have no inclination to divert from my person any share of the clamor but I will not [explain the inadequacies of this office] to the public." Melville firmly told Wellington that when he had taken office in 1812, the Royal Navy had had ninety fewer frigates and smaller ships than in 1809. Melville also informed Wellington that since then, the global war against France and the American War had continued to drain the navy of ships and men. He assured

Wellington that "by considerable exertion and speed, though with less durability," the navy had built twenty new frigates and sloops in the past six months. The problem was not building new ships, however, but finding the men to sail them. Melville added, "You will naturally ask, why don't you raise more men? To which I reply that nothing short of a strong legislative measure could produce the number required within the period of which they are required." Melville warned Wellington that any levy on manpower would assuredly take away soldiers from the army, and therefore "he had much rather have to encounter ten times the abuse for want of naval exertion than the evil of really cramping our military exertions." Using Wellington's past reluctance to part with any of his own troops against him, Melville suggested an unacceptable proposal: "The employment of a large body of troops to destroy the shipping in some of the enemy's ports in France or America would liberate a large portion of our naval force, but would you think that we were acting wisely [by drawing those troops away from you] in the Peninsula?"[93] It was a proposition that Wellington of course rejected.

Melville included a disposition of all available naval forces that supported the Peninsular War. Because of the nature and unpredictability of the American navy and privateer threat, the number of available ships in the squadrons of Admirals Martin and Collier had decreased, but their area of responsibility surrounding the peninsula had increased. Furthermore, Melville cited several examples of ship captains being forced to pursue pirates outside their area of responsibility. These operations added to the difficulty of the fleets supporting the army. He left Wellington with an assessment that reflected the difficulty of the navy's ability to counter the privateer threat:

> You have occasionally complained the coast of Spain and Portugal is unprotected, and the safety of your naval communications endangered, because privateers have been seen and have made some captures of vessels sailing, in defiance of law and without convoy. On that subject, I shall only state that during nearly twenty years of war, no Board of Admiralty has been able to guard the coasts of England from annoyance of that description and from capers much more numerous in proportion to the extent of trade than have ever taken place on the coast of Portugal. Ten times the amount of Ad-

miral Martin's force could not give that entire area protection against an active and enterprising enemy as we now face in the case of the American privateers."[94]

Melville also scolded Wellington for his condemnation of the effectiveness of the blockade by citing a letter to Lord Bathurst in which Wellington claimed that "the fact of the communication between San Sebastián and the Ports of France is notorious to the whole world."[95] Melville told Wellington, "These are assertions which surprised me a good deal, because I had not heard the same account from any naval officer, and am still at a loss how to account for it that the enemy's naval force in the Bay of Biscay is superior, and can drive off Sir George Collier whenever they please. I should be very much astonished if Lord Keith or Sir George Collier were of that opinion." Melville concluded, "I certainly think that you have formed erroneous opinions on some points, and have been misinformed on others; but I do not complain of your making those representations to the Secretary of State or myself. . . . However, appeals to subordinate officers against their superiors are not customary in either branch of service, and they can produce no good, and are injurious to the public interest." In an ineffective attempt to mend the situation, Melville added, "I feel no predilection for this paper warfare [to continue]. You and I have the same object in view." However, he concluded by once again chastising Wellington: "I will take your opinion in preference to any other person's as to the most effectual mode of beating a French army, but I have no confidence in your seamanship or nautical skill."[96]

Wellington deflected Melville's criticism: "What I have written [about inadequate naval assistance] has been founded on my sense . . . and I assure you that I neither know nor care what has passed, or may pass, in Parliament, or in the newspapers on the subject. . . . I know nothing of the cause of the evil. . . . I state the facts which nobody will deny; and leave government to apply a remedy or not as they may think proper." In response to Melville's comparison of the security of the coasts of Portugal and England, Wellington stated,

> The circumstances of the coast of Portugal and Spain are very different from those of the Channel . . . and for many reasons are much easier to guard. . . . The inconveniences also to which the public service is exposed from the want of secure navigation of the coast of Portugal and Spain by the army are

of a far greater magnitude than those suffered by a want of security on the coasts of the channel. If the security should be of any considerable duration it will affect the army in its bread and corn; and the truth is that the delay of any one ship, or loss of some particular ships loaded with ordnance or military stores would go to impede all the operations of the campaign.

He concluded, "I assure you that there is not an hour in the day in which some statement does not come before me of the inconvenience resulting from the want of naval means; and even while writing this letter the Commissary-General has been here to complain that his empty provision ships are detained at Santander for want of a convoy!"[97]

The Admiralty responded to Wellington's criticism of the blockade with private disdain. Lord Melville wrote, "Our Military officers on the frontiers of Spain do their duty most admirably, but they seem to consider a large ship within a few hundred yards off the shore of San Sebastián as safe in its position and as immovable by the winds and waves as one of the Pyrenean Mountains." In belittling Wellington's assessment of the blockade, Melville cited the rigid seniority-based system, which governed the chain of command in the Royal Navy as in the army. Melville declined repositioning any ships because Collier, much like Wellington in 1808, would be superseded by the new commander of those vessels. He rationalized that "Wellington would rather forgo the line of battle ships than change the active commander of the squadron at the most critical period of the campaign." As a result, Melville informed Lord Keith that no additional warships would be dispatched to Wellington.[98]

The Admiralty did not yield to Wellington's criticism, and it defended Collier and his squadron's actions, by claiming that Wellington had been evasive in his expectations of naval support prior to beginning the campaign. Melville argued that because Wellington had not informed Collier of his expectation to blockade San Sebastián, they were not to blame. In sum, he told Wellington, "Unless we are apprised in due time of what is expected of us, there is no such superfluity of force at our disposal as to render it practicable for us to do more to provide for the ordinary and foreseen contingencies of the service." Melville also claimed that the Admiralty had not received

Wellington's request for blockade operations, only that they should provide security for his transports: "There would not have been any hesitation in affording you whatever naval assistance you might have required. If it could have been provided by no other means, which I have no doubt it could, it might have been a question with government to determine what other object, the Baltic for instance, or a portion of the American squadron should have been given up; but you would have been secured in what you wanted in the first instance."[99]

Wellington was angry that the Admiralty refused to accept responsibility for its failures and refuted his claims that the French resupplied the fortress to any great extent. He was justified in his anger when the Admiralty publicly refuted these claims and privately claimed success. Wellington's frustration can be gleaned from the contemporaneous *Naval Chronicle* of 1813. The *Chronicle* records not one mention of the supply operation on the north coast of Spain. From the record it is clear that the Admiralty was more concerned with its operations worldwide. For example, the 1 June 1813 action between HMS *Shannon* (38) and the USS *Chesapeake* (30) is chronicled at length, as are the operations off the East and West Indies, the Baltic, the Channel and North Sea, and inevitably, the operations of the Mediterranean Fleet under Adm. Sir Edward Pellew. Of the operations in the Bay of Biscay, there is hardly a mention, except for the navy's blockade of Ushant and Brest. Naval support for Wellington's army rates only peripheral mention, with two accounts of occasional "cutting out" expeditions by Royal Marines and maritime bombardments, such as the action of Collier's flagship HMS *Surveillante* off Guitaria on 1 July. While certainly not glamorous, there is no mention whatsoever of resupply operations for the peninsula.[100]

Perhaps the most significant of all correspondence in the *Chronicle*, which accurately measures the true importance of Wellington's operations to the Admiralty, was submitted by the pseudonymous correspondent "AFY." On 6 August he wrote, The Royal Navy "must not be dazzled by these splendid victories of Lord Wellington ... so as to lose sight of the truly British axiom: Britain's best bulwarks are her wooden walls."[101] On 2 September he again attacked Wellington: "Wellington's victories must not blind us to Britain's real bastions," referring to the ships of the Royal Navy.[102] A day later, Melville boasted, "The naval blockade has not to any considerable degree been broken." In response to Wellington's claims that French resupply ships regularly eluded the blockade, Melville claimed that if so, the ships carried "nothing more than letters or few eggs and fowls."[103]

The interservice warfare continued for several months. Another source of contention against Wellington in the Admiralty was the undersecretary, John Wilson Croker. A well-established political essayist and reviewer for the London *Quarterly Review*, Croker assessed Wellington's overstated expectations of Lord Keith: "Our good friend the *Great Lord* [Wellington] is a little unreasonable. He is not satisfied with beating all the French Marshals one after another, but like Hermes he wishes to enchain the winds and waves."[104] Bathurst informed Wellington of Croker's comments, but added, "You must not read Croker's compositions, as [you] would those of any other official person. He has a talent for writing sharply and with great facility. When this is coupled together, it is a great misfortune in an official person.... His style is often what it should not be... at least I have found it so, but I have not taken any notice of it, for I know he does not mean anything by it—as for you, you are the God of his Idolatry."[105] Despite his anger, Wellington did not publicly respond to Croker. Instead he informed his brother, "I have heard nothing more from the Admiralty [concerning my operations] excepting that Lord Bathurst has told me that Mr. Croker is in the habit of writing impertinent letters and that I ought to not mind them."[106]

In addition to incomplete naval support and a bruised ego, Wellington also suffered from the ineptitude of the Ordnance Board and Transport Board. The inability of these organizations to coordinate their efforts in London to supply his army with adequate siege artillery had plagued him in his first attempt to besiege Badajoz in 1812. The same problem persisted the previous winter, when Popham had unsuccessfully attempted to transport naval guns to Wellington. In January 1813, in anticipation of another siege of Burgos, followed by perhaps a siege of San Sebastián, Wellington had requested a shipment of heavy guns and ammunition to the peninsula. In his request, Wellington had claimed that his army had fewer heavy artillery guns, "than any army in Europe... and below the scale which I have ever read of for an army of such numbers."[107] To prevent the delays that caused him such misery the previous fall, Wellington requested that the Ordnance Board send the guns and ammunition to Coruña, where they could be moved to his army without delay.[108] When Burgos fell without a siege as the allied army advanced up the coast, Wellington requested that the Transport Board amend his previous instructions and instead ship the guns to Santander, where they would be more useful. After several months, Wellington complained bitterly to Bathurst that the Transport Board had delayed his shipment at Portsmouth for more than two months and could not give him an estimate of when his supplies would be shipped from England. Out of ammunition and without heavier siege guns, Wellington was forced to use captured French 12-pound field pieces to bombard the enemy's fortifications. Not surprising, the light field pieces were of limited effectiveness against the thick walls of the fortress.[109]

As Wellington prepared to besiege the fortress, Bathurst told his general, "There has been an unaccountable confusion between the Transport Board and the Ordnance Board respecting the second battering train . . . which will be delayed a few days." Like Wellington, Bathurst was frustrated by his inability to gain an accurate assessment of the status of siege materials. He told Wellington, "There has been so much misunderstanding between the Ordnance Board and Transport Board that I have found it necessary to send down a clerk last night expressly for the purpose of ascertaining the truth of the case. By one report, the [siege train] sailed, but this has been contradicted."[110]

Bathurst was not alone in his criticism. Col. Henry Torrens at the Horse Guards notified Wellington: "Believe me . . . nothing connected with executive government of the country requires reform more than the Ordnance Board. It is the greatest clog about the state. It is a mélange of jealousy, intrigue, and stupid prejudice; the neglect of the Board is the [cause of the] failure in your supplies." Torrens warned Wellington, "There are two powers in the Ordinance Department always acting in opposition and in contradiction to each other; the one is the Master-General himself and the other is the Board and their secretary. They are jealous of each other. . . . The constitution of the whole thing is radically bad."[111]

Irrespective of Wellington's newfound moral support in London, his troops still faced the difficult task of taking San Sebastián without adequate firepower and ammunition. On 25 July, Wellington, thanks largely to Whitehall's overcomplicated and arcane bureaucracy, was forced to suspend operations because his men were out of ammunition.[112] In addition to an ineffective blockade, he blamed the shortage of musket and cannon ammunition for his failure to take the fortress.

Wellington also claimed to Bathurst that if the French mounted an attack to relieve San Sebastián, he doubted that his troops had the ammunition necessary to repel it. His message to Bathurst was prophetic: the French attack came on the same day that Wellington ordered his assault on the fortress.[113]

After Joseph's defeat at Vitoria, Napoleon took action to strengthen his forces in Spain. Furious at the ineptitude of his brother and Marshal Jourdan, Napoleon replaced them with the venerable Marshal Nicholas Soult. Dispatched from Dresden with sweeping powers to reorganize the three French armies along the Pyrenean frontier into one army with one headquarters, Soult took command of the *armée d'Espagne* in early July.[114]

Soult inherited a difficult task. He should have had control of the 120,000 French troops in Spain; however, because Marshal Suchet's force of nearly 45,000 men contained Murray's diversionary operations in eastern Spain, only 75,000 men were under Soult's direct control.[115] Even though his army outnumbered Wellington's, he had a couple of significant disadvantages the British general did not face. First, the French army was composed of inexperienced recruits and national guard levées. Second, it lacked artillery after losing 151 guns during the retreat from Vitoria. Soult replaced the majority of his guns from the magazines at Bayonne, but the loss of nearly 415 ammunition and supply wagons and their horses during the previous campaign had a greater adverse effect on limited logistics operations. Despite these disadvantages, Soult planned to attack Wellington and relieve the fortresses of Pamplona and San Sebastián. With only four days of rations and very little hope of acquiring any more, Soult marched against Wellington.[116]

Wellington expected Soult to attack along the coast to relieve San Sebastián.[117] However, the veteran French commander recognized the strength of Wellington's defenses along the Biscay coast and avoided them. Instead, Soult attacked through the inland mountain passes of Roncesvalles and Maya, in the direction of the besieged fortress of Pamplona. His rationale was sound. A blow against the lightly defended eastern flank of Wellington's army offered several advantages. If Soult could dislodge Wellington's right flank, he could threaten to envelop the entire allied line. Furthermore, a successful drive in the east might preclude assistance from Marshal Suchet's forces in Catalonia (which Wellington feared because of Murray's failed diversionary operation).[118] At the strategic level, Napoleon hoped that a French victory over Wellington in Spain might influence the allied armistice negotiations in central Europe to consider a more favorable peace.[119]

Collectively known as the Battle of the Pyrenees, Soult's offensive was characterized by nine days of heavy fighting along a twenty-mile front of mountainous terrain, which resulted in very few French gains.[120] Although the direction of Soult's attacks surprised Wellington, the British, Portuguese, and Spanish troops repelled each attack, inflicting heavy French losses.[121] Wellington restored his defensive line by assaulting and defeating Soult at the bloody battle of Sorauren from 28 to 30 July.[122] Soult's failed offensive resulted in nearly thirteen thousand French casualties. Though Wellington's army was proportionately mauled, suffering over seven thousand casualties, he prevented Soult from relieving the sieges of San Sebastián and Pamplona.[123] Wellington did not suffer to the same degree from shortages, but his forces were spread thin and the battle was not decided until Soult was forced to withdraw.

A fortunate and exhausted Wellington described the Battles of the Pyrenees as "bludgeon work."[124] In a letter to Pole, he recalled, "Never did I see such hard fighting as we have had. The 28th was hell. I escaped as usual unhurt; and I began to believe that the finger of God is upon me. You will perceive that my Generals are Gallant Officers in every sense of the word, but if I had been two minutes later, the entire position would have been lost."[125] His brother responded, "I believe the whole public thinks [your recent achievements] surpass infinitely all you had ever before. I agree with you that the finger of God is upon you but I shudder at the risks you run.... I believe you are safe but for the sake of Europe and of us all you ought not to run unnecessary risks."[126]

Unable to relieve the fortresses, Soult's army returned to France. Wellington did not pursue. Instead, he chose to resume the sieges of San Sebastián and Pamplona. His strategic decision was based on the ongoing diplomatic overtures to Napoleon in central Europe. Above all else, Wellington feared a premature allied advance into France followed by a peace proposal in the north that would require him to withdraw. He also feared that any allied retreat would signify weakness and bring about reprisals from the local inhabitants of the area and his own soldiers. He told Bathurst, "So far as the immediate invasion of France . . . I have determined to consider it only in reference to the convenience of my own operations."[127]

Wellington's decision was also based on logistics and his operational situation. His army was far from its primary supply point, the port of Pasajes, and the siege of San Sebastián continued to suffer from lack of naval resources. Nevertheless, the siege continued. The allies launched three major attacks against the fortress during the month of August that cost them more than two thousand casualties and failed miserably.[128]

As the casualties mounted on the allied side, conditions within the fortress deteriorated. The commander of the French garrison, Gen. Louis-Emmanuel Rey, had requested assistance from Marshal Soult via blockade runners. Without adequate rations or proper bridging equipment, but pressured by Napoleon to attempt to relieve the garrison, Soult launched another offensive to break through the allied lines.[129]

Soult led forty-five thousand men across the fog-shrouded Bidassoa River on 31 August and attacked the Spanish-held portion of the allied line between Irun and Vera. Soult's army had only a short distance to cover to reach the fortress, but the attack was delayed a day while bridging equipment was brought forward to span the Bidassoa. The French main attack consisted of three divisions, supported by reserves. The French under the command of Gen. Honoré Reille attacked the Spanish situated on the heights of San Marcial. The Spanish commander, Gen. Manuel Freire, had a firm grasp of Wellington's defensive scheme and led an effective defense that broke the French advance. It was the greatest Spanish victory since Baylen in 1808.[130]

Wellington was complimentary of the Spanish defense. He told Bathurst, "I cannot sufficiently applaud the conduct of Freire. . . . He ensured the success of the day."[131] Furthermore, he told his brother Henry, "The Spanish should be pleased with San Marcial. . . . Their troops behaved remarkably well. They were a little desirous of being relieved towards the end of the day; but I saw that the enemy were done and I would not relieve them."[132]

Heavy rains and stiff allied resistance forced Soult to abandon his relief operation, and on 1 September, he withdrew his force back into France. During the defense, the allies suffered in excess of 2,500 casualties. Soult lost more than 3,800 men in the failed relief attempt;

however, unlike Wellington, whose reinforcements now arrived frequently from England, Soult's losses, due to Napoleon's deteriorating situation in central Europe, were not replaced. After the defeat at San Marcial, the French could do nothing for the trapped garrisons of San Sebastián or Pamplona.[133]

The repulse of Soult's offensive doomed the defense of San Sebastián. After three weeks of fierce fighting, the British heavy guns opened a breach in the walls and on 31 August, British troops stormed the town. General Rey and the surviving French garrison abandoned most of the town and its inhabitants to pillaging British soldiers and retreated into a final defensive position within the castle of La Mota. Rey attempted to dictate surrender terms, proposing a two-week truce. If the garrison was not relieved within a fortnight, the French would surrender. Sir Thomas Graham, commander of allied troops, rejected Rey's terms.[134]

Ultimately, allied artillery decided the fate of the garrison, as the castle of La Mota was virtually impregnable to an infantry assault. On September 8, Graham positioned fifty-nine guns, mortars, and howitzers to pummel the fortress and its defenders. After a two-hour barrage, Rey surrendered. The fall of San Sebastián was decisive because it left the inland fortress of Pamplona and the port of Santoña, already under blockade, as the only French possessions in northwestern Spain.[135]

While Wellington's operational situation improved, his standing with the Admiralty did not. In a belated attempt to facilitate coordination between the two services, the Admiralty dispatched Adm. Sir Thomas Martin, the commander at Plymouth, to Wellington's headquarters at Lesaca, where they met for two days. The stated purpose of Martin's visit was to "confer with Wellington on the general nature of his wants and expectations from naval assistance in the whole line of operations which [Wellington] may have in view."[136]

The visit was intended to mend the relationship between the two services; however, Wellington used it to voice his displeasure with the inadequacy of his naval support. Martin agreed that French reinforcements were smuggled past the blockade and told Keith, "I would be nothing in the least degree surprised if [the French] succeeded in [smuggling] supplies and reinforcements nineteen times out of twenty . . . with boats with muffled oars . . . there is scarce chance of their being intercepted." Martin confirmed Wellington's reports that the British maintained a precarious naval advantage in the Bay of Biscay. Compared with the French, who maintained several ships in nearby ports, to include a frigate in port at Bayonne, the only British warship that could counter the French was HMS *Surveillante*. In Martin's words, the *Surveillante* was in "a dismantled state," missing four of its guns, which had been taken ashore the previous winter.[137] While the likelihood of the French frigate leaving its port was not great, Martin's confirmation of the inadequate British naval force gave credence to Wellington's complaints.

In light of events at San Sebastián, Wellington asked Martin for increased support for future operations, including protection of his supply ships in the Bay of Biscay and a blockade of the port of Santoña. In preparation for the next phase of the campaign, he also asked Martin to reposition transports from Bentinck's command to the peninsula.[138] Martin agreed to process Wellington's request for transports; however, he could not guarantee that more ships would be sent to Collier's squadron to secure Wellington's supply lines.[139]

Unlike Wellington, Admiral Martin viewed his visit as beneficial for the two services. He felt that Wellington now recognized the Admiralty's shortcomings and the efforts they had undergone to fix them. In doing so, he relayed a complimentary message from Wellington about the support he received from the navy: "If anyone wishes to know the history of this war, I will tell them that it is our maritime superiority which gives me the power of maintaining my army, while the enemy are unable to do so."[140]

Wellington, however, was not satisfied. He viewed Martin's visit as a shrewd attempt by the Admiralty to justify the navy's mishandling of the entire situation. Although he had no personal grievance against Martin, he felt that the admiral's visit failed to correct the real problem. Martin offered only promises, not more ships. Wellington told Bathurst, "In the future, I am convinced that the best mode of proceeding is to confine myself strictly to the line of my own duty, which is to report to you any deficiency that may be felt by [this army] for want of naval assistance, leaving it to [the ministers] to take such measures as they may think proper to apply a remedy."[141]

Wellington did not make his grievances with the Admiralty or Transport Board public. Instead, he complained to Bathurst and adjusted accordingly as he could. Privately, however, his scorn for the Admiralty and Transport Board was obvious. In a letter to Pole, Wellington's frustrations surfaced: "There are two men in the present government who I think must go. I mean Lord Melville and Lord Mulgrave. Both have neglected [this army] shamefully."[142] Furthermore, he resented the Admiralty's assertions that the navy had performed admirably during the campaign. In September, he complained to Pole about Croker's "blackguard abuse" in his private letters;, and after an American privateer attack on a transport bound for Lisbon in November, which resulted in the loss of nearly £400,000 in specie, he told his brother "[I am] a little inclined to believe that [Melville and Mulgrave] think that I have done them as much good as I am likely to do them; and that they don't feel any great desire to put themselves out of their way to gratify any wish of mine."[143]

While his army suffered from reduced naval support and bureaucratic sloth, the difficult decision of whether or not to follow his victories at Vitoria and San Sebastián with a quick invasion of France loomed large. Wellington's coastal success created great optimism in London, but his achievements were always overshadowed by the greater struggle in central Europe. Wellington was cautious despite the pressure to pursue the French across the border. He knew that Marshal Soult would not concede France's frontier without a struggle. He was also speculative about invading France without securing his flank and rear areas. He told Bathurst, "The [British government and nation] forget that we have but one army and that same men who fought at Vimeiro and Talavera fought the other day at Sorauren.... If I am to preserve that army, I must proceed with caution." Wellington concluded by condemning the government's reaction to heavy casualties: "This becomes doubly necessary as I see that notwithstanding the fondness of the British nation for the sport, and their exultation upon our success, they began to cry out the other day upon the loss of 300 or 400 men the unsuccessful storm of San Sebastián."[144]

The opposition, which had been uncharacteristically silent since Vitoria, also privately doubted that Wellington could successfully invade France. In a private letter, Grenville wrote, "I shall not rejoice to hear our Field Marshal entering France. I am strongly persuaded that the frontiers of France will be vigorously defended and that we shall make there no substantial or real impression. As an insult to

France and Bonaparte I do not object to our alarming them with our light troops, and [the Spanish], but more than this would in my mind be desperate folly."[145]

Wellington was forced to consider the impact on his operations of the explosive diplomatic and military situation in central Europe. At risk was the re-entry of Austria into the war, and any premature advance into southern France might force Napoleon and the French into a protracted struggle, which no one in Europe desired, except perhaps the Prussians. He told Bathurst, "As for the immediate invasion of France, from what I have seen of the state of negotiations in Northern Europe, I have determined to consider it only in reference to the convenience of my own operations. . . . If peace should be made by the powers of North, I [would be forced to] withdraw into Spain."[146]

On the home front, the ever-pessimistic opposition in London, unable to mount serious parliamentary dissension, exchanged private letters expressing their fears that an invasion of France would unnecessarily lengthen the war. One opposition leader wrote, "If I were in government, I would determine to connect the interests of this country with the Alliance in peace as well as in war, and therefore to propose to Napoleon a peace on very moderate terms. . . . Peace is attainable!"[147] The *Chronicle* remained resolute about rapprochement with Napoleon: "A proud moment for us is to hold forth an olive branch to Bonaparte . . . and offer moderate terms. . . . An invasion of France without such an overture, would in our minds only serve to strengthen the hands of the French Emperor, and condemn us to the most ruinous prolongation of the war."[148] The opposition party and the press's hopes for a peaceful conclusion were overly optimistic, since the allied peace offer to Napoleon was largely symbolic and promptly rejected. The temporary vision of a negotiated settlement with Napoleon disappeared as quickly as it was tabled. As the war in central Europe grew larger, Wellington's operations would remain further on the periphery to a general European conflagration and an invasion across the Rhine. As a result, his operations were, in the eyes of Parliament, the government, and the press, less important.

Ultimately, the Admiralty never accepted responsibility for its inability to protect his lines of communications and to isolate the fortress of San Sebastián. Instead, they blamed their poor performance on the weather, the shortage of available ships, and Wellington's failure to inform them of his expectations.[149] The Transport Board and the Ordnance Board also failed the general; not processing and shipping the requested siege train cost Wellington several months of valuable time and thousands of casualties in failed assaults.[150]

Despite these operational obstacles, the campaign of 1813 moved Wellington and his army onto the cusp of victory. What had begun only nine months before in Portugal after the misery of the previous winter now had Wellington and his troops in position to be the first allied troops to cross the French frontier. His victory at Vitoria had strengthened the government at a critical time and had effectively silenced parliamentary opposition. While his achievements should not be diminished, they remain secondary in importance to the one event that changed the scope of his long campaign. Napoleon's cataclysmic defeat in Russia changed the fortunes of the struggle; French armies without the prospect of reinforcements and resources could no longer control Iberia. In late fall of 1813, Wellington moved his army into position to bring the war to French soil.

9

THE FINAL ACT: THE INVASION OF FRANCE, 1813–1814

> I am quite certain that the government are tired of me and my operations and wish both to the devil.
>
> Wellington to Wellesley-Pole, 9 January 1814

After the fall of San Sebastián in September, the last major French possessions in northwest Spain were the port at Santoña and the inland fortress at Pamplona. Because both places were either blockaded or surrounded, Wellington was free to move the remainder of his army north along the coast toward the French border.[1]

He kept his army close to the coast to facilitate the Royal Navy's efforts to supply them. As he advanced, he received news from central Europe that reinforced his decision to exploit the momentum gained by the success at Vitoria and San Sebastián with an invasion of France. From captured French newspapers, Wellington learned that peace negotiations aimed at preventing war with France had been abandoned and that Austria had declared war on France. With the combined mass of the Prussians, Russians, Swedes, and Austrians now bearing down on Napoleon in central Europe, the emperor would be forced to use the majority of available French troops to defend France. Unable to reinforce Marshal Soult and the *armée d' Espagne*, the allies could invade southern France and apply pressure on Napoleon from two fronts. There were operational advantages associated with a quick invasion as well. If Wellington's troops could catch Soult before he established strong defensive positions in the Pyrenees, they could break through the French defenses and exploit their success by dispersing out in southern France.[2]

Given the clear advantages to be gained by an aggressive pursuit of Soult's forces into France, Wellington remained concerned about securing his rear and vulnerable right flank. The French still maintained a tenuous hold on the fortress of Pamplona, and several thousand French troops under Marshal Suchet occupied portions of Catalonia in eastern Spain. Although they had little chance of success against a strengthened Wellington, their presence and potential could not be ignored.

Wellington told Bathurst, "I shall put myself in a position to make a serious attack [when I hear] that the Allies have been successful [in Germany] or when Pamplona [falls.][3] . . . I see that, as usual, the newspapers on all sides are raising the public expectation, and that the Allies are very anxious that we should enter France, and that our government have promised that we should, as soon as the enemy should be finally expelled from Spain; and I think I ought and will bend a little to the views of the Allies, if it can be done with safety to the army, notwithstanding that I acknowledge I should prefer to turn my attention to Catalonia, as soon as I shall be secured this frontier."[4] Unwilling to rush into a premature invasion due to the expectations and exhortations of British or Spanish press, Wellington told a fellow officer, "Such extravagant expectations are excited by the excessively wise and useful class of people, the editors of newspapers. If I had been at any time capable of doing what these gentlemen expected, I should [have] been on the moon . . . or at least to Bordeaux [by this time]."[5]

Perhaps the most compelling reason for him to wait was the disposition of the French army that opposed him. After Marshal Soult's repulse at San Marcial in August, Soult ordered his engineers to construct a series of defensive lines along the mountainous French-Spanish border. A veteran opponent of Wellington in 1809–10, Soult hoped to contain Wellington's army in the mountainous border region.[6]

Similar to Wellington's construction of the Lines of Torres Vedras in 1809–10, Soult used the terrain to enhance the effectiveness of his defense. He blocked the limited number of roads that led through the

Pyrenees Mountains and fortified the banks of the major rivers that flowed throughout the region. The first line of defenses paralleled the Bidassoa River, which ran from the Pyrenees to the coastal town of Fuenterrabia. The second defensive line followed the Nivelle River from St. Jean de Luz on the coast to the town of Ascain. At Ascain, the second defensive line turned south to Modarrain Massif in the Pyrenees. The third and final protective barrier to contain the allied army was a defensive line along the Nive and Adour rivers. This line began at the fortress of St. Jean Pied de Port at the base of the mountains and ran south along the Nive River to the juncture of the city of Bayonne and the Adour River. It then followed the Nive River into the ocean. The cornerstone of this defensive line was the fortress city of Bayonne.[7]

Despite its depth, the strength of Soult's defense was limited by the vast size of the area and the size of his force. Soult had only fifty-nine thousand troops to cover more than thirty miles of mountainous territory. He was further hindered by the presence of the Royal Navy, which maintained the ability to conduct amphibious operations along his flank and provided logistics to Wellington's army.[8]

With the advantage of mobility, Wellington planned to bypass the majority of Soult's defenses along the Bidassoa River and outflank the veteran French commander.[9] Wellington took advantage of Soult's thin defensive lines and paid Spanish fisherman to sound the river to determine possible fording sites. Three sites were deemed appropriate, and Wellington used this information to ford the river. On 7 October, his forces attacked and routed Soult's weakly defended right flank. Soult's force retreated in disarray. The passage of the Bidassoa was brilliantly conceived and executed, and allied casualties were light. Wellington did not pursue Soult's force. Instead, due to logistics and the presence of the French garrison at Pamplona that determinedly held out under siege, Wellington cautiously advanced into France. Soult took advantage of Wellington's delay and occupied a second defensive line along the Nivelle River. Wellington spent the next few weeks monitoring the diplomatic events in central Europe and prepared for the next phase of the operation.[10]

The first good news to greet Wellington upon entry into France was the arrival of Gen. Sir John Hope. The Horse Guards dispatched the senior officer, who, since Wellington's promotion to field marshal in June 1813, was free under the restrictions of the regimental system to serve on Wellington's staff in the peninsula.[11] A veteran of the Peninsular War, Hope left command of the British forces in Ireland in September and arrived on the peninsula on 5 October 1813.[12] He arrived in time to witness the allied crossing of the Bidassoa River, and immediately following the successful offensive, Wellington replaced Sir Thomas Graham with Hope as the commander of the left wing of the allied army.[13]

Before proceeding with the campaign, Wellington asked Bathurst for assistance in remedying an old problem. For some time the disparity in pay of general officers to officers in the navy had concerned Wellington. A year earlier, he had complained about his pay. At the time, Wellington earned £10 a day; after taxes, it was less than £8 a day. He told Bathurst, "I believe there is no service in which a Commander in Chief of such a charge is so badly paid as in the British [Army]."[14] In October 1813, he readdressed the problem. This time, he told Bathurst, "The General Officers of the British Army are altogether very badly paid.... They receive less than they did fifty years ago, while their expenses are doubled." Wellington noted that because the British army's general officers "were obliged to keep tables for their Staff [officers]," their expenses were far greater than those of admirals.[15] He cited Sir Thomas Graham as an example, who despite his private fortune in England was disadvantaged because of his staff's size and the "unfavorable rate of exchange" at which he was forced to draw his money. Wellington stated that due to these problems, Graham was "frequently in distress" financially in the peninsula.[16]

Although Wellington knew it was impossible to raise the pay of all the general officers in the army, he requested that the government make a special consideration for his two senior officers, Sir John Hope and Sir Rowland Hill. Because of their positions of responsibility, Wellington requested that both men draw pay equal to the second in command in Sicily or to the commanding officer in Cadiz. Bathurst could not promise a raise in pay, but he promised to look into the matter.[17]

Wellington's complaint about senior officer pay was ironic. He was by far the best-paid British officer in Europe, and with every title he had received since 1809 came the benefit of an additional annual stipend, or pension. Wellington received pensions for victories after the battle of Talavera in 1809, after the defense of Portugal in 1811, and after Vitoria in 1813. By 1814, his annual pensions from those victories alone totaled more than £100,000. Furthermore, there was no accurate method to judge the amount of private treasure he had accumulated while in the peninsula. Nevertheless, despite his personal concern for his officers, he did not advocate a reduction in his own pay for the senior officers on his own staff.[18]

While Wellington attempted to increase the pay of his generals, his army was forced to wait for their supply trains. He was also forced to do battle again with an old adversary, the British press. This time, the problem stemmed from failure of the press to recognize Portuguese contributions to the war effort. For some time, Forjaz and the Portuguese Regency Council in Lisbon had perceived that their contributions to the war effort were deliberately withheld in the peninsular dispatches. Forjaz felt that the slight was purposeful, and therefore the Portuguese contributions were unknown to the British people and the world. Charles Stuart relayed the Portuguese concern to London and to Wellington.[19]

Wellington was furious that the English newspapers had neglected to mention the Portuguese effort for he had always taken great care to highlight the achievements of both the Spanish and the Portuguese in his dispatches. Most recently, the Portuguese had served with distinction during the campaign of 1813. Their bravery during the battle of Vitoria induced Wellington to tell the prime minister, "Notwithstanding, that the Portuguese are now the *fighting cocks* of the army, I believe we owe their merits more to the care we have taken of their pockets and bellies, than to the instruction we have given them."[20]

The problem was that the Portuguese troops were amalgamated into British units and served under British officers.[21] Aside from the slight by the press, the Portuguese felt underappreciated, especially compared with the Spanish troops, who fought as a separate national corps and therefore received great publicity in both the Spanish and London newspapers. Charles Stuart reported to Wellington that within the Regency Council, there was a "general tone of recrimination against Great Britain" and that Forjaz and the Regency Council could threaten the alliance by withholding its support.[22] In reaction to the comments made by Forjaz, Wellington told Stuart, "Our newspapers do us plenty of harm by which they insert, but I never suspected that they could do us the injury of alienating from us a Government and a nation which we ought to be on the best of terms."[23]

These events coincided with Marshal Beresford's scheduled convalescent visit to England. The timing of Beresford's departure and of the war's transition to the security of northern Spain gave the Regency Council a window of opportunity to assert itself. In October, Forjaz and the council proposed that the Portuguese form a separate corps and that it be commanded by a Portuguese officer, Gen. Francisco Silveira.

Wellington empathized with the Portuguese. No one in the peninsula had a better appreciation of the burden endured by the Portuguese people than Wellington. He was responsible for a great measure of their suffering and for their success. Nevertheless, he could not afford to see the fruits of the Anglo-Portuguese alliance wasted over a claim that the newspapers did not recognize the actions of the Portuguese troops. A pragmatic Wellington instructed Stuart to relay his concerns to Forjaz. He told Stuart, "Forjaz is the ablest statesman . . . in the Peninsula; but I hope that he will not be induced, by such folly as the contents and omissions of our newspapers, to venture upon the alteration of a system which has answered admirably and has contributed in a principal degree to our great success."[24]

Regarding Forjaz's desire to separate Portuguese regiments under the command of a Portuguese general, Wellington warned, "If Forjaz will give me credit . . . if the Portuguese troops were separated from the British divisions [and if] the British departments did not assist the Portuguese [with food and equipment,] they could not field a respectable [force.]" Furthermore, he told Stuart, "The Portuguese government would incur ten times the expense they now incur." In regard to Silveira personally, Wellington told Stuart, "My opinion of Silveira is very much altered. He possesses not one military quality; and he has been repeatedly guilty of . . . courting popularity with the common soldiers, by flattering their vices, and by impunity from their misconduct. Such a man will not do in this army."[25]

He also addressed the catalyst of the strained Anglo-Portuguese relationship. Wellington attacked the English newspapers for not publishing his glowing accounts of the merits of the Portuguese army and for giving the Portuguese a venue to vent their dissatisfaction: "All that I can say is that if we are to begin to disagree about such nonsense as the contents or omissions of the newspapers, I quit the Peninsula forever."[26]

While his anger was outwardly directed at the newspapers, Wellington's true concern was with the gradual insistence of the Portuguese regency to demand a greater influence in the affairs of the Portuguese troops in his army. Since the start of the Peninsular War, the Portuguese people had undergone great hardship to preserve their independence. For its support of the war and for supplying Wellington with thirty thousand troops, in 1808 the British government had increased its annual subsidy to the Portuguese regency from £900,000 to £2 million. In addition to the subsidy, the British also agreed to supply uniforms, weapons, and training. The agreement benefited both nations and Wellington, since the Portuguese were fighting three hundred miles from their homeland.[27]

Despite the infusion of British money, the Portuguese government operated with a budget deficit. By the end of 1810, the government's revenue totaled £1.7 million, while the army's expenses alone totaled more than £2.8 million. After deduction of the subsidy and donations, Portugal was left with a deficit of £1 million for 1810, a figure that did not include the £1 million carried over from the previous year.[28]

Through the reforms established by Charles Stuart and Forjaz in the fall of 1812, the situation had improved by 1813. In May 1813, Castlereagh changed the subsidy agreement to include the value of uniforms and equipment, which decreased the overall subsidy amount available to the regency; however, increased customs receipts, a revision of the *décima* (or 10 percent income tax), and the sale of crown lands offset the loss.[29]

Furthermore, in December, after the Portuguese commissariat failed to supply its troops, Wellington further reduced the Portuguese burden by assuming responsibility for the supply of independent Portuguese units.[30] Nevertheless, due to supply and shipping shortages, Forjaz complained that the Portuguese troops were eight months in arrears and that the Regency Council did not have the funds necessary to pay its troops.[31]

The changing course of the war provided additional tensions between Portugal and Spain. By the autumn of 1813, it was clear that Portugal was secure and that the war effort had shifted to the security of Spain. Unsurprisingly, tensions arose between the Portuguese and Spanish governments over the future of the Iberian Peninsula. In addition to a long-standing grievance between both countries over the border region of Olivenza, the summer of 1813 brought out fresh insinuations that each country owed the other war debts. Both conflicts threatened the tenuous Portuguese and Spanish alliance that existed primarily due to British diplomacy, Wellington's leadership, and a common enemy.[32]

The situation was not improved by the presence of a large number of Spanish troops who were not called to the front and therefore were available for action in the interior of the country. Because the majority of available Portuguese soldiers served with the British in northern Spain, the Regency Council threatened to recall the Portuguese troops from the Wellington's army.[33]

Wellington solved the problem with skillful diplomacy and brute persuasion. First, he addressed the problem caused by the newspapers. To reassure the Portuguese and gain official recognition of their efforts, he asked his government for assistance. In October, Lord Castlereagh, the foreign secretary, issued a statement that seemed to praise the Portuguese government's contribution to the war effort: "His Royal Highness [applauds] those British troops along with their Portuguese and Spanish brothers [who] have shared the glory and expelled the enemy from the Peninsula. . . . [He] trusts nothing is wanting but perseverance on the part of the Allies, indissoluble union, and an uninterrupted application of the same courage and discipline in battle which have so eminently marked their conduct."[34] Castlereagh's sentiment was echoed by the Prince of Wales, who delivered a speech to both houses of Parliament in which he praised the "steadiness and unconquerable spirit . . . displayed by the troops of the three nations united under [Wellington's] command."[35]

Wellington also agreed to do a better job in his dispatches of highlighting the achievements of his Portuguese troops. He told Beresford, Forjaz's complaint "is a fair one, that in mentioning the Portuguese army, whether in Parliament or elsewhere, it should be considered distinct. In short, the Portuguese should have the reputation of possessing a [better] army, to a greater degree, than they have. I shall do everything in my power to impress the government with [Forjaz's] wishes."[36]

While Wellington attempted to solve the distraction of Portuguese recognition, a more serious crisis loomed. The Portuguese Regency continued to resist its increased involvement in the war unless the situation with Spain could be solved. The Portuguese threatened withdraw troops from service in Wellington's army to prepare itself for a postwar struggle with Spain. The issue culminated in January 1814, when Wellington dispatched eight troop transports to Lisbon to bring Portuguese reinforcements northward. Due to a disagreement with the Spanish over aid to wounded Portuguese soldiers in Spanish hospitals, the Regency Council refused to embark more than nine thousand replacement troops.[37] Wellington told Stuart, "The Portuguese Government should recollect, that their engagement to keep 30,000 men in the field is not with the Spanish Government, but with His Majesty. . . . [The Regency Council] should not allow a paltry discussion upon a trifle . . . in the existing state of Spain. . . . The Spanish Government has no power to prevent the Portuguese from keeping their army complete at this critical moment."[38]

To remedy the crisis, Charles Stuart proposed that the mandatory age of induction into the Portuguese army be lowered to seventeen.[39] To aid Stuart, Wellington dispatched Marshal Beresford to Lisbon to enforce conscription and to apply pressure on Portuguese officials.[40] Beresford's weakened health limited his actions, but Stuart's work to remedy the crisis in October 1813 led to a substantial rise in recruits by November. Exemptions from service formerly observed in the case of the servants of nobles and clergy were waived. Most important, however, Wellington threatened to reduce the Portuguese subsidy in proportion to the number of Portuguese troops in the ranks.[41]

Forjaz and the Regency Council relented under the pressure of Stuart and Wellington. In January the Regency Council dispatched 1,000 troops and sent another 2,700 to Wellington in March 1814.[42] Despite his success in forcing the Portuguese to honor its agreement, Wellington's relations with the Portuguese remained tense for the remainder of the war.[43]

Wellington was also forced to address a story published in the English newspapers that claimed British troops had looted and burned the city of San Sebastián after they stormed it in September. Both the *Chronicle* and the *Times* published several Spanish newspaper accounts in early November that accused British soldiers, with the consent of their commanders, of setting fire to the town, looting homes and businesses, and murdering Spanish inhabitants before and after the French garrison surrendered.[44]

A month before the story was published in London, Henry warned Wellington that his soldiers had been implicated for the behavior by two Spanish newspapers: "The calumnies against British Troops for their conduct at San Sebastián has reached new heights."[45] The reports of British atrocities were originally published in the liberal Spanish paper *El Duende de los Cafées*. Although the paper had longstanding hostility toward British involvement in the Peninsular War, Henry suspected that the editor—who was employed by the Spanish regency minister of war, Gen. Juan O'Donoju—claimed that Wellington had ordered San Sebastian destroyed to remove it as a threat to British commerce and had published the reports to incite Spanish uprisings against the British. Henry Wellesley claimed that O'Donoju intended to increase hostile sentiment toward the British and induce the Cortes to strip Wellington of his command of the Spanish armies.[46]

In an attempt to protect his brother and preserve the reputation of the British army, Henry asked a more conservative Spanish newspaper, the *Consisco*, to publish the report of a British officer, Major Smith, who was present during the storming of San Sebastián, to vindicate the actions of the British soldiers and commanders present. After refuting the *Duende* with the British officer's version of events, Henry told his brother that the officer's statement "produced a good effect" in Cadiz.[47]

Wellington was outraged by the insinuation that either he or his senior commander, Thomas Graham, had ordered the destruction of the city. He accused the Spanish press of libel and of deliberately attempting to derail the war effort. Although he did not deny that British soldiers had looted the city, he rejected the claim that the British had set fire to it. He informed Henry that the commander of the French defense at San Sebastián, Gen. Emmanuel Rey, had even noted that the city was on fire in five or six places before the British stormed the town.[48] Furthermore, he told Henry, "I never saw such libel as in the *Duende*. . . . If it is published in England, I shall prosecute the printer. . . . I think it would do no harm if you were to hint occasionally that all this will tend to put people in England very much out of humor with the Spanish alliance. . . . I do not know whether the conduct of the soldiers in plundering San Sebastián, or the libels of the *Xefe Politico* and *Duende* made me most angry." In an attempt to downplay the events, he concluded, "What can be done with such libels, and such people, excepting despise them, and continuing one's road without noticing them?"[49]

Despite his efforts, Henry was not successful in downplaying the story. The magistrates of San Sebastián used the Spanish press to question Wellington about the role his soldiers played in the destruction of their city. In return for the misconduct, they requested financial assistance from Wellington to rebuild San Sebastián. Wellington replied,

> I am very sorry that it is not in my power to be any use to the town of San Sebastián.... The course of operations of the war rendered necessary the attack of the town.... It was the subject of the utmost concern to me to see that the enemy wantonly destroyed it.... The infamous libels upon the subject in which the destruction of the town has been attributed to the troops under my command, by order of their officers (notwithstanding that it was in great part burned ... before they [stormed] the city) render it a matter of delicacy for me.... I am very desirous not to be applied to again, and not to have to write upon it.[50]

Wellington was also unsuccessful in keeping the story from reaching London. On October 29, the *Chronicle* published the *Duende*'s accounts of atrocities committed by British troops upon the Spanish populace of San Sebastián. While it could not confirm the reports of these atrocities, the newspaper felt obligated to publish the *Duende*'s account. The paper stated, "The precious blood of the Spaniards poured forth with impunity at San Sebastián loudly calls for the punishment of the aggressors.... The People of Spain expect Lord Wellington complete satisfaction for so scandalous an outrage, which cannot be concealed from the other powers of the continent.... [The Spanish] government cannot fail to demand it."[51] The *Duende* published a letter from a Spanish civilian who claimed to have witnessed British troops looting, pillaging, murdering, and raping. In one instance, the letter writer said, "With regard to examples of personal violation ... a personal friend was in his house endeavoring to protect an innocent daughter of 12 years old. In order to rescue himself of being a witness to her infamy he purchased her safety with 12 dollars.... It is impossible to ascertain the numbers of martyrs to purity who paid the forfeit of life.... They are burnt and buried beneath the ruins of their dwellings."[52]

The *Duende* was substantiated by other sources. British officers within Wellington's army published letters claiming they too had witnessed the atrocities committed by British soldiers. They accused Sir Thomas Graham of failing to prevent the looting and destruction of San Sebastián by not gaining control of his troops.[53]

The published Spanish reports had a resounding impact on the public. For the next several days, the *Chronicle* published multiple letters from Britons, who were both angry and supportive of their troops. In one letter, a peninsular veteran wrote, "The excesses alleged committed at San Sebastián are doubtless revolting. . . . Indeed judging from the probabilities, I must confess their committal seems [likely.] But in the name of candor is the general character of the British soldier to be aspirated and vilified by a mere divulgation of the fact that his conquests are not absolutely free from all those horrors which are inseparable from the bloody trade of death and misery?" He defended the British soldiers by portraying the difficulties associated with capturing a fortress like San Sebastián:

> Let us consider what the horrors of a capture by storm intrinsically are, and allow the [person blaming the British soldiers and officer] to be himself the infuriated soldier, rushing on to the assault, but too fortunate in escaping destruction from the cannon's mouth and borne on to conquest literally over the dead and mangled carcasses of his comrades—perhaps a father or a brother! Heated with anger and revenge, alike regardless of friend or foe, and in all probability, under the additional influence of excessive intoxication, I would ask whether in such a situation, and under such circumstances, any reasonable person, possessed of the slightest knowledge of human nature can suppose that any officer, however high his rank or strong in his authority, to interpose effectually in endeavoring to curb those licentious excesses among the soldiers which are the invariable concomitants of an attack by storm?[54]

The veteran's sentiment was echoed by the government. Bathurst also pledged his support to Wellington and his troops. He told Wellington, "There are many [officers in the peninsula] who like to complain, or who like to write flourishing letters of what is going on.

I am inclined to believe [the commander's report] of what is going on."⁵⁵ Bathurst believed Graham, who denied any wrongdoing, and praised British soldiers for sparing the lives of several hundred French defenders, who by the laws of warfare could have been put to the sword.⁵⁶

Reports of British misconduct could have had a strategic impact on the war. Wellington wanted to prevent a civil uprising in southern France, but reports of British violence against civilians could raise the level of French resistance in cities such as Bayonne and Bordeaux. Increased resistance would lead to more casualties and therefore could have a disastrous effect on the allied invasion of France. If the reports were accurate, they would also present the struggling opposition party in Britain with needed ammunition to attack the ministry for its aggressive stance toward France. Referencing the paper's claims that would assuredly be followed by questions in Parliament, Bathurst told Wellington, "The charge against the conduct of British troops has made a sensation here."⁵⁷

Despite publication of the condemning reports, Wellington and the Liverpool ministry were aided by the fortuitous timing of a much larger story from central Europe: Napoleon's defeat at Leipzig in October. The allied victory at Leipzig superseded the story of British atrocities at San Sebastián and was a distraction Bathurst and Castlereagh effectively used to deflect the negative reports from Spain. Bathurst told Wellington, "We are all so delighted that this charge is for the present almost forgotten."⁵⁸

Despite the news of Leipzig, the ministry was reluctant to let the charges against Wellington and his men go unanswered. Instead, at the next meeting of Parliament, Bathurst and Castlereagh delivered speeches in both houses to refute the reports.⁵⁹ On 8 November, Bathurst told the House of Lords, "One of the charges was that the British troops were accused of robbing churches. Now certainly all Spain must be aware that the French had hardly ever entered or remained in a town without sacking the churches." Bathurst claimed that the charge that the troops had plundered the town was "doubly false." Instead, he praised the troops: "There was one charge that the British Troops would plead guilty. And that was the charge of having saved the lives of six hundred Frenchmen, when by the laws of war; they might all have been put to the sword. When the place was stormed these men threw down their arms and implored mercy. . . . British soldiers, though heated by the ardor of attack, smarting as they were under the pain of their wounds, or scorched with the flames of houses burning around them, spared the lives of those who threw themselves on their mercy."[60]

Bathurst reaffirmed his trust in Wellington and his commanders, especially Sir Thomas Graham, and moved for a vote of thanks to Wellington for the Vitoria campaign. The majority of the House of Lords agreed. One member of Parliament even argued to withhold money from public works and instead erect statues to Wellington and his commanders for their gallantry.[61] Bathurst registered his faith in Wellington and for the prospect of victory in the war: "What had distinguished [Britain from France] during [the Peninsular War]? It was not merely the greatness of her exertions, nor was it the skill of [Wellington]. . . . It was the firmness and perseverance with which the country had maintained the contest and the pertinacity with which it upheld the independence of the Peninsula, under every aspect of fortune, thus holding up a pillar of fire amidst the surrounding darkness, which marked out to other nations the path to the promised land—to the haven of safety and independence."[62]

The defense of Wellington and Graham could have cost Castlereagh and Bathurst their political reputations. Nevertheless, with momentum gained by the allied victory at Leipzig and Wellington's successful crossing of the Bidassoa, the two men undoubtedly felt it was worth the risk. The public vote of confidence in Wellington had the desired effect; the issue of British misconduct at San Sebastián was never raised in Parliament again.

While the charges of misconduct against British troops were answered in London, a more serious problem for Wellington surfaced in the peninsula. This problem concerned the composition of his army and the role that Spanish troops would play in the invasion of France. During the fall of 1813, the Spanish Cortes attached twenty-five thousand Spanish troops to Wellington for the invasion of France. Wellington had to consider the implications of invading France with Spanish troops that may or may not harm the allied cause by seeking revenge on the French.[63]

Invading France with Spanish troops who were neither paid nor properly fed by their government was of grave concern to Wellington. He was also concerned about Spanish generals who would not enforce discipline and would allow their troops to seek retribution for the destruction of their country. If this occurred on a large scale, he feared that his army would find a similar situation to that which the French had encountered in Iberia, where bands of Spanish bandits roamed the countryside killing French couriers and ambushing supply trains, which would "set the whole country against [the allies]."[64] Because virtually every French male citizen had served in either the army or national guard, Wellington told General Hope, "If we were five times stronger than we are, we could not venture to enter France, if we cannot prevent our soldiers from plundering."[65]

In July Wellington issued a general order: "To revenge [the French misconduct in Spain and Portugal] on the peaceable inhabitants of France would prove unmanly and unworthy of the nations [in this army]. . . . They would also be highly injurious to the public interests." Nevertheless, Spanish generals who incited and encouraged violent reprisals countered him. One Spanish general officer, Conde del Abisbal, called for a "just revenge" on the premise that "the very devastation which we shall have to pass to get to the Pyrenees is a living monument to the barbarism of our invaders."[66]

Since many of the Spanish units were not properly supplied with adequate provisions, Wellington also feared that starvation would be another motivation to plunder and loot France. His fears were realized after the crossing of Bidassoa, when the Spanish soldiers began looting French towns.[67] In response, Wellington instructed his subordinates to court-martial violators and to use cavalry patrols to round up stragglers.[68]

On 31 October, after five weeks of relative inactivity, Wellington received the news that the French garrison in Pamplona had surrendered. With the fall of the last major French possession in Spain, Wellington resumed offensive operations. On 10 November, Wellington's troops assaulted Soult's defensive line on the Neville River. Compared with the crossing of the Bidassoa River, the crossing of the Neville was considerably more costly. In the victory, Wellington's troops captured fifty-one French guns; however, they suffered nearly twice the casualties of Bidassoa.[69]

After his victory, Wellington was still without money to pay or food to supply his Spanish troops. The Spanish responded by continuing to plunder, and on 12 November, the violence escalated when the Spanish divisions under generals Francisco Longa and Pablo Morillo destroyed the French villages of Ascain and Espelette.[70] Wellington was furious with the Spanish generals who permitted the behavior and ordered the execution of Spanish soldiers. Unwilling to allow the Spanish troops to continue inciting French resistance, Wellington sent General Longa back to Old Castille and sent the entire Spanish Army of the Reserve under Gen. Pedro Girón as well as the majority of the Fourth Spanish Army back into cantonments in Spain.[71]

Several of the Spanish generals, including the "hero of San Marcial," Gen. Manual Freire, objected to Wellington's decision to withdraw the Spanish force. He argued that the marauding was the work of a few individuals, and to punish the entire Spanish force was a "gross injustice . . . [Especially] when the disorders of [his] unit were common to every army, none of which lack for marauders and miscreants."[72] Wellington responded by telling the Spaniard, "I have not come to France to pillage. . . . I have not caused the death and wounding of thousands of officers and soldiers so the survivors can pillage the French. On the contrary, it is my duty and the duty of all, to put a stop to pillage, especially if we want to subsist our armies on the resources of the country."[73]

Torn between military necessity to maintain order and anger that the Spanish government was unable to support its soldiers, Wellington told Bathurst,

> I despair of the Spaniards. They are in such a miserable state, that it is really hardly fair to expect that they will refrain from plundering a beautiful country, into which they enter as conquerors; particularly adverting to the miseries which their own country has suffered. I cannot bring them into France unless I can feed and pay them. . . . If I could now bring forward 20,000 good Spaniards, paid and fed, I should have Bayonne. If I could bring forward 40,000, I do not know where I should stop. . . . Without pay and food, [the Spanish] must plunder; and if they plunder they will ruin us all.[74]

Wellington also asked Bathurst to consider an increase to the Spanish subsidy to pay the Spanish troops: "I think I can make an arrangement of the subsidy to cover the expense of 20,000 Spaniards. . . . If we could only get the money." Regardless of his desire to pay the Spanish troops, Wellington knew that his government did not have the money or time necessary to act fast enough to curb the violence. A frustrated Wellington told Bathurst, "It is impossible for me to [get the money] from Lisbon, as they can buy no Commissariat debts, or very little, for the draughts on the Treasury, and the Yellow Fever has put a stop to the communication with Cadiz and Gibraltar; [even] with three million dollars, we could not get a shilling for want of ships to bring it."[75]

Wellington had little choice but to take on the added burden of supplying the Spanish troops with the British commissariat. To feed them, Wellington decided to withhold the Spanish subsidy from Spanish units that were not actively deployed with his army on the French frontier. He told his brother Henry, "It is obvious that when it comes to food, pay, maintenance, and means of transport, [the subsidy] will not support half the number of men that could be supported by it paying [only the Spanish troops] for our future objects." This meant stopping all payments to the three Spanish divisions that were not attached to his army. Furthermore, Wellington proposed that the Spanish government provide for the Spanish garrisons of Ciudad Rodrigo and the depot at Cadiz.[76]

Henry responded by telling Wellington that he would pursue any course of action that Wellington requested concerning the disposition of the subsidy. However, he advised that in light of the Cortes's scheduled move from Cadiz to Madrid, it would be best to wait until the new government was established. In the wake of the most recent crisis with the Cortes, Henry advised a cautious approach. He told Wellington that there would assuredly be changes in the government structure, and therefore, "there would be less danger of their misinterpreting what you propose in Madrid than at Cadiz."[77]

After withdrawing the majority of Spanish troops from France, Wellington followed his brother's advice but made one exception that cost him dearly. Despite previous misconduct of General Morillo's troops toward French civilians, Wellington allowed his division to remain in France. Because of the threat of Marshal Suchet's troops in eastern Spain, Wellington ordered Morillo and his troops to guard the allied right flank.[78] In early December, Wellington received reports of atrocities carried out by Morillo's troops on French citizens. Morillo blamed the conduct of his men on the failure of the British commissariat to supply his troops. He claimed that the commissariat was not providing the amount of food necessary to feed his troops, and therefore, they were forced to take from the French. Wellington castigated the Spaniard for allowing his troops to pillage the French: "I did not lose thousands of men to bring the army under my command into French territory, in order that the soldiers might plunder and ill treat the French peasantry . . . I prefer to have a small army that will obey my orders and preserve discipline, than a large one that is disobedient and undisciplined."[79] He ordered General Freire to ensure that Morillo's troops withdrew from France to a position close to a British magazine. He also ordered Freire to guard Morillo's troops to ensure they did not loot.[80] Despite personal anger toward Morrillo, Wellington saw some merit in the Spanish complaints. With his own supply system stretched thin along the coast, he recognized the limitations of the commissariat to push supplies out to the extreme right flank that Morillo's troops occupied. Nevertheless, he ordered the commissariat to ensure the delivery of rations for the Spanish troops. The entire situation forced Wellington to remind the Spanish that despite their bravado and numbers, they could not succeed without British help. He told General Freire, "If [the Spanish] did not care for the provisions which he provided, [they] were welcome to invade France [on their own.]" Without British help, Wellington predicted, "they could not remain in France for fifteen days."[81]

As Wellington prepared future operations, his relations with the Spanish reached a breaking point. Earlier in the year, Wellington had disagreed with the policies of Cortes regarding Spanish clergy and had removed several Spanish generals from their commands. In reaction, the Cortes had disapproved of his recommendations for promotion of Spanish officers and had threatened to strip his command of the Spanish armies.[82] Fortunately for Wellington, through the work of his brother Henry, the crisis was avoided. Nevertheless, the situation induced Wellington to comment to his brother, "These [Spanish] fellows are sad vagabonds, but we must have patience with them, for the state of Europe, and of the world, and of Spain in particular requires that I maintain command of the Spanish armies."[83] Nevertheless, these events were quickly followed by the charge of British atrocities at San Sebastián and an absurd assertion that Wellington, in exchange for his conversion to Catholicism, had been offered the throne of Spain.[84] His decision to reprimand the Spanish generals and deny Spanish troops their moment of victory stemmed from frustration and an inability to provide his Spanish troops with money and supplies. Unfortunately, the decision to withdraw the Spanish troops plagued Wellington for the remaining months of the war, as the French fought desperately to defend their homeland.

For the next five weeks the two armies faced one another across the Nive River. Soult was resolved to improve his defensive line, and Wellington was forced to delay due to weather and logistics. Prior to launching the last phase of the campaign, Wellington attempted to facilitate the task of transporting supplies to his army by transferring his forward logistics port to Santander. Despite his plan to use the ocean and rivers to bring supplies as far forward as possible, he was hampered by the navy's inability to secure his supply lines from privateers. His logistics were also delayed because the Admiralty and Transport Board failed to coordinate the departure of his supply convoys with their naval escorts. In particular, Wellington complained that his supplies, which were shipped from Lisbon or Porto, were being delayed in Coruña and were not being brought forward to Santander.[85]

Wellington feared the delays would affect his army's capacity to survive the upcoming winter campaign. As an example of the navy and Transport Board's failure to develop plans, Wellington told Bathurst of a particular convoy loaded with tents and heavy winter coats that had been delayed at Coruña for nearly two weeks, waiting for an escort and about two ships, carrying needed supplies for the army, that had sailed past the British blockade of Santoña and mistakenly docked at the French-held town, where they were subsequently captured. "It is extraordinary that a vessel in the public service should run into any port excepting to which it is bound. . . . I have suggested to Admiral Collier to instruct the officers who command those vessels that Santoña is an enemy port, and he should warn them to keep away from it."[86]

In the wake of the problems at San Sebastián, Wellington was also angry that the Admiralty had not increased the number of ships that supported his army. Instead, he asked Bathurst to question the Admiralty concerning the numbers of vessels on station, and told him, "whatever may be the number employed, they do not perform the service."[87]

The problem for the navy was that no predictable supply convoy system existed. Supply ships departed at irregular intervals from multiple ports, including Gibraltar, Cadiz, Lisbon, and Coruña, bound for multiple destinations along the Biscay coast. Unable to determine which ships required escort, the understrength naval squadrons often delayed entire convoys until escorts could be found. Furthermore, Wellington was angry that despite Admiral Martin's "good faith" visit to assist Wellington in September, the Admiralty had not increased the number of ships in Collier's squadron, and therefore the same problems that had affected his operations at San Sebastián were now delaying his invasion of France. As Wellington advanced north along the coast, the task of supplying the army became increasingly difficult as pirates continued interrupting his supply lines amid worsening weather.[88]

In Wellington's mind, the solution was simple: increase the number of warships available to escort the transports and reduce the number of ports utilized. However, the Admiralty viewed events quite differently. Although the first lord of the Admiralty admitted there was a problem, he proposed a solution that infuriated Wellington. Rather than accepting responsibility for the Admiralty's inability to plan predictable convoys, Melville suggested that Wellington assume the burden of planning his logistics and assign a senior army officer from within his staff to coordinate the convoys with Admiral Collier's headquarters.[89]

Wellington perceived Melville's solution as an attempt to force the army to fix a problem that it did not create and that was outside the bounds of its expertise. Furthermore, he refused to send an officer to Collier's headquarters, fifteen miles from his own. Wellington responded, "There is a great difference between the service in this country and those on which Admiral Keith has been employed. . . . This is no joint service. All that is required from His Majesty's navy is to convoy the supplies for the army coming from England and elsewhere, and to convoy back the empty transports, or those with wounded soldiers and prisoners."[90] Instead, Wellington proposed that the supply convoys sail from their ports at predictable intervals, using only Lisbon for outgoing supplies and Santander for incoming shipments. Wellington's proposal was forwarded to the Admiralty; however, no action was taken in time to prevent the delays that characterized joint operations for the remainder of the war.[91]

The navy did seek to remedy the problem between Wellington and Collier. In a sign of Wellington's increased stature and of the navy's diminished role in the war, Rear Admiral Charles Penrose replaced Collier as commander of the Biscay squadron in January 1814.[92] While health was the stated reason for Collier's removal, he was transferred back to England and assigned to command a fifty-gun frigate. Despite their stormy relationship, prior to his departure, Collier sent Wellington a barometer with which he could take atmospheric readings and thanked Wellington for his support.[93]

Collier was never blamed for the string of conflicts between Wellington and the navy, but his demotion was clearly a sign that the navy at last realized Collier was not the right man for the difficult task of providing security and supplies for Wellington's army. Although Collier never maintained the number of ships required for the job, his greatest misfortune was that he followed two men, admirals Cotton and Berkeley, who possessed a greater grasp of joint operations as well as the most coveted of qualities—Wellington's admiration and respect.[94]

After Wellington had removed Spanish troops from his force and again settled affairs with the senior service, his next target was Bayonne, a city known for its loyalty to the emperor. To reach the town, the allies began crossing the Nive River at dawn on 9 December. Soult counterattacked as the allies crossed the river. What followed was four days of intense fighting known as the battles of Nive and St. Pierre. Despite Soult's attempt to stop Wellington's advance, the allies forced the French to retreat to its entrenched defensive positions around the city of Bayonne. On 13 December, the allies invested the city. A week later, as winter weather descended on his exposed troops, Wellington ordered his exhausted army into its winter cantonments.[95]

Prior to halting the offensive, Bathurst notified Wellington that the government had dispatched an expedition under command of Sir Thomas Graham to Holland to seize the fortresses of Antwerp and Bergen-op-Zoom. In his dispatch, Bathurst told Wellington that in accordance with communications with the Russians, the British were to assist the Dutch "in the infancy of their exertions against the French."[96] Despite his intentions to send over eight thousand British troops to the Low Countries, Bathurst asked Wellington, "Would it not be wise for the British to throw our whole force to cooperate with Allies in the Netherlands, than in the divided manner, in which they now acted?" Concerned about control of the Low Countries in a postwar treaty, Bathurst told Wellington "that such an operation would grant England substantial influence on the Dutch frontier, something that England lost the moment that it left the [Low Countries.]" Bathurst did not advocate abandoning the British position in the peninsula because he feared Spanish and Portuguese fighting over the border fortresses of San Sebastián and Pamplona; however, he requested Wellington's approval for the operation in the Low Countries. Bathurst had an ulterior motive for seizing the great French naval base at Antwerp: "Our great object is Antwerp. We cannot make a secure peace if [Antwerp] is left in the hands of France. In this the allies feel no common interest with us. Some absurdly jealous of our maritime power, may even wish Antwerp remain with France."[97]

Wellington was angry at Bathurst's insinuation that another force in another location could affect the course of the war to a greater extent than his army in southern France. He was also pained that once again, the Admiralty had influenced British strategy against him. He told Bathurst, "I am already farther advanced into the French territory than any of the allied powers; and I believe that I am better prepared than any of them to take advantage of any opportunities which may offer of annoying the enemy than any of the allies." Upset by what he felt was another attempt by his government to decrease the size of his army for an unsuccessful and wasteful operation in the Low Countries, he candidly told Bathurst, "By having kept 30,000 men in the Peninsula, the British government has given employment to at least 200,000 Frenchmen. And it is ridiculous to suppose that either the Spaniards or Portuguese could have resisted for a moment if the British force had been withdrawn." Wellington added,

> As of right now, there are 100,000 Frenchmen opposing me, with 100,000 forming in Bordeaux in reserve. Is there any man weak enough to suppose that one third of that number would be employed against the Spaniards and Portuguese, if [my army] were withdrawn? . . . If I could put 40,000 Spaniards into the field, I should have my posts on the Garonne River. Does any man believe that Napoleon would not feel that such an army in such a position [was more harmful, especially with a strong Bourbon party in southern France,] than he would 30,000–40,000 British troops laying siege to one of his fortresses in Holland? [In terms of men, money, and reputation he would lose,] it will do ten times more to procure peace than ten more armies in Flanders.[98]

In regard to keeping an army in the peninsula and deploying another in Holland, Wellington again lectured the secretary for war: "You cannot maintain military operations in the Peninsula and in Holland with British troops; you must give up either the one or the other, as, if I am not mistaken, the British establishment is not equal to the maintenance of two armies in the field." As for helping the Dutch, Wellington was blunt: "Whenever you extend your assistance to any country, unless at the same time fresh means are put into action, the service is necessarily stinted in all its branches at the old stage, particularly the naval branch, and those supplies which necessarily come from England."[99]

Despite his objections, a British force was deployed to Holland on 14 December 1813. True to Wellington's predictions, the expedition was a military disaster. The British troops were poorly trained, and the French were well prepared. After a series of attacks on Antwerp and Bergen-op-Zoom, and a long-range bombardment of the French fleet, Graham was forced to lay siege. The forts, after gaining Prussian assistance in the spring of 1814, resisted all of Graham's attempts to capture them. In the end, the entire operation gained very little as Napoleon's troops were able once again to keep a large British force immobilized in the Low Countries. In retrospect, it is hard to blame the cabinet for pursuing a strategic port such as Antwerp in 1814. Possession of the port undoubtedly would have helped Britain's postwar strategy for the Low Countries. Nevertheless, the entire episode demonstrated the cabinet's struggle to formulate its strategy and once again placed the burden on Wellington and his troops in the decision phase of the war.[100]

Wellington's army was also forced to halt due to a money shortage. Although Bathurst and Herries had made a great effort to provide Wellington with £100,000 monthly, Wellington did not receive the December payment on time. Furthermore, due to the nature of his operations and the increasing number of soldiers under his command, the monthly subsidy was not enough. The troops-to-supply ratio was not a new issue for Wellington. When his brother Richard had attacked Liverpool for not sending reinforcements in 1812, Wellington had remarked, "How foolishly people will talk of matters with which they are not acquainted. Had an addition of 10,000 men been made to my army, they [would have] starved. Circumstanced as I was I could not have found provision for them."[101] By January 1814,

Wellington's army, not including the Spanish troops he was obligated to feed, numbered nearly sixty thousand men.[102] These numbers quickly overburdened the supply and transportation systems designed for an army half this size.

The problem was twofold. First, the extensive magazine and transportation system established by Wellington from 1809 to 1812 was too inefficient and costly to sustain his operations in 1813. His army had simply outdistanced the large magazines, such as the one established in Lisbon, and therefore had to find an alternate method of bringing wheat and corn to the army. Shipping the supplies to Santander and beyond was both quick and cheap since the transport cost could be paid in England.[103]

The new commissariat system of supplying Wellington's army from forward bases by sea and then transporting supplies along the coastal roads by mule brigades into the Pyrenees was also less expensive than the previous arrangements, because Wellington's area of operations was reduced after 1812. The winter weather and mountainous roads prevented the mule drivers from providing a complete supply from the rear; thus, Wellington augmented the muleteers with private contracts. Nevertheless, because most supplies were purchased in and shipped from England, the system costs were still far lower than with previous methods.[104]

Unfortunately, this supply system, which extended along the coast to St. Jean de Luz and ultimately to Bordeaux, proved more difficult to support during the invasion of France in the closing months of the war. Moving away from the coastal depots forced upon the commissariat the added expense of paying the local French businessmen and farmers for supplies received. Without his December shipment of money, Wellington was unable to pay his commissariat officers, and he refused to issue the French credits. Therefore, Wellington halted his operations until the money was received, telling Bathurst in exasperation, "I am prepared in every respect, excepting money, to push the enemy to the Garonne during the winter . . . but I cannot move at all . . . as the army is paralyzed for want of money." Wellington complained, "My posts are already so far distant, that the transport of the army is daily destroyed in supplying the troops, but there is not a shilling in the military chest to pay for anything. . . . Our credit is already gone in this country."[105] All these events led an exhausted Wellington to tell his brother, "I am quite certain that the Government are tired of me and my operations; and I wish both to the Devil."[106]

At this point in the war, given what he had achieved, Wellington's complaints seem excessive. Compared to Soult's tired and beleaguered army, Wellington's troops were well supplied. Nonetheless, even the venerable Sir Thomas Lawrence, who immortalized Wellington in several portraits, remarked about the change in Wellington's personality when he was informed of supply and pay shortages. In a letter to a friend, Lawrence recalled, "It has been observed that when [Wellington] thinks of Military movements, he has a habit of taking his left elbow in to his right hand and sitting in that posture, and that when he is dissatisfied with the management of the Commissariat or other concerns, he covers his nose with his hand, and on seeing this token of his disapprobation those officers who are concerned get out of his way as much they can."[107] Fortunately for Wellington and the officers on his staff, the pay shortage was temporary, and by February the supply of coin once again flowed and would continue uninterrupted for the remainder of the war.[108]

After a two-month winter encampment, Wellington decided that conditions were once again favorable for the offensive. He divided his force by detaching Sir John Hope and thirty thousand soldiers to continue the investment of Bayonne while the rest of the army pursued the French army across the Adour River. Soult took up a position near Orthez, and on 27 February, Wellington attacked and forced Soult again to withdraw. During the battle, Wellington was hit by a musket ball in the belt buckle. The wound was not serious, and after a six-day rest, his army continued pursuit of the French east toward the city of Toulouse.[109]

The situation was dire for the French. Nevertheless, Napoleon continued issuing instructions to his commanders to resist at all costs. To prevent Wellington's forces from capturing his naval squadron at Rochefort, Napoleon ordered it to sail for Toulon, Brest, or Cherbourg.[110] Soult, meanwhile, prepared a final defense at Toulouse. Wellington decided again to divide his army. On 8 March he detached Marshal Beresford with twelve thousand men to occupy the city of Bordeaux.[111]

The decision to send Beresford to Bordeaux was a political move. The fourth largest city in France, Bordeaux was also the home of many Bourbon royalists. Wellington was under considerable pressure to recognize Bourbon claims, having received Louis Antoine de Bourbon, Duc d'Angoulême, the nephew of Louis XVIII, at his headquarters in February.[112] Furthermore, he had received intelligence that the mayor of Bordeaux, Jean Baptiste Lynch, would surrender the city if Wellington sent troops.[113]

The problem for Wellington was that the government could not officially recognize the Royalist claims of independence at the same time they conducted negotiations with Napoleon. To do so would jeopardize any peace overture the allies made toward the emperor. In turn it might also ignite anti-British feelings throughout the country. Wellington viewed the Royalists as an untapped military resource that should be exploited, but he was powerless to act. He told Bathurst, "I can tell you that if I were a [Bourbon Prince], nothing should prevent me from coming forward, not in a good house in London, but in a field in France; and if Great Britain would stand by him, I am certain he would succeed."[114] He echoed similar concern to the prime minister, "I find the sentiment in the country still more strong against the Bonaparte dynasty and in favor of the Bourbons. . . . Any declaration from us would raise such a flame in the country as would soon spread from one end of it to the other, and would infallibly overturn [Napoleon]."[115]

Wellington did not approve of the government's refusal to solicit Royalist support, but he complied with its orders, instructing Beresford to take careful measures to distance himself and the British from pro-Royalist activities.[116] Despite his compliance, he told Liverpool, "I cannot discover the policy of not hitting one's enemy as hard as one can, and in the most vulnerable place. I am certain that he would not so act by us, if he had the opportunity. [Napoleon] would certainly overturn the British authority in Ireland if it was in his power."[117]

In the north, the French situation was much worse as Napoleon's empire rapidly collapsed. While Wellington pursued Soult to the east, the allied armies of Prussia, Austria, and Russia were driving west into France. A brilliant defense of the French frontier by Napoleon and his armies could not compensate for numerical inferiority. Furthermore, his subordinates were unequal to the energy of their emperor, and the allies defeated the venerable French marshals one after another. The allies captured Paris on 31 March and both sides agreed to an armistice. Napoleon abdicated his throne on 6 April 1814.

Unfortunately, news of the armistice and Napoleon's abdication did not reach Wellington and Soult before their armies clashed again. In the last acts of the Peninsular War, Wellington and Soult fought a bloody battle at Toulouse on Easter Sunday, 10 April, and the British forces under Sir John Hope repelled a large French sortie at Bayonne on 14 April.[118] Following these two engagements, Wellington and Soult were both notified of the cease-fire and abdication. In accordance with the cessation of hostilities in the north, Soult and Wellington signed the Convention of Toulouse on 18 April 1814, effectively ending the Peninsular War.[119]

Concerned over the unnecessary loss of so many of Wellington's men, Bathurst blamed Napoleon's supporters for the "unwarrantable delay" in communicating the restoration of the monarchy in Paris. He also called the battles of Toulouse and Bayonne "the last effort of an expiring cause, consistent in evil, to protract the miseries which its supporters had occasioned, and to postpone as long as possible the return of that harmony and peace which they had for upwards of twenty years too successfully labored to disturb."[120] Bathurst informed Wellington that he would be promoted to duke, and five of his most senior officers were to be made peers.[121]

The last remaining obstacle for Wellington was the extraction of his army from France. Prior to his departure, however, he was notified by Castlereagh that he had been recommended for the post of ambassador to Paris. In uncharacteristically humble fashion, Wellington accepted the responsibility: "I am very much obliged and flattered by your thinking of me for such a position for which I never have thought myself qualified."[122] On 14 June, Wellington bid farewell to his army at Bordeaux.

Before assuming his post in Paris, on 23 June 1814, after five years and two months of continued service in the peninsula, Wellington returned home. Wellington had departed England in 1808 as temporary commander of an expeditionary force to an uncertain destination with an unsure objective. In 1814, he returned as the liberator of the Iberian Peninsula and a hero of his nation. His two-front war was over.

Conclusion

Wellington's victory in the peninsula was a major factor in the ultimate defeat of Napoleon's forces and should not be underestimated. In terms of men, resources, and will to fight, the Peninsular War drained Napoleon and France. It was truly a "bleeding ulcer" that deprived France of its most valuable commodities: manpower, gold, and glory. This war was also the proving ground for a man who would become one of England's greatest generals. Dispatched to Spain as a temporary commander of an expeditionary force, Sir Arthur Wellesley, the future Duke of Wellington, soon bore the weight of a nation on his shoulders.

Wellington's brilliant military campaigns from 1808 to 1814 are noteworthy in themselves; however, they are also the result of less visible achievements that must be addressed in totality to understand his great victory. Deemed by some in London as the "Prince of Grumblers," Wellington not only fought the French on the battlefield, he also waged a protracted campaign in the ministries at Whitehall and in the cloakrooms of Westminster. A determined and entrenched civil and military bureaucracy, and an often shortsighted press, caused Wellington nearly as much angst as the military forces arrayed against him. He also fought for control of the Spanish and Portuguese armies, whose governments resisted nearly all his efforts to liberate their countries from French control. For Wellington, it was indeed a two-front war.

In fairness to the many ministers who labored in tiny London offices far from the battlefield and who felt the sting of Wellington's pen, expeditionary warfare in 1808 remained a challenge for a parliamentary monarchy. The difficulties of supplying and fighting an army on foreign soil while placating the Parliamentary "mob" influenced by public opinion were overwhelming. Nevertheless, Wellington used the opportunity that presented itself in 1808 to test his mettle against the greatest army in the world, and in doing so placed himself in the path of political opposition in London.

The first half of the war was fraught with challenges, highlighted by Marshal André Masséna's invasion of Portugal in 1810. Masséna's failed invasion determined the fate of Portugal and became the highwater mark of Napoleon's westward expansion and domination of the Iberian Peninsula. During these early years of the war, Wellington encountered his greatest challenges and developed his irresistible urge for complaining to his government for help. He had good reason.

Almost immediately upon landing in 1808, Wellington was handicapped by his government's struggle to plan a strategy for victory. Although Canning and Castlereagh dispatched him to the peninsula, it was Wellington who determined that Portugal, not Spain, offered the greatest opportunity. It was he, not the cabinet, who ultimately determined the course of the war.

Meanwhile, an army bureaucracy characterized by a seniority-based promotion system had a stifling effect on Wellington's operations. Best exemplified by politics within the Horse Guards, this system led to his removal from command and the forfeiture of gains in the battles of Roliça and Vimeiro. It also led to the Convention of Cintra, an armistice that fractured public and political support for the war.

Another millstone imposed by the Horse Guards was the assignment of incompetent general officers to Wellington's army. Choosing officers solely based on political patronage and the arbitrary date of rank to lieutenant colonel, the Horse Guards sent them to command in Wellington's army regardless of talent or ability. Of course, it would be naïve to suggest that Wellington had attained his own status in the British armed services solely on merit; he was born into wealth and status in Ireland and had a privileged childhood. Unlike many of the men sent to him, however, he was an experienced and successful soldier, driven by the high standards of military competence.

While Wellington was at the front, a sinister opponent also surfaced in London. The opposition Whig Party attempted to undermine Wellington's war efforts by using the newspapers to question the rationale of fighting such a costly war. Wellington was not the first, nor was he the last, general to feel harsh criticism of an uncontrolled, free press, but he was also willing to use it to his advantage. On the one hand, he despised disloyalty and the anonymous attacks from within his own ranks, but on the other, he hastened to use the press to influence and inform the public of his victories. On balance, the soldier who thinks that the press is his friend is foolhardy because the nature of a free press is incongruous with a structured, disciplined military force.

Wellington did become more accustomed to dealing with the press as the Peninsular War dragged on, but he also had to ensure that he had allies on the home front to help ameliorate the sting of partisan editors. His lasting lesson, and that of countless other generals and politicians, was that one can never have the last word against a man armed with a barrel of ink.

Wellington also suffered from the cabinet's inability to define a clear strategy for victory. The two men responsible for providing Wellington with general guidance and support during the first half of the war, Castlereagh and Liverpool, ultimately gave him the financial and logistical support required to maintain his army. Neither man, however, gave Wellington's army strategic priority until Masséna's withdrawal from the Lines of Torres Vedras in 1811, when victory in Portugal was almost assured.

In 1809, while Wellington, who struggled to feed and pay his army, killed or captured thousands of French soldiers at places such as Porto and Talavera, Castlereagh, out of economic desperation and military miscalculation, pursued a disastrous operation in Holland. Liverpool followed suit by suggesting diversionary expeditions to Spain that had no strategic purpose nor basis on sound principles of war. Liverpool also gave Wellington contradictory signals by pledging support and sending reinforcements, while warning Wellington not to fight unnecessary battles or risk the army's safety.

Another demand on Britain's precious finances was the necessity to subsidize the allied coalitions against France. In its attempt to substitute money for what Britain lacked in manpower, the cabinet must be given credit for persisting with an aggressive strategy in the teeth of a global specie shortage. Most of its efforts were lost on Wellington, who was reduced to pleading for the resources he required for his campaigns in Portugal. He had to resort to revolving debt, promising to pay the various merchants and vendors for supplies to keep his army in the field, while awaiting shipments of gold and silver coins from England.

Had it not been for the skills of two British diplomats—Charles Stuart, in Lisbon, and Wellington's brother Henry, in Cadiz—and the minister of defense and marine in Lisbon, Dom Miguel Forjaz, Wellington would have been unable to stabilize the political situation in both Portugal and Spain. These men manipulated the political situations and economic markets of the corrupt and often incompetent Iberian governments with subsidy payments. And in the end, despite the parsimonious British government, these men helped preserve Wellington's legitimacy in the eyes of the Portuguese and Spanish people.

There were some successes in the first half of the war. The most important of these was Wellington's ability to conduct joint operations with the Royal Navy, not through the cooperation of the Lords of the Admiralty, who dispatched the ships and sailors to accomplish the task. The success of the operations was due largely to the personalities and professionalism of two men who made Wellington's army a priority, admirals Charles Cotton and George Berkeley. Both men consistently risked their careers by expounding on their orders from London to support Wellington.

Wellington was not without fault in the first half of the war. After his victories at Roliça and Vimeiro, he signed the notorious Convention of Cintra, an error that resulted in his recall to England and near abolishment to the bottom of the army list. Upon the death of Sir John Moore in January 1809, Wellington was fortunate to gain a second chance. He returned to the peninsula, resolving to keep the British press in the dark concerning his defensive strategy. It worked to perfection, but it also kept the ministers uncertain of the depth and construction progress of the Lines of Torres Vedras. Although the true strength of the lines remained a secret to all, including the French, this secrecy left him vulnerable and unable to answer Liverpool's incessant questions concerning an exit strategy in 1810.

Despite his problems and personal shortcomings, Wellington's defeat of Marshal Masséna in 1811 led Napoleon to look east, where he would ultimately encounter his greatest loss in Russia. Thus Wellington's victory over Masséna was undoubtedly the beginning of the end for the Napoleonic Empire. Masséna's withdrawal marked a British transition to strategic offense and a clear dividing line between a desperate and a sometimes pedantic Wellington. After the spring of 1811, Wellington was never pushed to the brink of defeat again. Nevertheless, his criticism of the government did not diminish in proportion to his problems.

In May 1811, the ministry finally granted Wellington unprecedented authority to plan offensive and defensive operations throughout the entire Iberian Peninsula. This ushered in a significant shift in the government's policy toward Wellington and the Peninsular War. For the first time since the government had formed in 1809, Wellington was granted the operational and strategic flexibility to look past the defense of Portugal and to protect the peninsula as a whole. While the merits of the ministry's decision would not be realized until 1813, when Wellington moved his combined army into a position to invade France, the results of their renewed pledge of support validated Wellington's strategic vision of forming a single powerful army under his command. Of course, this was not readily apparent to the government at the time, and they continued to question the cost of the war and of supplying the Portuguese and Spanish with subsidies.

Nevertheless, over the course of the next two years, as more and more British troops were dispatched to the peninsula and Wellington gained increased control, the decision of May 1811 formed the nucleus of the winning strategy. By 1813, the government's decision had also made Britain, with the help of its Spanish and Portuguese allies, a significant continental military power.

Despite being granted operational freedom, Wellington was still hindered throughout the second half of the war by a global gold shortage. But with the help of Lord Bathurst, he was able to procure enough money from abroad and from within the peninsula to survive.

The financial crisis of 1812 also signified the government's renewed resolve to help Wellington, although Liverpool and Bathurst managed the fiscal crisis in contrasting ways. As the secretary for war under Perceval, Liverpool was forced to adhere to Perceval's conservative fiscal policy. The primary problem was that Perceval viewed Wellington's army as only one of Britain's strategic priorities and therefore chose to subsidize the continental powers instead of Portugal and Spain. In addition, Wellington countered the stifling influence of opponents such as John Herries, who from his office in London continually suppressed Wellington's suggestions concerning the issuing of British securities traded at the peninsular markets as well as increasing the subsidies to Portugal and Spain. As a result, Wellington blamed Liverpool, perhaps unjustly, for failing to produce the money necessary to win the war in 1812.

After Perceval's assassination, Liverpool, as prime minister, not only named Bathurst secretary for war, but also supported Bathurst's plans to provide Wellington the necessary gold, even if it meant challenging the Bank of England to do so. As the prime minister in the summer of 1812, Liverpool supported Wellington's operations despite events in Russia, where it seemed Napoleon would emerge victorious. He also supported Wellington's disastrous decision to besiege the fortress city of Burgos. Liverpool bore the brunt of criticism in England as the failed siege of Burgos tested the public's patience in Liverpool's government at a vital time. Had Napoleon defeated the Russians, Liverpool's decision to empty Britain's coffers to supply Wellington's army might have been costly. Nevertheless, Wellington gained substantially from his prime minister's support. This of course did not stop Wellington's rants in 1813 concerning money; however, they were related more to the breakdown of his logistics support than to a substantial fiscal shortage.

Despite his thrifty approach to the Peninsular War, Spencer Perceval's assassination brought great consternation to Wellington. The prime minister's death in May 1812 forced Wellington to choose between the love of his family and the continued support of the ministry. His brothers Richard and Pole, always seeking increased prestige, attempted to form a new ministry with Wellington's help. Unwilling to trade the support of Liverpool and the fledgling cabinet, however, a pragmatic Wellington chose to support his government. His decision helped preserve the Liverpool ministry at a crucial time, but it also effectively removed Richard from the apex of power and relegated Pole to a minimal role in government.

By 1812, two old foes clashed again. The insistence of the Horse Guards to send inexperienced recruits in exchange for veteran troops stressed Wellington's command authority. He had successfully defended Portugal from several of Napoleon's ablest generals, including marshals Masséna, Soult, and Marmont, and deserved better than the continuing interference of the Horse Guards in the selection of his senior commanders. The emerging style of warfare favored the commander who could make quick decisions of character and competence as well as the military autocrat, like Napoleon, who knew his senior officers intimately. The refusal of the Horse Guards to subordinate their authority not only hindered Wellington's operations, it forced him to divert precious energy away from defeating the French. Victory rarely brings reform, and despite his constant struggles with the Horse Guards and the army bureaucracy that governed the army of the day, Wellington—who served as the master general of the ordnance and twice served as the commander in chief of the army, the last period from 1842 until his death in 1852—never oversaw sweeping reforms of the army. Only the disasters of the Crimea War and Sepoy Mutiny of 1857 would bring about the impetus to implement the Cardwell and Childers reforms of the late nineteenth century. Long overdue, these reforms not only modernized the army's organizational structure and abolished the sale of commissions, but they also streamlined the administration of the War Office and commissariat.

Nevertheless, problems with the Horse Guards and commissariat paled in comparison to the inadequate naval support Wellington received along the Biscay coastline in 1813 and 1814. Since 1809, while Wellington and the British army had assumed the burden of defending Portugal, the Royal Navy had served in a supporting capacity. This fact was not lost on their powerful lordships, who no doubt felt a animosity in their supporting role to the army. The Admiralty too readily turned to the outbreak of hostilities with the United States in 1812 to once again assert themselves as Britain's preeminent force. By the fall of 1813, the navy was treating Wellington's operations with benign neglect, providing inadequate naval resources to protect Wellington's lines of communications and failing to adequately blockade French strategic targets along the Biscay coastline. Paper warfare developed between Wellington and the first lord of the Admiralty, Lord Melville. Personal in nature, their incessant complaints not only diminished the positive relationship that had developed between the two services, but had operational consequences as well. Lacking proper naval support, Wellington's operations came to a grinding halt in the fall of 1813.

Overall, the war with America was rightfully viewed by Wellington as a great distraction that strained the precious commodities on which he relied—warships and transports to keep men and supplies flowing. Unfortunately, the Treaty of Ghent, signed in December 1814, came too late and provided little relief. For the Admiralty, the war with America demonstrated its inability to balance the strategic expectations of supporting Wellington's army on the continent and defeating America on the high seas with the operational realities of a finite number of resources to do both. In the end, both ventures suffered, and the painful consequences were endured most by Wellington and his men.

As in the first half of the Peninsular War, Wellington was not without fault in the second half. A control freak by modern standards, there was no aspect of his army's operations that did not consume him, and therefore his decision to leave his best troops under Gen. Rowland Hill in Madrid in the summer of 1812 and pursue Marmont's shattered army without an adequate siege train cost him time and men during the failed siege of Burgos. Moreover, his inability to control his own men after the battle of Vitoria and the sieges of Badajoz, Ciudad Rodrigo, and San Sebastián cost him valuable time and troops, as well as nearly costing him the support of his Spanish allies and the British public. However, Wellington's errors were dwarfed by Napoleon's defeat in Russia. This watershed event marked a distinct transition in the Peninsular War. From the fall of 1812, the ministers, particularly Bathurst, sensed blood in the water and relinquished a great deal of command and diplomatic authority to Wellington.

Bathurst's faith in Wellington was the result of five years of successful campaigning. The series of victories in the peninsula had made Wellington an extremely powerful political force. By 1813, he had gained control of the Spanish and Portuguese armies, and his personal decisions steered the politics and economies of both countries. Furthermore, his relations with his superiors, including Prime Minster Liverpool, were based on respect and admiration. After 1813, Wellington was no longer a general to whom orders could be sent to be carried out without at least his tacit approval. Promoted to field marshal, Wellington had become a powerful presence, whose views were not limited to the Peninsular War; his opinions on British global strategy were considered before any decision was made.

With increased responsibility came increased burdens, and Wellington had to reinvent a method of supplying his army during the ensuing invasion of France. He was also forced to curtail the number of troops he could carry into France, because he could no longer support the Spanish with needed gold and food. While Bathurst struggled to send Wellington the gold to accomplish the task, both men were aided once again by Napoleon's defeat in Russia. The French defeat opened the Baltic ports and Hanseatic cities to British trade, thus giving England access to German investors and banks. It also gave Wellington supplies of badly needed wheat from Russia. Once again, disaster at one end of Napoleon's empire contributed to his defeat at the other. So Wellington took advantage of the situation by importing a higher percentage of his required food, thus becoming less reliant on the peninsular and American markets.

Wellington's personality also had an effect on the prosecution of the war. Forced to fight for prioritization from a government that initially did not understand the war, Wellington also carried the burden of an unpredictable Spanish ally. The cumulative strain would have broken a lesser man. His dispatches and letters unsurprisingly reflected his frustrations. While the majority of his anger was directed toward the disjointed political situation in Cadiz, history has proven that his blanket condemnations of the Spanish army were unwarranted. While the army was not effective in pitched battle, the cumulative effect of the Spanish effort is telling. The Spanish army inflicted nearly 50 percent of overall French losses in the peninsula. Compared to 30 percent inflicted by the Anglo-Portuguese troops under Wellington and another 20 percent by irregular, or Spanish guerilla, forces, the Spanish armies were essential to victory. Nevertheless, Wellington remained disdainful of their contributions and when made public, his dispatches often fueled opposition at home and made him a target of the Spanish politicians and generals on whom he depended for support.

Wellington's Iberian campaign was a bridge into modern expeditionary operations. Much like modern commanders, Wellington served many masters. Not only was he an overburdened chief executive and a battlefield commander, but he was also the senior ambassador for his country and a principal adviser to the cabinet. Under this political burden, Wellington found his greatest challenges and labored while his soldiers carried the government's anti-Napoleonic policy on their bayonets.

While enduring great distractions and frustrations with those in Britain and Iberia for whom he fought, Wellington never lost sight of the first principle of war—objective. As with Cato centuries before in the Roman senate, who ended his speeches with "Carthage must be destroyed," Wellington was driven to defeat the French. It was his mission, and nothing superseded it. Although others in Britain would have withdrawn from the Iberian Peninsula, ceding it to Napoleon, Wellington understood the strategic gains by killing French in the peninsula. Therefore, his broad strategic vision was one of his enduring traits. At Waterloo, Napoleon would later personally discover the same resolve and determination that Wellington's opponents had witnessed for six years in the peninsula. It was through sheer tenacity and an indomitable spirit that Wellington won his two-front war.

Appendix A

Cabinet Positions with Strategic Responsibility, 1808–1814

Prime Minister

Duke of Portland	March 1807–September 1809
Spencer Perceval	October 1809–May 1812
Earl of Liverpool	June 1812–

Secretary for War and Colonies

Viscount Castlereagh	March 1807–September 1809
Earl of Liverpool	October 1809–May 1812
Earl of Bathurst	June 1812–

Foreign Secretary

George Canning	March 1807–September 1809
Earl Bathurst	October 1809–December 1809
Richard, Marquess of Wellesley	December 1809–March 1812
Viscount Castlereagh	March 1812–

First Lord of the Admiralty

Lord Mulgrave   March 1807–April 1810
Lord York   April 1810–May 1812
Viscount Melville (R. Dundas)   June 1812–

Master General of the Ordnance

Earl of Chatham   March 1807–April 1810
Lord Mulgrave   April 1810–

Appendix B

French Army Commanders in Spain, 1810–1813

Army of the South

Marshal Nicolas Soult, Duke of Dalmatia	January 1810–March 1813
General Honoré Gazan	March 1813–July 1813

Army of Portugal

Marshal André Masséna, Prince of Essling	May 1810–May 1811
Marshal Marmont, Duke of Ragusa	May 1811–July 1812
General Baron Bertrand Clausel	July 1812–September 1812
General Souham	September 1812–November 1812
General Jean-Baptiste Drouet, Count D'Erlon	November 1812–January 1813
General Honoré Reille	January 1813–July 1813

Army of the North

Marshal Bessières, Duke of Istria	January 1811–July 1811
General Jean-Marie Dorsenne	July 1811–May 1812
General Marie-François Caffarelli	May 1812–January 1813
General Baron Bertrand Clausel	January 1813–July 1813

Army of the Center

General Jean-Baptiste Drouet, Count D'Erlon	January 1813–July 1813

(Before January 1813, the Army of the Center was commanded directly by King Joseph Bonaparte.)

In July 1813, the four armies were merged into the *armée d'Espagne* under the command of Marshal Soult.

Appendix C

Chronology of the Peninsular War

1807

18 October	French troops cross Franco-Spanish Border
30 November	French troops occupy Lisbon

1808

23 March	French troops occupy Madrid
May–June	Insurrections against the French occur throughout Spain
1–8 August	Sir Arthur Wellesley lands his army in Portugal
17 August	Battle of Roliça
21 August	Battle of Vimeiro
10 December	Sir John Moore's army advances from Salamanca
24 December	Moore's army retreats toward Coruña

1809

16 January	Battle of Coruña (Moore is killed)
22 April	Wellesley takes command of British forces in Portugal
12 May	Battle of Oporto
3 July	Wellesley's army enters Spain
28 July	Battle of Talavera
20 October	Defensive preparations of the Lines of Torres Vedras begin

1810

10 July	The French Army under Masséna takes Ciudad Rodrigo
27 September	Battle of Bussaco

1811

3 March	Masséna withdraws from Santarém
3–5 May	Battle of Fuentes d'Oñoro
16 May	Battle of Albuera
23–25 June	Battle of Caia
28–30 September	Battle of the upper Côa

1812

19 January	Wellington takes Ciudad Rodrigo
6 April	Wellington takes Badajoz
22 July	Battle of Salamanca
12 August	Madrid falls to Anglo-Spanish forces
22 October	Wellington raises siege and retreats from Burgos
19 November	Wellington's army begins winter encampment at Ciudad Rodrigo

1813

22 May	Wellington's final offensive in Spain commences
21 June	Battle of Vitoria
25 July–1 August	Battle of Pyrenees
31 August	San Sebastián falls to the Allies
7 October	Wellington crosses the Bidassoa
25 October	Pamplona falls to the Allies
10 November	Battle of Nivelle
9–13 Dec	Battles of the Nive

1814

27 February	Battle of Orthez
10 April	Battle of Toulouse
14–18 April	French forces opposing Wellington capitulate

Notes

ABBREVIATIONS USED IN THE NOTES

BL   British Library, London
PRO   Public Record Office (National Archive) of Great Britain, Kew Gardens, London
RP   Raglan Papers, Gwent County Record Office, Cwmbrân
WD   Wellington's Dispatches (published)
WP   Wellington Papers, Hartley Library, University of Southampton
WSD   Wellington's Supplementary Dispatches (published)

INTRODUCTION

1. Two works stand out in the assessment of British strategy during the Napoleonic Wars: Muir, *Britain and the Defeat of Napoleon*, and Hall, *British Strategy in the Napoleonic Wars*. For monetary matters, see Sherwig, *Guineas and Gunpowder*, 143–65. See also Silberling, "Financial and Monetary Policy."

2. Wellesley to the Duke of Richmond, 1 August 1808, Wellington, *Supplementary Dispatches*, 6:95 (hereafter WSD); Muir, *Britain and Defeat of Napoleon*, 37–46. Wellesley's force sailed from England on 20 July 1808. An additional 5,000 men under Gen. Brent Spencer joined him in Portugal on 6 August 1808.

3. Clode, *Military Forces of the Crown*, 1:90–91.

4. Silberling, "Financial and Monetary Policy," 214–18; Hall, *British Strategy*, 15–16. See also Muir and Esdaile, "Strategic Planning," 1:2.

5. R. Glover, *Peninsular Preparation*, 147–51.

6. Ward, *Wellington's Headquarters*, 10–13.

7. Stephen and Lee, *Dictionary of National Biography* (hereafter *DNB*), 19:991–93.

8. Fortescue, *History of the British Army*, 7:419; Glover, *Wellington as Military Commander*, 24–28.

9. R. Glover, *Peninsular Preparation*, 46–110; Muir and Esdaile, "Strategic Planning," 18–19.

10. Clode, *Military Forces of the Crown*, 1:194–97; R. Glover, *Peninsular Preparation*, 35–36.

11. Palmerston to Fanny Temple, October 1809, MS 62, BR 24/1, Palmerston Papers (hereafter cited as WP), Hartley Library, University of Southampton; *DNB*, 19:497. Henry John Temple, Viscount Palmerston (1784–1865) assumed his duties in the War Office on 27 October 1809 and held his post until 1828. He was an excellent administrator, and throughout the Peninsular War, he worked tirelessly to increase the War Office's proficiency.

12. Weller, *Wellington in the Peninsula*, 27–28.

13. Wellesley to the House of Commons, 3 June 1808, *Cobbett's Parliamentary Debates*, (hereafter *Parliamentary Debates*) 11:814–15.

14. Four works stand out in their scope and analysis of the naval war around the Iberian Peninsula: Krajeski, *In the Shadow of Nelson*; McCranie, *Admiral Lord Keith*; Hall, *Wellington's Navy*; and DeToy, "Wellington's Admiral." See also Horward, "British Seapower," 56.

15. Ward, *Wellington's Headquarters*, 4–6; Weller, *Wellington in the Peninsula*, 27–28.

16. *DNB*, 8:576–79. Baron William Wyndam Grenville (1759–1834) served as prime minister (Ministry of All Talents, 1806–1807) following the death of William Pitt the Younger in 1806. However, Grenville lost his position and ministry when he attempted to force King George III to make a decision concerning Catholic emancipation. The king subsequently dismissed the ministry and appointed the Duke of Portland as prime minister. After Grenville's fall from power, he returned to Parliament to lead the Whig opposition in the House of Lords.

17. Muir and Esdaile, "Strategic Planning," 21.

18. Weller, *Wellington in the Peninsula*, 27–28. From 1809 to 1814, Wellington's military secretary was Captain Lord Fitzroy Somerset, the future Lord Raglan.

19. Grey to Gordon, 3 March 1810, Add. MSS 49477, Gordon Papers, British Library, London (hereafter BL); Grey's Board of War consisted of a first lord, four lord commissioners, a public secretary, and an undersecretary. Subordinate to these officials would be the army's adjutant general, quartermaster general, lieutenant general of the ordnance, paymaster, treasurer of the ordnance, barracks master, and medical board officer. Grey's proposal would eliminate the offices of the secretary for war and colonies, secretary at war, master general of the ordnance, and the commander in chief. Grey estimated that the new Board of War would cost far less to maintain. He felt the board's greatest advantage would be "to give the army a better government." To this end, Grey maintained that the first lord should stand "in the authorization to the king as a Secretary of State, so that he could receive His Majesty's orders

without [interference] from another minister and thereby communicate [his instructions] to the board."

20. Evidence on the Civil Administration of the Army, 1837, reprinted in Ward, *Wellington's Headquarters*, 5; also cited in Clode, *Military Forces of the Crown*, 1:219.

21. Croker, *The Croker Papers*, 1:342.

22. Ibid.

23. Weller, *Wellington in the Peninsula*, 21–22; M. Glover, *Wellington as Military Commander*, 26. Wellesley successively commanded British troops during the expedition to the Low Countries in 1794, but his greatest success came in India. During these campaigns in 1803, Wellesley led Sepoy troops to several victories over the French-trained Mahratta armies at the battles of Assaye and Argaum and stormed the large fortress of Gawilghur. At Assaye, Wellesley's army of 4,500 troops, of which only 1,500 were British, destroyed an army of 40,000 men, including 10,000 infantry and 100 guns.

CHAPTER 1. ROOTS OF THE STRUGGLE

1. Weller, *Wellington in the Peninsula*, 30–34. Gen. Henri-Francois Delaborde and Gen. Henri Loison at Roliça and Gen. Jean-Andoche Junot at Vimeiro commanded the French armies.

2. Hall, *Wellington's Navy*, 29–31; Weller, *Wellington in the Peninsula*, 39–57.

3. M. Glover, *Wellington as Military Commander*, 24–28.

4. M. Glover, *Britannia Sickens*, 59–60.

5. Duke of York to Wellesley, 14 June 1808, Arthur Wellesley, Duke of Wellington, *Dispatches of Field Marshal*, 4:10–12 (hereafter WD).

6. Wellesley to the Duke of Richmond, 1 August 1808, WSD, 6:95.

7. Duke of York to Dalrymple, 21 July 1808, WD, 4:32–33.

8. Moore, *Diary of Sir John Moore*, 2:239–45.

9. Muir, *Britain and Defeat of Napoleon*, 44–47; M. Glover, *Britannia Sickens*, 60–61. Sir Hew Dalrymple's only year of active service was in 1793, when he commanded a battalion of grenadier companies at the battle of Farmars and at the sieges of Valenciennes and Dunkirk.

10. Glover, *Britannia Sickens*, 62–64.

11. Ibid., 62–66. Officers in the artillery, engineers, and marines were not considered capable of commanding infantry and cavalry regiments. In addition, foreign officers or officers currently serving abroad in India, in the West Indies, or in diplomatic missions were also not considered for command. Due to the urgent time constraint only officers currently serving in England or Ireland were considered for command. Sir Harry Burrard was fifty-eight years old at the time of his appointment. His brigade in 1796 command captured by the French and returned through prisoner exchange after the Helder Expedition of 1799.

12. Castlereagh to Wellesley, 15 July 1808, WD, 4:30.

13. Wellesley to Castlereagh, 1 August 1808, WD, 4:55.

14. Wellesley to the Duke of Richmond, 1 August 1808, WSD, 6:95.

15. Wellesley to Wellesley-Pole, 19 August 1808, Wellington A/5, Lord Raglan Papers, County Gwent Record Office, Cwmbrân, Wales (hereafter RP).
16. Wellesley to Burrard, 8 August 1808, WD, 4:66–71.
17. Wellesley to Burrard, 21 August 1808, battlefield quote reprinted in Fortescue, *History of the British Army*, 6:231.
18. Burrard to Castlereagh, 21 August 1808, WD, 4:108.
19. Wellesley to Castlereagh, 21 August 1808, WD, 4:107.
20. Wellesley to Castlereagh, 22 August 1808, WD, 4:115–16.
21. Wellesley to Wellesley-Pole, 22 August 1808, Wellington A/6, RP.
22. Evidence of Sir Arthur Wellesley, in Great Britain, Board of General Officers, *Proceedings upon the inquiry*, 100; M. Glover, *Britannia Sickens*, 132–33.
23. M. Glover, *Britannia Sickens*, 129, 131–35.
24. Wellesley to Castlereagh, 23 August 1808, WSD, 6:123–24.
25. Ibid.
26. Wellesley to Wellesley-Pole, 24 August 1808, Wellington A/7, RP.
27. The genius behind the popularity of the *Morning Chronicle* was its editor, James Perry (1756–1821). By 1810, the newspaper made enough money for Perry to hire England's best radical journalists, including William Hazlitt and Charles Lamb. He was a continual target of the Tory government. For more information on the British newspapers of the day see, Aspinall, *Politics and the Press*.
28. *Morning Chronicle*, 21 September 1808.
29. Ibid., 29 September 1808.
30. Ibid.
31. Wellesley to Richmond, 10 October 1808, WSD, 6:151.
32. Severn, *Architects of Empire*, 229–30.
33. Ibid., 229–31.
34. *Times*, 4 January 1809.
35. Holmes, *The Iron Duke*, 124–25.
36. Weller, *Wellington in the Peninsula*, 32–33.
37. Ibid.
38. Wellesley to Castlereagh, 8 August 1808, WD, 4:72–73.
39. Wellesley to Wellesley-Pole, 19 August 1808, Wellington A/5, RP.
40. Wellesley to Castlereagh, 8 August 1808, WD, 4:72–73.
41. Castlereagh to the House of Commons, 21 February 1809, printed in the *Times*, 22 February 1809.
42. Hall, *Wellington's Navy*, 34–37.

CHAPTER 2. A SECOND CHANCE

1. Muir, *Britain and defeat of Napoleon*, 65–74; Fortescue, *History of the British Army*, 6:291–95; Severn, *Architects of Empire*, 232–34. Adding to his problems was the British representative to the Spanish Supreme Junta, John Hookham Frere, who pledged broad Spanish support and urged Moore to advance into central Spain. See also Frederick Black, "Diplomatic Struggles."

2. Moore to Castlereagh, 24 November 1808; Moore, *Narrative*, 260–61.

3. Muir, *Britain and Defeat of Napoleon*, 73–78; Moore, *Narrative*, 204–10, 217–24.

4. Bruno, "Sir John Craddock," 74–78.

5. Vichness, "Marshal of Portugal," 116, 120–26.

6. For an excellent analysis of the British strategic alternatives in 1808, see Hall, *British Strategy*, 174–79.

7. *Times*, 2 February 1809.

8. "Thirtieth Bulletin of the Army of Spain," 21 January 1809, *Times*, 5 February 1809.

9. *Times*, 6 February 1809.

10. Muir, *Britain and the Defeat of Napoleon*, 80–81.

11. "Substance of a Communication," 2 December 1808, and reply 24 December 1808, Vienna, 7/89, Foreign Office (hereafter FO), National Archive (formerly Public Record Office, London, hereafter PRO) ; Sherwig, *Guineas and Gunpowder*, 208–10. Not only was Canning uncertain that England could provide the amount the Austrians requested, but he also did not favor the arrangements of their request. Unlike William Pitt, Canning did not favor granting an initial demand for preparations followed by monthly subsidies. He considered this practice outdated, and he did not want to repeat the mistakes of the past. Instead, he favored granting an initial sum of £250,000 and the establishment of a "military chest" of between £750,000 and £1 million on the island of Malta for Austria's use in the event of war.

12. Severn, *Architects of Empire*, 233–36; *Times*, January–March 1809.

13. Wellesley, Memorandum on the Defense of Portugal, 7 March 1809, WD, 4:261–63; Hall, *British Strategy*, 18–20.

14. Ibid.

15. Severn, *Architects of Empire*, 243–48.

16. Castlereagh to George III and his reply, 26–27 March 1809, King George III, *Correspondence*, 5:3844.

17. Ibid.

18. Earl of Buckinghamshire to the House of Lords, 14 April 1809, *Parliamentary Debates*, 14:29–30.

19. Castlereagh to Wellesley, 2 April 1809, WSD, 6:210–12.

20. Ibid.

21. Castlereagh to Wellesley, 3 April 1809, Vance, *Castlereagh Correspondence*, 7:49–50.

22. Memorandum by Sir Arthur Wellesley, 11 April 1809, WSD, 6:221.

23. Wellesley to Castlereagh, 12 April 1809, WSD, 6:223–24.

24. Castlereagh to Wellesley, 11 April 1809, WSD, 6:225.

25. Castlereagh to Wellesley, 13 April 1809, WSD, 6:225–26.

26. Wellesley to Wellesley-Pole, 13 April 1809, Wellington A/11, RP.

27. Hall, *Wellington's Navy*, 78–85; DeToy, "Wellington's Admiral," 2:406–408.

28. Wellesley to Castlereagh, 24 April 1809, WD, 4:269–70; Wellesley to Castlereagh, 27 April 1809, WD, 4:271–72.

CHAPTER 3. THE TRIALS BEGIN

1. Wellesley to Castlereagh, 24 April 1809, WD, 4:269–70.
2. Wellesley to Castlereagh, 12 May 1809, WD, 4:322–26. A British major general, William Carr Beresford, who had accepted the local rank of marshal of the Portuguese army in February 1809, commanded the Portuguese troops. For more on Beresford's role, see Vichness, "Marshal of Portugal," 137–57.
3. Wellesley to Berkeley, 7 June 1809, 21 June 1809, WD, 4:390–92, 441–42. For more on Admiral Berkeley's effort to resupply Wellington during his march, see Hall, *Wellington's Navy*, 87–94, and DeToy, "Wellington's Admiral," 2:460.
4. Wellesley to Cuesta, 22 May 1809, 30 May 1809, 10 June 1809, WD, 4:353–55, 371–72, and 407. See also Weller, *Wellington in the Peninsula*, 86.
5. Wellesley to Castlereagh, 29 July 1809, WD, 4:532–40; See also Oman, "The French Losses," 682–83. Oman uses the comprehensive analysis of A. Martinien's *Tableaux Officers Tués et Blessés pendant les Guerres de L'Empire, 1805–1815*, to collect his data on French casualties. For an order of battle of both armies, see Weller, *Wellington in the Peninsula*, 104–109. At Talavera, Wellesley's army numbered approximately twenty thousand men; Victor's approximately forty-six thousand; and Cuesta's approximately thirty-four thousand. British casualties numbered 5,365 compared to Victor's 7,268, including 266 officers killed or wounded. Spanish losses, due to its premature withdrawal, were negligible. For more on Wellesley's victory at Talavera due to his renovation in tactics, see, Cornell "Wellington and the Transformation of Warfare."
6. Moore to Frere, 10 November 1808, reprinted in Oman, *History of the Peninsular War*, 1:475.
7. Moore to Castlereagh, 24 November 1808, reprinted in Moore, *Narrative*, 262.
8. Wellesley to Villiers, 31 May 1809, WD, 4:374. Wellesley's disdain for the conduct of his men is well documented and never improved during the war, particularly during siege operations. This topic will be covered in much more detail in chapters 7–9.
9. Ward, *Wellington's Headquarters*, 92. Large civilian contractor bills could be settled with Treasury bills, which could be used for exchange, and small privateers, such as muleteers, could sometimes be paid with receipts or vouchers, known as *vals*.
10. Wellesley to Villiers, 31 May 1809, WD, 4:374.
11. *DNB*, 10:323–26. William Huskisson (1770–1830) assumed the duties of chancellor of the Exchequer in April 1807.
12. Wellesley to Huskisson, 5 May 1809, WD, 4:302. The ship that carried the money was the *Surveillante*, the same ship that had carried General Craddock to Gibraltar. In Cadiz, Craddock had delayed the return of the *Surveillante* for approximately two weeks for personal reasons, thereby further delaying the time it took to reach Wellesley.
13. Ibid.
14. Schaumann, *On the Road with Wellington*, 158–59.

15. Villiers to Wellesley, 30 May 1809, WP 1/261.
16. Wellesley to Villiers, 1 June 1809, WD, 4:382–83.
17. Ibid.
18. Wellesley to Huskisson, 30 May 1809, WD, 4:373.
19. Wellesley to Castlereagh, 31 May 1809, WD, 4:380.
20. Wellesley to Villiers, 31 May 1809, WD, 4:374.
21. General Order 180, 29 May 1809, WSD, 6:270–71.
22. Wellesley to Huskisson, 30 May 1809, WP 1/263.
23. Wellesley to Castlereagh, 11 June 1809, WD, 4:413–14.
24. Wellesley to Villiers, 11 June 1809, WD, 4:412–13; Wellesley to Wellesley-Pole, 1 July 1809, Wellington A/13, RP.
25. Wellesley to Huskisson, 28 June 1809, WP 1/266.
26. Huskisson, Memorandum on War Finance, 13 August 1809, Add. MSS. 37416, Huskisson Papers, BL. For complete analysis of Huskisson's viewpoint from the treasury see Muir, *Britain and the Defeat of Napoleon*, 110–13.
27. Extraordinary expenses were the costs of maintaining an army overseas as opposed to garrisoning the same number of men in Britain or Ireland.
28. Huskisson, Memorandum on War Finance, 13 August 1809, Add. MSS. 37416.
29. Perceval to King George III and his reply, 6 December 1809, King George III, *Correspondence*, 5:465–66.
30. Castlereagh to Wellesley, 11 July 1809, *Castlereagh Correspondence*, 7:95–96; Hall, *British Strategy*, 21–22.
31. Grey to Grenville, 25 May 1809, Historical Manuscripts Commission, *Report on the Manuscripts of J.B. Fortescue*, 9:308 (hereafter HMC *Fortescue*).
32. Wellington to Villiers, 21 June 1809, 1/266, WP.
33. Wellesley-Pole to Wellesley, 2 August 1809, Wellington B/91, RP.
34. *Times*, 3 August 1809.
35. Ibid., 2 August 1809.
36. Wellesley to Wellesley-Pole, 1 July 1809, Wellington A/13, RP.
37. Ibid.
38. Wellesley-Pole to Wellesley, 2 August 1809, Wellington B/91, RP.
39. Wellesley to Wellesley-Pole, 1 July 1809, Wellington A/13, RP.
40. Wellesley-Pole to Wellesley, 2 August 1809, Wellington B/91, RP.
41. *Times*, 15 August 1809.
42. Wellesley-Pole to Wellesley, 22 August 1809, Wellington B/93, RP.
43. Wellington to Wellesley-Pole, 13 September 1809, Wellington A/20, RP.
44. Duke of York to Gordon, 14 August 1809, Add. MSS. 49473, Gordon Papers, BL.
45. Wellesley to Wellesley-Pole, 1 August 1809, Wellington A/16, RP.
46. Wellesley-Pole to Wellington, 22 August 1809, Wellington B/93, RP.
47. Wellington to Wellesley-Pole, 13 September 1809, Wellington A/20, RP.

48. For the definitive work on the Walcheren Expedition, see Bond, *The Grand Expedition*. The British invasion force comprised 237 combat ships and 301 transports that carried 43,297 troops. The expedition was poorly prepared for the conditions it faced upon landing, and more British troops were lost to an outbreak of "Walcheren fever" than were lost in combat action. British casualties exceeded 4,000 dead, and some 12,000 more were incapacitated due to illness.

49. King George III, *Correspondence*, 5:474. The council called for a rigid, impartial, and general inquiry into the Walcheren Expedition and the peninsula.

50. Wellington to Liverpool, 2 January 1810, MS Loan 72, vol. 20, Liverpool Papers, BL.

51. Wellington to Wellesley-Pole, 4 January 1810, Wellington A/28, RP.

52. Wellington to Villiers, 2 January 1810, WD, 3:670–71.

53. Milton to the House of Commons, 1 February 1810, *Parliamentary Debates*, 15:280.

54. Tarleton to the House of Lords, 25 January 1810, ibid., 250.

55. Wellington to Liverpool, 1 March 1810, WD, 3:759–62.

56. Wellington to Craufurd, 4 April 1810, WD, 4:1–2.

57. For more on Wellesley's use of dispatches for propaganda and political purposes, see Woolgar, "Writing the Dispatch," 13–15.

CHAPTER 4. WANING SUPPORT

1. Horward, *Napoleon and Iberia*, 5–8; Muir, *Britain and the Defeat of Napoleon*, 125–26.

2. Severn, *A Wellesley Affair*, 106–108.

3. Wellington to Castlereagh, 25 August 1809, WD, 5:82–90.

4. Wellington to Wellesley-Pole, 29 August 1809, Wellington A/19, RP.

5. Horward, "Wellington's Peninsular Strategy," 47–49.

6. Esdaile, *Duke of Wellington*, 12–16. See also Herson, "Siege of Cadiz."

7. For a complete account of Wellington's defensive preparations, see Muir, *Britain and the Defeat of Napoleon*, 126–28.

8. Ibid.; Horward, "Wellington's Peninsular Strategy," 49–51. The Lines of Torres Vedras consisted of three lines. The first two, twenty-nine and twenty-two miles respectively, stretched between the Tagus River and the Atlantic Ocean. The third line, a final protective barrier, was a two-mile line covering the port of São Julião, from which the army could evacuate if necessary. Each line consisted of a series of mutually supporting strong points, covered by abatis and escarpments, which would make the capture of each strongpoint very costly for the French. In addition, the lines were manned by second echelon forces, which allowed the main allied army to commit against any forces that penetrated the defenses.

9. Wellington to Fletcher, 20 October 1809, WD, 5:234–39; M. Glover, *Wellington as Military Commander*, 162–63.

10. Wellington to Castlereagh, 25 August 1809, WD, 5:82–90.

11. Severn, *Architects of Empire*, 267–70; Muir, *Britain and the Defeat of Napoleon*, 105–107.

12. *Parliamentary Debates*, 23 January 1810, 15:13–37. Fortunately for Perceval, the period between October 1809 and January 1810 gave his cabinet time to prepare for the Whigs' attacks on Walcheren and the costs of the war. Had the Whigs come to power, they would have undoubtedly evacuated the peninsula and pursued rapprochement with Napoleon. For Parliamentary papers relative to the Walcheren inquiry, which were issued during the debates, see *Parliamentary Debates*, vol. 15, appendix 1.

13. Knight, "Lord Liverpool and the Peninsular War," 53–96.

14. Wellington to Wellesley-Pole, 6 October 1809, Wellington A/24, RP. With the change in government, Wellesley-Pole resigned his post as secretary to the Admiralty and replaced Sir Robert Dundas as chief secretary for Ireland. As a result of Pole's move to Dublin, most of Wellington's letters to his brother from October 1809 through March 1810 went unanswered until the summer of 1810.

15. Wellington to Wellesley-Pole, 22 October 1809, Wellington A/25, RP16. Liverpool to Wellington, 10 September 1810, WSD, 6:593–94.

17. Liverpool to Wellington, 20 October 1809, MS Loan 72, vol. 20, BL.

18. Wellington to Liverpool, 14 November 1809, WD, 5:280–81.

19. Wellington to Liverpool, 28 November 1809, WD, 5:317.

20. Wellington to Wellesley-Pole, 29 November 1809, Wellington A/27, RP. The Memorandum of Operations in 1809 was sent to London on 9 December, and it included a detailed synopsis of all military operations that took place from May to November 1809. It also included details concerning Wellington's repeated attempts to caution the Spanish about openly confronting the French. It is found in WD, 5:347–64.

21. Liverpool to Wellington, 1 November 1809, Add. MSS. 38325, Liverpool Papers, BL.

22. Liverpool to Wellington, 21 November 1809, MS Loan 72, vol. 20, BL.

23. Ibid., Knight, "Lord Liverpool," 74–75.

24. Liverpool to Wellington, 15 December 1809, Add. MSS. 38325, BL.

25. Liverpool to Wellington, 2 January 1810, War Office (WO) 6/34, PRO.

26. Memorandum of Operations in 1809, 9 December 1809, WD, 5:347–64. Wellington had ordered his army to withdraw from Spain into Portugal on 9 December.

27. Wellington to Villiers, 25 January 1810, WD, 5:452–57.

28. *Morning Chronicle*, 7 August 1809.

29. Wellington to Villiers, 4 September 1809, WD, 5:180.

30. Wellington to Liverpool, 14 November 1809, WD, 5:275.

31. Wellington to Villiers, 14 January 1810, 25 January 1810, WD, 5:424, 453. Forjaz asked Villiers to secure advances of the first £350,000 through various arrangements with the commissary general. Villiers rejected his proposals because of the scarcity of funds for the British. In March 1810, the regency requested a loan of £2,000,000 from London, which was also rejected because London felt they could exert a greater influence over how the Por-

tuguese spent the money if it was supplied through subsidy. For more on Forjaz's role in securing the Portuguese subsidy in 1809, see Francisco De La Fuente, "Dom Miguel Pereira Forjaz," 276–83.

32. Wellington to Villiers, 6 December 1809, WD, 5:338.

33. Notes on Finance by George Rose, 11 November 1809, Add. MSS. 31237, Rose Papers, BL.

34. Ferguson to House of Commons, 9 March 1810, *Parliamentary Debates*, 16:15.

35. Bankes to House of Commons, 9 March 1810, *Parliamentary Debates*, 16:16. The Portuguese subsidy was approved 204 votes to 142. In February, Parliament had also debated issuing Wellington its "thanks" for his actions at Talavera. The measure passed on 16 February by a vote of 213 to 106; however, once again, every measure for the war effort in Portugal was contested.

36. Liverpool to Wellington, 15 December 1809, Add. MSS. 38325, BL.

37. Ibid.

38. Wellington to Stuart, 3 March 1810, WD, 5:544.

39. Wellington to Stuart, 17 March 1810, WD, 5:576–77. See also Fryman, "Charles Stuart and the Common Cause: The Anglo-Portuguese Alliance, 1810–1814," 362–458.

40. Wellington to Liverpool, 24 January 1810, WD, 5:448.

41. Wellington to Liverpool, 20 March 1810, WD, 5:581–83.

42. Wellington to Liverpool, 2 April 1810, WD, 6:6; Liverpool to Campbell, 21 December 1809, Add. MSS. 38244, BL. Liverpool also questioned the defensibility of Gibraltar. In December, he instructed General Colin Campbell, the garrison commander at Gibraltar, to reinforce the existing fortifications between the British and Spanish in case the French attacked.

43. Liverpool to Wellington, 13 February 1810, MS Loan 72, vol. 20, BL; Taylor to Bunbury, no date, November 1809, Add. MSS. 38244, BL. The origin of Liverpool's proposal to evacuate the army to Cadiz was the king's secretary Lt. Col. Herbert Taylor. Taylor had served with Liverpool's undersecretary, Henry Bunbury. In November, Taylor inform Bunbury, "The superior importance of Cadiz must be acknowledged. . . . [Cadiz's] port actually contains the concentrated naval means of Spain. [Lisbon] offers no comparative advantage."

44. Liverpool to Wellington, 13 March 1810, Add. MSS. 38325, BL.

45. Wellington to Liverpool, 31 January 1810, WD, 5:478–82.

46. Ibid.

47. Wellington to Liverpool, 2 April 1810, WD, 6:6.

48. Ibid.

49. Wellington to Liverpool, 1 March 1810, WD, 5:540.

50. Wellington to Wellesley-Pole, 6 April 1810, Wellington A/30, RP.

51. Ibid.

52. Wellesley-Pole to Wellington, 5 April 1810, Wellington B/102, RP.

53. Wellington to Liverpool, 2 April 1810, WD, 6:5–10.

54. Wellington to Berkeley, 7 April 1810, WD, 6:22. See also Horward, "British Seapower," 54–71.

55. Wellington to Wellesley-Pole, 9 May 1810, Wellington A/32, RP.
56. Memorandum for the Defense of Portugal, 7 March 1809, WD, 4:263. In March 1809, Wellington had warned that "as soon as [dispositions for offensive operations in Portugal] are done, the General and Staff officers should [be deployed] as it may be depended upon that as soon as the newspapers shall announce their departure for Portugal, the French armies in Spain will receive orders to make their movements towards Portugal."
57. Wellington to Liverpool, 21 November 1809, WD, 5:305–306.
58. Ibid.
59. Liverpool to Wellington, 16 February 1811, Add. MSS. 38325, BL.
60. Wellington to Liverpool, 16 March 1811, WD, 7:368–69.
61. Elizabeth Longford, *Years of the Sword*, 219.
62. *Times*, 7 August 1810.
63. Wellington to Croker, 20 December 1810, *Croker Papers*, 1:40–42.
64. Horward, *Napoleon and Iberia*, 114–15.
65. Liverpool to Wellington, no date, May 1810, Add. MSS. 38325, BL.
66. Taylor to Liverpool, 21 April 1810, WSD, 6:515.
67. Liverpool to Wellington, 25 April 1810, WSD, 6:517–18.

CHAPTER 5. THE CRUCIBLE

1. Imperial Decree, 17 April 1810, Napoleon, *Correspondance Ier*, 16385, 20:338. The *armée du Portugal* (Army of Portugal) consisted of three corps, which formerly composed a portion of the Army of Spain: II Corps, commanded by Gen. Jean Louis Reynier; VI Corps, under Marshal Michel Ney; and VIII Corps, under Gen. Andoche Junot.
2. Napoleon to Masséna, 18 April 1810, reprinted in Horward, "Logistics and Strategy," 355–56. Napoleon promised Masséna over 140,000 men; however, the Army of Portugal never numbered more than 65,000.
3. Napoleon to Berthier, 29 May 1810, Napoleon, *Correspondance Ier*, 16519, 20:447–49. Napoleon's decision to invest the fortresses was a critical error because Wellington used the time to finish preparing the defenses at Torres Vedras.
4. Horward, *Napoleon and Iberia*, 177–80, 300–303. During the siege of Almeida, Masséna received his one piece of luck for the entire campaign, when a cannonball ignited the fortress' main powder magazine. The explosion killed more than 800 men inside the fortress, and it resulted in the fortress' capitulation.
5. *Morning Chronicle*, 1 October 1810.
6. Wellington to Liverpool, 27 June 1810, WD, 6:227; Wellington to Liverpool, 11 July 1810, 6:257; WD, 203–09. Brig. Gen. Robert Crauford commanded the light infantry division that defended Almeida. However, on 24 July, the division was nearly cut off and destroyed by Ney's corps at the Côa River, two miles from Almeida.
7. Horward, *The Battle of Bussaco*, 36, 60–61, 159–175. Wellington's strength at Bussaco was 61,454 men. Prior to the battle, his army had been augmented by the arrival of a division of infantry (10,371 men) under Gen.

Rowland Hill. The battle was indecisive but costly. The French suffered 4,487 casualties, and the allies (British and Portuguese) had 1,252 men killed, wounded, or captured.

8. Ibid., 97–113, 127–28. Despite possessing more troops, the French attacks were poorly coordinated and faced formidable opposition. For an excellent account of the campaign from the French perspective, see Horward, *The French Campaign in Portugal*.

9. Horward, *Napoleon and Iberia*, 321–24; *The French Campaign in Portugal*, 279–85, 507; Oman, *History of the Peninsular War*, 4:202–205. The reinforcements only made Masséna's task more difficult, because the men brought only limited supplies, and therefore their numbers further burdened the existing task of feeding the army.

10. Wellington to Liverpool, 19 August 1810, WD, 6:369–70.

11. Ibid.

12. Liverpool to Wellington, 24 April 1810, WP 1/308; Wellington to Liverpool, 14 January 1811, BL Add. MSS. 38246. The issue of finding men to fill the needs of the British army is amply covered in Hall, *British Strategy*, 1–9; see also Knight, "Lord Liverpool," 172–83. The reinforcements were to be drawn from six battalions currently abroad in Sicily, Malta, and Halifax. These would be joined by 2,500 fresh drafts sent from England.

13. Wellington to Liverpool, 11 July 1810, WD, 6:255.

14. Wellington to Liverpool, 14 July 1810, 1 August 1810, and 8 August 1810, WD, 6:269, 315, 343. Liverpool to Wellington, 2 August 1810; Henry Wellesley to Wellington, 16 August 1810, WSD, 6:567–69, 574; Oman, *History of the Peninsular War*, 3:429–30.

15. Wellington to Liverpool, 19 August 1810, WD, 6:369–70.

16. Wellington to Wellesley-Pole, 5 September 1810, Wellington A/34, RP.

17. Liverpool to Wellington, 10 September 1810, Add. MSS. 38325, BL.

18. Ibid.

19. Liverpool to Wellington, 14 December 1810, Add. MSS. 38325, BL.

20. Wellington to Wellesley-Pole, 11 January 1811, Wellington A/39, RP.

21. Wellesley-Pole to Wellington, 1 February 1811, Wellington B/111, RP.

22. Liverpool to Wellington, 20 February 1811, WP 1/324.

23. Wellington to Liverpool, 23 March 1811, WD, 7:388–92.

24. Horward, "Logistics and Strategy," 355–56. The Battle of Fuentes d'Oñoro was fought because Masséna attempted to break through the allied line to relieve the besieged French garrison at Almeida. His attempt failed, and the French were forced to withdraw.

25. For more information concerning the effect of Berkeley on Wellington's 1810–1811 campaign see, Hall, *Wellington's Navy*, 93–104, and Horward, "Wellington, Berkeley, and the Royal Navy," 92–93. For the definitive work on the career of Berkeley, see DeToy, "Wellington's Admiral."

26. Wellington to Wellesley-Pole, 26 January 1810, Wellington A/29, RP.

27. Ibid. The term "Leopards," referring to British troops, originated with Napoleon, who addressed his soldiers in 18 September 1808 by stating, "Soldiers I need you, the presence of the hideous Leopard contaminates the

country of Portugal and Spain, the Leopard will flee in terror at your approach." Proclamation of Napoleon enclosed in Napoleon to Berthier 18 September 1808, Napoleon, *Correspondance Ier*, 14338, 17:607.

28. Wellington to Wellesley-Pole, 26 January 1810, Wellington A/29, RP.
29. Wellington to Wellesley-Pole, 6 April 1810, Wellington A/30, RP.
30. Wellesley-Pole to Wellington, 7 March 1810, Wellington B/101, RP.
31. Berkeley to Wellington, 2 May 1810, cited in DeToy, "Wellington's Admiral," 481–82.
32. Ibid., 519. See also Horward, "Admiral Berkeley and the Duke of Wellington."
33. Wellington to Berkeley, 17 October 1810, WD, 6:518.
34. Wellesley to Berkeley, 15 May 1809, WD, 4:337.
35. Wellington to Berkeley, 4 November 1810, WD, 6:585.
36. Berkeley to Stuart, 4 November 1810, WP 1/319.
37. Wellington to Stuart, 6 November 1810, WD, 6:592–93.
38. Wellington to Berkeley, 13 November 1810, WD, 6:618.
39. Berkeley to Croker, 16 November 1810, WP 1/320.
40. Barrow to Berkeley, 3 December 1810, WP 1/320; *DNB*, 1:1225–27.
41. Transport Board (George Ambrose-Boyle) to Croker, 6 December 1810, WP 1/320.
42. Barrow to Bunbury 3 December 1810, WP 1/320; Liverpool to Wellington, 8 December 1810, WP 1/320.
43. Liverpool to Wellington, 4 January 1811, WO 6/29, PRO.
44. Wellington to Liverpool, 5 January 1811, WD, 7:111.
45. Wellington to Berkeley, 30 June 1811, WD, 8:62–63.
46. Wellington to Berkeley, 25 June 1811, WD, 8:50; DeToy, "Wellington's Admiral," 2:525–26.

CHAPTER 6. THE TIDE TURNS

1. Wellington to Henry Wellesley, 10 April 1811, WD, 7:455.
2. Wellington to Wellesley-Pole, 15 May 1811, Wellington A/41, RP. Wellington's wrath was centered on Gen. William Erskine for not delivering a set of orders on time. See also, Oman, *History of the Peninsular War*, 4:350–55.
3. For a detailed account of the battle of Albuera and of the operations preceding and following the battle, see Vichness, "Marshal of Portugal," 390–433; see also Oman, *History of the Peninsular War*, 4:390–99, 634–5.
4. Wellington to Arbuthnot, 28 May 1811, Arbuthnot, *Correspondence*, 6.
5. Wellesley-Pole to Wellington, 16 June 1811, Wellington B/114, RP.
6. Ibid.
7. Wellington to Wellesley-Pole, 2 July 1811, Wellington A/43, RP. Wellington claimed that the French had outnumbered him three to one.
8. Beresford to Wellington, 17 May 1811, WP 1/330; Beresford to Wellington, 18 May 1811, WP 1/330. See also Woolgar, "Writing the Dispatch," 1–25.
9. Wellington to Wellesley-Pole, 2 July 1811, Wellington A/43, RP.

10. Beresford to Wellington, 17 May 1811, WP 1/330.
11. Beresford to Wellington, 18 May 1811, WP 1/330. Both the original and amended dispatches exist at the Hartley Library in Southampton. Although the revised dispatch is in the handwriting of Fitzroy Somerset, it contains Beresford's signature at the bottom. Wellington's practice of amending dispatches and casualty figures was not uncommon.
12. Wellington to Beresford, 19 May 1811, WD, 7:573.
13. Stanhope, *Notes of Conversations*, 67; Vichness, "Marshal of Portugal," 431–32.
14. Oman, *Wellington's Army*, 162.
15. Liverpool to Wellington, 30 May 1811, WO 6/50, PRO.
16. Liverpool to Wellington, 29 May 1811, WSD, 7:144–45.
17. Wellington to Richard Wellesley, 26 January 1811, WD, 8:192–93.
18. Wellington to Stuart, 18 March 1811, WD, 8:372–73.
19. Wellington to Stuart, 6 September 1811; Wellington to Liverpool, 11 September 1811, WD, 8:260–62, 268–69.
20. Wellington to Stuart, 6 October 1810, WD, 6:494. For more on the problems within the Portuguese commissariat see, Fryman, "Charles Stuart," 2:215–25.
21. Ponsonby to the House of Commons, 18 March 1811, *Parliamentary Debates*, 19:394–98.
22. Tarleton to the House of Commons, 18 March 1811, ibid., 19:399.
23. Auckland to Grenville, 7 March 1811, HMC *Fortescue*, 10:126–27.
24. Liverpool to Wellington, 20 February 1811, WSD, 7:68–70.
25. Wellington to Wellesley-Pole, 31 March 1811, RP, Wellington A/40.
26. *Times*, 27 March 1811.
27. J. H. Doyle to Sir Charles Hastings, 9 April 1811, *HMC Hastings*, 3:288–89.
28. Liverpool to Wellington, 26 March 1811, WP 1/326. Vote on the Portuguese subsidy, 11 May 1811, *Parliamentary Debates*, 19:393, 453, 1169. See also Horward, "Wellington and Defense of Portugal," 46, 50–51
29. Liverpool to Wellington, 11 April 1811, WP 1/327.
30. Lord Grey to the House of Lords, 26 April 1811, *Parliamentary Debates*, 19:767.
31. Wellesley-Pole to Wellington, 16 June 1811, Wellington B/114, RP.
32. Grey to Grenville, 1 September 1811, HMC *Fortescue*, 10:168; Grenville to Grey, 28 January 1812, ibid., 10:199.
33. Wellington to Stuart, 18 July 1811, WD, 7:653.
34. Wellington to Liverpool, 20 January 1812, WD, 8:549–57. See Horward, *Napoleon and Iberia*, 180–81. See also, Pelet, *The French Campaign in Portugal*, 80–82.
35. Wellington to the Duke of Richmond, 29 January 1812, WD, 8:579–80.
36. Memorandum for the Attack of Badajoz, 6 April 1812; Wellington to Liverpool, 7 April 1812, WD, 9:32–44. Peninsular historians treat the events surrounding the sacking of Badajoz very differently. Oman and Fortescue spend very little time discussing the events or actions of the troops. Fortescue states, "It is useless to waste words in condemning the behavior of the

troops." *History of the British Army*, 8:403. Others condemn the actions. Jac Weller states that the pillage of Badajoz was "no temporary lapse in discipline but a beastly mutiny." *Wellington in the Peninsula*, 204. For a condemning account of Wellington and the conduct of his men after Badajoz, see Meyer, "Wellington and the Sack of Badajoz," 251–57. For more on Wellington's inadequate siege train and the efforts of the Royal Navy to transport guns more than one hundred miles from Porto to Lisbon and then inland to Badajoz, see Brian DeToy "'A Busy Meddling Folly,'" 184–195.

37. Report of British soldier at Badajoz, *Peninsular Sketches*, 1:285–86.
38. Bell, *Soldier's Glory*, 28.
39. Wellington to Liverpool, 7 April 1812, WD, 9:39.
40. Liverpool to the House of Lords, quoted in the *Times*, 27 April 1812.
41. Wellington to Henry Wellesley, 11 April 1812, WD, 9:53–56.
42. Bentinck to Liverpool, 25 January 1812, Liverpool to Bentinck, 4 March 1812, WSD, 7:290–91, 300; Oman, *History of the Peninsular War*, 5:342–47.
43. For the most complete account of the battle, see Muir, *Salamanca, 1812*. See also Sarramon, *La Bataille des Arapiles*, 195–290; Oman, *Peninsular War*, 5:469–71; Fortescue, *History of the British Army*, 8:504–506; There are no reliable sources for the total number of French casualties at Salamanca. However, Wellington reported that Marmont and four of his eight division commanders were wounded, two mortally, and that the allies had captured two regimental eagles and over twenty cannons. The allies were hurt badly and suffered nearly five thousand casualties, including the loss of Gen. John La Merchant and the wounding of several of Wellington's generals.
44. Wellington to Bathurst, 24 July 1812, Wellington to Bathurst, 25 July 1812, WD, 9:308–309, 312–13. Wellington's pursuit failed because the Spanish general Carlos de España evacuated a blocking position and bridge at Alba de Tormes without informing Wellington, allowing the French to escape. Nevertheless, some units, including the King's German Legion, successfully engaged the French rear guard at Garcia Hernandez. On 25 July, unable to catch Marmont, Wellington called off the pursuit and reconstituted his forces. For the impact on Anglo-Spanish relations following the Talavera campaign see Esdaile, *Duke of Wellington and the Command of the Spanish Armies*, 33–36.
45. Henry Wellesley to Wellington, 6 August 1812, WP 1/350.
46. Auckland to Grenville, 25 August 1812, HMC *Fortescue*, 10:293.
47. Ward, *Wellington's Headquarters*, 93; Oman, *Wellington's Army*, 161.
48. Bills of exchange were issued by His Majesty's Treasury in London and therefore were negotiable instruments payable in London, normally at thirty days after they were presented.
49. Wellington to Berkeley, 4 November 1810, WD, 6:584–5; Wellington to Sampaio, 28 November 1810, WD, 7:11; Wellington to Berkeley, 3 October 1810, 6:482; Redgrave, "Wellington's Logistical Arrangements," 110. Villiers felt that more than one agent was needed in Cadiz and therefore proposed that several agents be employed to increase activity. Wellington disagreed and defended Duff's actions. In his letters to Admiral Berkeley, he

stated, "Duff got as much money as can be procured and I should doubt that two or three shops would sell more bills than one."

50. Wellington to Stuart, 11 September 1810, WD, 6:427; Redgrave, "Wellington's Logistical Arrangements," 111–12. In the summer of 1810, the exchange rate fell sharply in the financial panic produced by the fall of Almeida and the advance of Masséna's army; however, by December 1810, the exchange rate returned to its previous level. In Lisbon, Charles Stuart was largely responsible for maintaining economic order. For an account of Stuart's actions, see Fryman, "Charles Stuart," 228–61.

51. Sherwig, *Guineas and Gunpowder*, 254–55, 237–39.

52. For an example of the negative influence of this relationship, see Wellington to Gordon, 6 November 1810, WD, 6:594–95. Oman, *Wellington's Army*, 161–62, 307–19; Ward, *Wellington's Headquarters*, 93; *DNB*, 9:706–707.

53. Wellington to Beresford, 13 July 1811, WD, 8:102.

54. Wellington to Stuart, 22 July 1811, Wellington to Liverpool, 1 August 1811, Wellington to Stuart, 18 August 1811, 8:135, 160, 208. See also Fryman, "Charles Stuart," 2:362–45.

55. Liverpool to Wellington, 23 August 1811, WO 6/50, PRO; Wellington to Stuart, 23 August 1811, WD, 8:223; Sherwig, *Guineas and Gunpowder*, 199. See also, Officer, *Between the Dollar-Sterling Gold Points*.

56. Wellington to Liverpool, 13 November 1811, WD, 8:400–401.

57. Liverpool to Wellington, 23 August 1811, WSD, 7:210. Wellington to Stuart, 6 September 1811, Wellington to Liverpool, 11 September 1811, WD, 8:260–62, 268–69. For more on the efforts to subsidize the Portuguese, see Horward, "Wellington and Defense of Portugal," 46, 50–5; Wellington's primary adversary in Lisbon was the Portuguese minister of war, Dom Miguel Forjaz. For an excellent account of Forjaz and Wellington's relations, see De La Fuente, "Dom Miguel Pereira Forjaz," 251–75.

58. Liverpool to Wellington, 23 August 1811, WSD, 7:210.

59. Wellington to Liverpool, 11 September 1811, WD, 8:268–69.

60. Liverpool to Wellington, 18 December 1811, ADD. MSS. 38326, BL. For a complete account of Liverpool's role in the financial crisis of 1811–1812, see Knight, "Lord Liverpool," 127–39.

61. Wellington to Liverpool, 12 February 1812, WD, 8:607–608.

62. Herries, Memorandum of Financial Resources, 23 March 1812, Add. MSS. 57393, Herries Papers, BL; Wellington to Liverpool, 11 September 1811, WD, 8:268–69.

63. Liverpool to Wellington, 11 March 1812, ADD. MSS. 38326, BL; Wellington to Liverpool, 2 May 1812, WD, 9:103–105.

64. Herries to Perceval, 27 March 1812, Add. MSS. 57393, BL.

65. For examples of Wellington's continuing problems with generating currency, see Wellington to Liverpool, 4 December 1811, Wellington to Stuart, 2 January 1812, WD, 8:434–36, 526–27.

66. Oman, *Wellington's Army*, 307–19; Ward, *Wellington's Headquarters*, 70–75. Bissett was acting in the place of his superior, Robert Kennedy, commissary general in the peninsula from 1810 to 1814. Kennedy was on leave for the majority of 1812. Commissary officials served under the Trea-

sury's jurisdiction for accountability of funds, but were also responsible to the expeditionary force commander for obtaining supplies, specie, and so forth.

67. Wellington to Liverpool, 2 April 1812, WD, 9:25-26.

68. Wellington to Liverpool, 22 April 1812, WSD, 7:318-19. In his dispatch, Wellington named a ship, the *Standard*, which brought the $400,000 purchased at Gibraltar for the reduced rate. However, in support of his brother, Henry, who Wellington claimed, "received the disapprobation in appropriating a part of a previous shipment from America" at a reduced rate, Wellington stated, "I have not thought it proper to request him to send me any part of this money."

69. Overture for Peace from France, 21 July 1812, *Parliamentary Debates*, 23:1124-56.

70. Grey to Grenville, 8 May 1812, HMC *Fortescue*, 10:243.

71. Wellington to Stuart, 6 May 1812, WD, 9:121-22.

72. For more on Bathurst's policies, see Thompson, *Earl Bathurst*,; *DNB*, 1:1328.

73. Bathurst to Wellington, 31 August 1812, WSD, 7:412-13; Bathurst to Wellington, 7 September 1812, 7:413-14, Bathurst to Wellington, 9 September 1812, 7:457-58.

74. Herries, *Memoir of J. C. Herries*, 126.

75. Thompson, *Earl Bathurst*, 59.

76. Bathurst to Harrowby, 16 September 1812 and reply 17 September 1812, Historical Manuscripts Commission, *Manuscripts of Earl Bathurst* (hereafter HMC *Bathurst*), 213-14; *DNB*, 17:531-32.

77. Bathurst to Wellington, 13 October 1812, WSD, 7:457-58; Thompson, *Earl Bathurst*, 59-60.

78. For the details on the scheme to fund Wellington through the Rothschilds, see Knight, "Lord Liverpool," 133-35, and Corti, *Rise of the House of Rothschild*, 117.

79. The last date when specie was sent to Lisbon rather than to Coruña was 15 July 1813. During this period, Wellington also received about £500,000 from Gibraltar and £280,000 from Cadiz, which combined with the British subsidies totaled nearly £2 million—probably about one-quarter of the army's expenditure for an eight-month period.

80. Stuart to Wellington, 3 November 1810, WP 1/319; DeToy, "Wellington's Admiral," 544-47.

81. Berkeley to Wellington, 2 May 1810, WP 1/310. Wellington to Berkeley, 4 December 1811, WD, 8:433. For the circumstances behind Berkeley's promotion and replacement, see DeToy, "Wellington's Admiral," 593-96.

82. Wellington to Liverpool, 12 February 1812, WD, 8:606; DeToy, "Wellington's Admiral," 596-97.

83. Wellington to Bathurst, 13 August 1812, WD, 9:356-57.

84. Melville to Bathurst, 7 September 1812, WSD, 7:419.

85. Wellington to Bathurst, 10 September 1812, WSD, 7:419.

86. Wellesley to the Prince Regent, 17 February 1812, George IV, *Letters* 1:9-10. Wellesley had tendered his resignation in January; however the prince

regent, wishing to postpone ministerial changes until the restrictions of his powers were reviewed, convinced him to remain in office. However, when Perceval's premiership was confirmed on 15 February, Wellesley declared that he could continue to serve in the administration. Furthermore, Wellesley urged the prince regent to place his friend Lord Moira at the head of a new government, which should not be opposed to Catholic emancipation and which should include both Castlereagh and Canning. On 17 February the cabinet unanimously decided to resign unless Wellesley's resignation was accepted, and on 19 February, Wellesley resigned his office.

87. Lord Holland, *Further Memoirs of the Whig Party, 1807–1821, with some Miscellaneous Reminiscences*, 115–16.

88. Wellesley-Pole to Wellington, 20 April 1811, Wellington B/113, RP.

89. Wellington to Wellesley-Pole, 6 April 1810, RP, Wellington A/30.

90. For the best and most complete account of the spring 1812 political crisis between Wellington and his brother Richard, see Severn, *Architects of Empire*, 348–58.

91. Liverpool to Wellington 20 January 1812, WSD, 7:256–57; Perceval to Wellington, 22 January 1812, and Perceval to Henry Wellesley, 23 January 1812, as printed in Spencer Walpole, *Life of Spencer Perceval*, 2:261, 242.

92. Wellesley-Pole to Wellington, 12 February 1812, RP, Wellington B/116.

93. Wellington to Richard Wellesley, 20 January 1812, WSD, 7:256–7; Severn, *Architects of Empire*, 348–53. Wellington also complained to Richard about the appointment of his replacement. Wellington did not like that Lord Castlereagh, who had overseen the war until 1809, and who Wellington believed was better suited for the War Department, took Richard's post at the Foreign Office.

94. Wellington to Wellesley-Pole, 29 June 1812, RP, Wellington A/47.

95. Minutes of a conversation between Lord Wellesley and Lord Liverpool, 17 May 1812, *Parliamentary Debates*, vol. 23, appendix 2; Severn, *Architects of Empire*, 354–56.

96. Bathurst to George Rose, 24 May 1811, Rose, *Diaries and Correspondence*, 510–11.

97. Lord Holland, *Memoirs of the Whig Party*, 137–38; Severn, *Architects of Empire*, 356–57.

98. Wellesley-Pole to Wellington, 12 February 1812, Wellington B/116, RP; Wellesley-Pole to Wellington, 12 April 1812, Wellington B/118, RP.

99. Liverpool to Wellington, 7 October 1812, WP 1/352. For the background to Liverpool's offer, see Wellington to Wellesley-Pole, 29 June 1812, Wellington A/47, RP; Wellington to Wellesley-Pole, 27 August 1812, Wellington A/50, RP; Wellington to Liverpool, 7 September 1812, WD, 9:401.

100. Wellesley-Pole to Wellington, 30 June 1812, RP, Wellington B/119; Wellesley to the House of Lords, 1 July 1812, *Parliamentary Debates*, 23:813–868; Severn, *Architects of Empire*, 363–64.

101. Severn, *Architects of Empire*, 360–61. See also *Parliamentary Debates*, vol. 23.

102. Wellington to Wellesley-Pole, 7 September 1812, Wellington A/51, RP.

103. Wellington to Liverpool, 7 September 1812, WD, 9:401; Severn, *Architects of Empire*, 369–70.

104. Wellesley to Arbuthnot, 5 July 1812, Arbuthnot, *Correspondence*, 7.

105. Severn, *Architects of Empire*, 364–66; Esdaile, *Duke of Wellington*, 39–45.

106. Lord Auckland to Lord Grenville, 7 June 1812, *HMC Fortescue*, 285.

CHAPTER 7. EXPLOITATION

1. Wellington to Bathurst, 13 August 1812, WD, 9:352–55; For the definitive work on the complexity surrounding the effort to secure Wellington's command of the Spanish armies, see Esdaile, *Duke of Wellington*, 47–56, 130–31. See also Muir, *Britain and the Defeat of Napoleon*, 210–13. For more on the siege of Cadiz, see Herson, "Siege of Cadiz."

2. Wellington to Bathurst, 7 September 1812, Wellington to Hill, 8 September 1812, WD, 9:403–405.

3. Wellington to Stuart, 11 August 1812, WD, 9:349; Hall, *Wellington's Navy*, 114. For a detailed analysis of Berkeley's effort to transport siege guns by river to Wellington, see DeToy, "'A Busy Meddling Folly,'" 184–95.

4. Several recent studies detail Popham's role in supporting Wellington's siege of Burgos. See Hall, *Wellington's Navy*, 200–206. Most recently, Kevin McCranie's *Admiral Lord Keith and the Naval War against Napoleon* is the definitive work on the role Popham's commander, Lord Keith, played in supporting the British army. For an excellent summary of the amphibious campaigns conducted throughout the campaign, see Paul Krajeski's thesis, "British Amphibious Operations during the Peninsula War," 138–45, and Richard Herzog's article, "The Royal Marine and Insurgent Operations in the Salamanca Campaign, 1812."

5. Hall, *Wellington's Navy*, 200–201.

6. Popham to Keith, 30 May 1812, Perrin and Lloyd, *Keith Papers*, 3:267–68. For an excellent account of Popham's previous raids and subsequent operations in South America, see Vichness, "Marshal of Portugal," 30–62.

7. McCranie, *Lord Keith*, 353–56; Herzog, "Once More Unto the Breach," 33–39.

8. Ibid.

9. Popham to Keith, 30 May 1812, Perrin and Lloyd, *Keith Papers*, 3:267–68; Wellington to Liverpool, 10 June 1812, WD, 9:228–29.

10. Popham to Keith, 21 June 1812, Perrin and Lloyd, *Keith Papers*, 3:268–70; Hall, *Wellington's Navy*, 201–202.

11. Melville to Bathurst, 12 July 1812, *HMC Bathurst*, 186–87.

12. Hall, *Wellington's Navy*, 202–206.

13. Ibid.

14. Wellington to Popham, 4 August 1812, WD, 9:332–33.

15. Wellington to Popham, 26 September 1812; Wellington to Popham, 5 October 1812, ibid., 9:450 and 471.

16. Wellington to Mulgrave, 27 September 1812, WD, 9:454; Douglas to Wellington, as cited in Oman, *History of the Peninsular War*, 6:40–41.

17. Wellington to Popham, 2 October 1812, WD, 9:464–65.

18. Conversation between Burgoyne and Wellington, September 1812, *Burgoyne's Correspondence*, 1:234; Oman, *History of the Peninsular War*, 6:41; Wellington to Burgoyne, 18 October 1812, WD, 9:502–503.

19. Plan for the attack of the exterior line of the Castle of Burgos, 22 September 1812, Wellington to Bathurst, 27 September 1812, WD, 9:447–49, 455–56,

20. Popham to Melville, 21 October 1812, HMC *Bathurst*, 218.

21. Wellington to Bathurst, 5 October 1812, WD, 9:472–74.

22. Wellington to Popham, 12 October 1812, WD, 9:486–87.

23. Wellington to Popham, 17 October 1812, WD, 9:494–95.

24. Keith to Popham, 20 October 1812, Perrin and Lloyd, *Keith Papers*, 3:286–87.

25. Bathurst to Wellington, 8 October 1812, WSD, 7:446; McCranie, *Lord Keith*, 354. Popham's squadron was reinforced with the *Abercrombie* (74) and a second battalion of marines.

26. Hall, *Wellington's Navy*, 206–208.

27. Wellington to Hill, 10 October 1812, WD, 8:485; Wellington to Hill, 12 October 1812, WD, 9:82; Oman, *Peninsular War*, 6:55–56.

28. Wellington to Popham, 21 October 1812, WD, 9:510–11; Memorandum on the Occurrences in Spain and Portugal from April 1810 to October 1812, WSD, 7:460–61.

29. Wellington to Bathurst, 19 November 1812, WD, 9:557–63; Oman, *Peninsular War*, 6:40–42.

30. Wellington to Maitland, 30 August 1812, Wellington to Liverpool, 23 November 1812, WD, 9:386, 574–75; Hall, *Wellington's Navy*, 182–85; Oman, *History of the Peninsular War*, 5:570–75. Despite the success gained by Popham's diversion, a similar diversionary operation was conducted along the Spanish east coast. Led by General Maitland, this operation, involving a British force dispatched from Sicily, met with disastrous results as King Joseph's retreating army marched to join French marshal Suchet's force in the region. The overwhelmed British troops landed without adequate transportation and were forced to withdraw from the peninsula.

31. Wellington to Liverpool, 23 November 1812, WD, 9:570–71.

32. Ibid.

33. Oman, *History of the Peninsular War*, 6:40–41; Fortescue, *History of the British Army*, 8:583.

34. Swabey, 21 November 1812, *Diary of the Campaigns*, 151.

35. Grey to Grenville, 1 November 1812, HMC *Fortescue*, 10:300.

36. Wellington to Liverpool, 21 December 1809, WD, 5:384–85.

37. Liverpool to Wellington, 9 January 1810, WSD, 6:468. The shortage of cavalry officers was a result of the home office's reluctance to deploy cavalry abroad because cavalry were an invaluable asset in quelling civil insurrection in Britain and Ireland. Liverpool did agree to dispatch generals William Stewart and Sir Thomas Picton to command the infantry divisions.

38. *DNB*, 6:863–64. During the defense before the Lines of Torres Vedras, Erskine was given command of Major General Craufurd's light division. During the subsequent pursuit of Ney's corps, Erskine continually demonstrated bravery to a fault, and on several occasions unnecessarily risked his men. At the battle of Sabugal, in April, Erskine nearly destroyed his division when he pursued Ney's troops into a fog, only to realize that Ney had occupied a strong defensive position. When Craufurd returned, Erskine was attached to Sir Rowland Hill's force in Madrid. During the withdrawal from Madrid, Erskine demonstrated signs of mental instability and was hospitalized in Lisbon. On May 14, 1813, he committed suicide by jumping out of a window. Holmes, *The Iron Duke*, 169.

39. Wellington to Liverpool, 15 May 1811, WD, 7:565–67. As a result of the French escape, combined with heavy casualties after Fuentes d'Oñoro, Liverpool refused to recommend to Parliament that it issue Wellington its thanks.

40. Wellington to Wellesley-Pole, 15 May 1811, Wellington A/41, RP.

41. Wellington to Torrens, 29 August 1810, WP 1/312.

42. Torrens to Wellington, 19 September 1810, WP 1/315.

43. Wellington to Torrens, 29 August 1810, WP 1/312.

44. For the merits of Sir Rowland Hill see Oman, *Wellington's Army*, 115–18. For an excellent analysis of Sir John Hope's contributions to the Peninsular War, see Reese, "In Defense of the Crown."

45. Torrens to Wellington, 19 September 1810, WP 1/315.

46. Wellington to Croker, no date, 1826, Croker, *Papers*, 1:343.

47. Liverpool to Wellington, 4 May 1810, Wellington to Spencer, no date, 1810, WSD, 6:520–21, 1:343–44.

48. Wellington to Wellesley-Pole, 5 September 1810, RP, Wellington A/34.

49. Wellington to Beresford, 10 December 1812, WD, 9:616–17.

50. Duke of York to Bathurst, 28 December 1812, WSD, 7:516–17.

51. Vichness, "Marshal of Portugal," 470–71; Fortescue, *History of the British Army* 9:86–87.

52. Mulgrave to Bathurst, 7 October 1812, HMC *Bathurst*, 216.

53. Ibid.

54. Wellington to Liverpool, 14 July 1810, WD, 6:270.

55. Wellington to Torrens, 6 December 1812, WP 1/355.

56. Wellington to Torrens, 6 December 1812, WD, 9:610–11.

57. Wellington to unknown lieutenant colonel, 7 September 1811, WD, 8:262.

58. Wellington to Torrens, 15 August 1811, WD, 8:201.

59. Wellington to Campbell, 13 August 1811, WD, 8:189.

60. Wellington to Torrens, 15 August 1811, WD, 8:201.

61. Swabey, 2 November 1812, *Diary of the Campaigns*, 151.

62. General order, 16 November 1812, WSD, 7:470.

63. Wellington to Torrens, 6 December 1812, WP 1/355. Stewart was in command of the First Division on the night of 17 November 1812 after succeeding Sir Edward Paget, who had been taken prisoner the previous night by

a French cavalry patrol that rode through his formation and grabbed the officer from his horse. The French later paroled him. Although Wellington did not name the "newcomers," the only inexperienced general officers in the First Division on 17 November were Gen. John Oswald and Gen. Lord James Dalhousie.

64. Ibid.

65. Wellington to the Officers commanding Divisions and Brigades, 28 November 1812, WD, 9:582–83.

66. Holmes, *The Iron Duke*, 173–74.

67. Wellington to Torrens, 6 December 1812, WP 1/355. In addition to Gen. Christopher Chowne, Gen. Stewart, and Gen. Frederick Robinson, Wellington asked for the recall of two German officers, Gen. Sigismund Löw and Gen. Von Bernewitz, from his army. About half of them were eventually sent home, but several were left with him for another campaign.

68. Wellington to Torrens, 22 January 1813, WD, 10:32–34.

69. Auckland to Grenville, 10 January 1813, HMC *Fortescue*, 10:322.

70. Wellington to Liverpool, 11 July 1811, WD, 8:91–94.

71. Wellington to Liverpool, 18 June 1812; Wellington to Bathurst, 14 July 1812, WD, 9:238–42, 283–86.

72. Henry Wellesley to Wellington, 11 March 1811, WSD, 7:80–81; 31 March 1811, WP 1/341. Esdaile, *Duke of Wellington*, 38–56, 130–31; Muir, *Britain and the Defeat of Napoleon*, 210–13.

73. Ibid.

74. Esdaile, *Duke of Wellington*, 50–56; Muir, *Britain and the Defeat of Napoleon*, 210–13.

75. Wellington to Carvajal, 25 December 1812, WD, 10:1–4.

76. Esdaile, *Duke of Wellington*, 134–37; Muir, *Britain and the Defeat of Napoleon*, 212–13.

77. Fortescue, *History of the British Army*, 9:14. This number is exclusive of foreign, veteran, and garrison regiments. It also does not include the Royal Artillery, which fell under the jurisdiction of the master general of the ordnance. With the deductions for boys and raw recruits, unfit for service, the number drops to approximately forty-five thousand.

78. Ibid.

79. Ibid., 14–16.

80. The King's German Legion was essentially a small army consisting of five cavalry regiments, ten infantry battalions, six artillery batteries, and a small detachment of engineers. For more on the effectiveness of the King's German Legion, see Gray, "The Services of the King's German Legion."

81. Wellington to Liverpool, 23 May 1811, WD, 7:597–98.

82. *Times*, 15 May 1812.

83. Minutes of Conversation between Lord Wellesley and Lord Liverpool, 21 August 1812, *Parliamentary Debates*, vol. 23, appendix I2; Fortescue, *History of the British Army*, 9:15–16.

84. Torrens to Wellington, 28 June 1811, WP 1/361.

85. Fortescue, *History of the British Army*, 9:16–17.

86. Wellington to Liverpool, 10 April 1812, WSD, 7:313.

87. Bathurst to Wellington, 22 August 1812; Bathurst to Wellington, 9 September 1812; Bathurst to Wellington, 12 October 1812, WSD, 7:406–407, 415–16, 455–56.
88. Bentinck to Bathurst, 31 August 1812, HMC *Bathurst*, 209–10.
89. Bunbury to Bathurst, 7 October 1812, ibid., 217.
90. Return of the Regiments arrived in the Peninsula in the Year ended 15 December 1812, Wellington Papers 1/359; General Result of Reinforcements sent to the Peninsula in 1812, WSD, 7:507–508; Fortescue, *History of the British Army*, 8:571–72.
91. Return of the casualties suffered by the Army under Wellington's command 15 December 1811, 14 December 1812, WP 1/359; Duke of York to Bathurst, 22 December 1812, WP 1/354.
92. Wellington to Bathurst, 27 September 1812, WD, 9:457–58.
93. Ibid.

CHAPTER 8. OPPORTUNITY ARRESTED

1. 29th Bulletin De La Grande Armée, 3 December 1812, Napoleon, *Correspondance Ier*, 19365, 24:325–29; Liverpool to Wellington, 22 December 1812, WSD, 7:502–503. After dictating the Bulletin in Malodetchna, Napoleon left the army in Russia for Paris on December 5. He arrived thirty-six hours after his bulletin reached Paris on 18 December. Smuggled out of the country, news of the bulletin and Napoleon's defeat reached Liverpool on 21 December. For the complete set of Napoleon's translated bulletins, see Markham, *Imperial Glory*, esp. 310–13.
2. Liverpool to Wellington, 22 December 1812, WSD, 7:502–503.
3. Bathurst to Wellington, 16 December 1812, WSD, 7:499; Wellington to Bathurst, 30 March 1813, WD, 10:163–64.
4. Herries, *Memoir*, 79; Bathurst to Wellington, 16 December 1812, WSD, 7:499.
5. Wellington to Bathurst, 30 March 1813, WD, 10:163–64.
6. Wellington to Bathurst, 9 August 1813, WD, 10:624.7. Memorandum on the Operation to be carried on the Eastern Coast of the Peninsula, Wellington to Murray, 14 April 1813, WD, 10:297–301.
8. Wellington to Bathurst, 10 February 1813, WD, 10:104–105; Wellington to Murray, 23 May 1813, Murray to Wellington, 14 June 1813, WSD, 7:622–22, 638; Bentinck to Wellington, 19 August 1813, WSD, 8:197. A veteran of the peninsula, having commanded a brigade of troops that crossed the Duero River at Porto in May 1809, Murray landed approximately sixteen thousand troops on 3 June near Tarragona. His troops were drawn from Sir William Bentinck's in Sicily. Despite having numerical superiority over the French garrison, Murray began deliberate siege operations of the city. Upon the receipt of intelligence concerning French relief columns, Murray abandoned the siege and re-embarked his force on 13 June, landing in Balaguer. However he lost the confidence of his men. Bentinck arrived and superseded Murray, ordering the force to sail south to Alicante. After Vitoria, Bentinck returned with his force to lay siege to Tarragona. For more on the allied diver-

sionary operations during 1813, see Krajeski, "British Amphibious Operations," 124–30.

9. The most prominent of the guerilla chiefs under Wellington's control were Francisco Longa, Julian Sánchez, and Espoz Miña. By 1813, all three held regular commissions in the Spanish army and did their best to obey Wellington's instructions. Although the armies led by these men were capable of fighting the French and seizing large, fortified places (Miña possessed the two 24-pound guns supplied by Popham the previous year), Wellington instructed them not to risk general battle but to continue to interdict supply and communications routes. For a complete account of the impact of the Spanish resistance, see Esdaile, *Fighting Napoleon*.

10. Clarke to Joseph Bonaparte, 4 January 1813, Napoleon, *Confidential Correspondence*, 2:244–45. In January 1813, Napoleon also replaced the commander of the *armée du Nord*, General Caffarelli, with Gen. Bertrand Clausel. Clausel's force numbered approximately thirty thousand men. The largest French force was Marshal Suchet's army (sixty-five thousand men) in Valencia, which was controlled by the threat of Murray's invasion. The three French armies in central Spain under Joseph and Jourdan were the armies of the South, under Theodore Gazan, the Center, under Jean-Baptiste Drovet (later Count D'Erlon), the Army of Portugal, under Charles Reille.

11. Napoleon to Clarke, 3 January 1813, Napoleon, *Correspondance Ier*, 19411, 24:360. Acting on poor intelligence, Napoleon also estimated that Wellington would detach twenty-five thousand troops to raid Holland or Hanover or perhaps land in the Vendée to support a Royalist insurrection. Most of this faulty intelligence came from spies in London who erroneously gave credence to the Royalists who lobbied Liverpool for support. For a list of the principal French armies that faced Wellington in 1813, see appendix C.

12. Wellington to Bathurst, 10 March 1813, WD, 10:177. Wellington reported that General Clausel had replaced Caffarelli. He also reported that an Italian Division under Palombini had occupied northern parts of Spain.

13. Wellington to Bathurst, 10 February 1813, WD, 10:104–105.

14. Wellington to Bathurst, 17 February 1813, WD, 10:104–105; Muir, *Britain and Defeat of Napoleon*, 266–68.

15. Wellington to the Prince Regent, 27 January 1813, King George IV, *Letters*, 215–16.

16. Anonymous letter to the Earl of Liverpool, *Times*, 8 December 1812.

17. Liverpool to Wellington, 17 February 1813, WSD, 7:555–56.

18. Thomas Grenville to Lord Grenville, July 1813, HMC *Fortescue*, 10:348–49.

19. Duke of York to Wellington, 30 May 1811, WP 1/331; State of the Infantry in the Peninsula, January 1813, WSD, 7:522–23.

20. State of the Infantry in the Peninsula, January 1813, WSD, 7:522–23. See also Oman, *Peninsular War*, 6:230–35.

21. Duke of York to Wellington 26 November 1812, WP 1/353.

22. Wellington to the Duke of York, 6 December 1812, WD, 9:609.

23. General order, 6 December 1812, WSD, 7:491–94.

24. Duke of York to Wellington, 13 January 1813, WSD, 7:524–25.

25. Ibid.
26. Wellington to Torrens, 2 February 1813, WD, 10:76–78.
27. Duke of York to Wellington, 17 February 1813, WSD, 7:552–53.
28. Wellington to the Duke of York, 27 April 1813, Wellington to the Duke of York, 25 May 1813, WD, 11:332–33, 400.
29. Duke of York to Wellington, 17 February 1813, WSD, 7:552–53.
30. General order, 13 March 1813, WSD, 7:581–84.
31. Bathurst to Wellington, 24 February 1813, Bathurst to Wellington, 16 March 1813, ibid., 7:559–61, 588.
32. Wellington to the Duke of York, 16 July 1813, WD, 11:532–33; general order, 13 March 1813, WSD, 7:581–84.
33. Liverpool to Wellington, 27 October 1812, WSD, 7:462–63.
34. Wellington to Bathurst, 7 November 1812, WD, 9:541–42.
35. Bathurst to Wellington, 12 October 1812, WSD, 7:455.
36. Bathurst to Wellington, 7 April 1813, WSD, 7:601–602.
37. Wellington to Bathurst, 20 April 1813, WD, 10:307.
38. Ibid.
39. Bathurst to Wellington, 12 October 1812, Liverpool to Wellington, 27 October 1812, WSD, 7:455–56, 462–64.
40. Wellington to Henry Wellesley, 11 April 1812, WD, 5:589.
41. Liverpool to Wellington, 19 August 1812, WSD, 7:401.
42. Bathurst to Wellington, 12 October 1812, Liverpool to Wellington, 27 October 1812, WSD, 7:455–56, 462–64.
43. Bathurst to Wellington, 12 October 1812, WSD, 7:455–56. For more on Bentinck and his attempt to overthrow the French in Italy, see John Rosselli, *Lord William Bentinck and the British Occupation of Sicily, 1811–1814*, 102–04.
44. Henry Bunbury, Memorandum on the Present State of Affairs and the Military Operations which might be Pursued, 31 December 1812, WSD, 8:459.
45. Wellington to Bathurst, 16 May 1813, WD, 10:384–85.
46. Wellington to Graham, 18 May 1813, WD, 10:386–88; *DNB*, 8:359–60. Despite his limited experience, having never commanded any unit larger than a battalion, Thomas Graham's appointment to command the second wing of the allied army surprised many. However, Graham, a Scotsman, possessed three qualities that Wellington coveted: competence, bravery, and obedience.
47. Murray, *Memoir Annexed to an Atlas*, 81–3. Murray fostered the deception by conducting reconnaissance rides on separate avenues of approach to "create uncertainty in the minds of the [French Cavalry patrols] as to the intended direction of the allied advance."
48. Wellington to Henry Wellesley, 4 June 1813, WD, 10:415; Weller, *Wellington in the Peninsula*, 257–59. Graham was able to outflank Jourdan's defensive line on the Douro River and compel the French to retreat to Burgos. Wellington and Graham's columns united on 3 June, and due to an unsuccessful attempt to repair damage to the fortress from the previous winter, Burgos fell on 12 June. Because his men were tired and Graham's column spread out, Wellington allowed the French to occupy the rectangular valley of Zadorra,

west of Vitoria. The valley was six miles wide and ten miles long. Mountains surrounded it, and several roads led into the valley, which allowed Wellington to divide his force into four columns and enter the valley from several directions.

49. Wellington to Graham, 21 June 1813, WSD, 8:1; Wellington to Henry Wellesley, 22 June 1813, WD, 10:454–55. Wellington claimed to have seized 120 pieces of artillery, all of their ammunition, baggage, provisions, money, and so forth. In addition to the baggage, Wellington also seized King Joseph's art collection, which Joseph had stolen from the Spanish. The collection is visible today at Apsley House in London. Sarramon, *La Battaille de Vitoria*, 173–237; Oman, *History of the Peninsular War*, 6:750–61. In all, the French lost around eight thousand men and 149 artillery pieces. Despite routing Joseph's army, the Allies captured only two thousand prisoners.

50. Prince of Wales to Wellington, 3 July 1813, WP 1/372; Bathurst to Wellington, 3 July 1813, WSD, 8:48–49.

51. Bathurst to Wellington, 14 July 1813, WP 1/372.

52. Wellington to Bathurst, 29 June 1813, WD, 10:472–73.

53. Ibid. In addition to the disruption caused by the raiding, Wellington was hindered by the presence of thousands of French camp followers that cluttered the roads and prevented an effective pursuit of the French army.

54. Wellington to Bathurst, 2 July 1813, WD, 10:495–96.

55. Wellington to Bathurst, 9 July 1813, WD, 10:519.

56. Bathurst to Wellington, 22 July 1813, WSD, 8:104–105.

57. Duke of York to Wellington, 22 July 1813, WSD, 8:106.

58. Wellington to Torrens, 3 July 1813, WD, 10:499–500.

59. Wellington communicated his position several times throughout the campaign. The first instance occurred before the battle of Vitoria. See Wellington to Collier, 6 May 1813, WD, 10:360–61.

60. Perrin and Lloyd, *Keith Papers*, 3:261–65; For a complete account of the siege of San Sebastián and subsequent operations, see Herzog "Once More Unto the Breach," 145–55. The French defended San Sebastián with 2,300 veteran troops under the command of Gen. Emmanuel Rey.

61. Jones, *Journals of Sieges*, 2:14–15; Herzog, "Once More Unto the Breach," 20–23.

62. Latimer, *1812: War with America*, 89.

63. Wellington to Bathurst, 17 February 1813, WD, 10:125; Fortescue, *History of the British Army*, 9:104.

64. Wellington to Bathurst, 7 April 1813, WD, 10:272–73.

65. Redgrave, "Wellington's Logistical Arrangements," 60–61. For the American contribution to the defense of Lisbon, see Galpin, "American Grain Trade," 25, 28.

66. Wellington to Bathurst, 10 July 1813, WD, 10:522–23; Latimer, *1812: War with America*, 88–9.

67. Latimer, *1812: War with America*, 84–87. The *Constitution* was one of three 44-gun frigates the United States built to overpower British frigates. Furthermore, because of their length and width, they carried stouter masts and rigging, which made them faster than most ships-of-the-line. In contrast to British frigates, which only carried 18-pound guns, the American

frigates carried 24-pound guns and 32-pound carronades. Furthermore, they had the added advantage of all-volunteer crews, which in contrast to the majority of "impressed" or foreign sailors on British ships were much better trained and motivated. As a result of the emergence of the larger American frigates, British frigates were forced to sail in pairs.

68. Wellington to Beresford, 6 February 1813, WD, 10:91–2.

69. Wellington to Collier, 22 April 1813, WD, 10:318.

70. Collier to Keith, 19 July 1813, Perrin and Lloyd, *Keith Papers*, 3:294. Collier replaced Admiral Popham in March 1813.

71. Collier led several amphibious operations in support of Spanish guerillas, including the raid on Bermeo in October 1811. Fortescue, *History of the British Army*, 9:104–106.

72. Melville to Keith, 21 May 1813, Perrin and Lloyd, *Keith Papers*, 3:290–91.

73. Keith to Popham, 11 December 1812, ibid., 3:289; Melville to Wellington, 28 July 1813, WSD, 8:146–47. For an excellent account of the actions of the admiral in charge of supporting Wellington, see McCranie, *Lord Keith*. The squadron off the coast of Spain consisted of only three frigates and three smaller vessels. Another factor in the reduction of squadrons off Lisbon and the Biscay coast involved ship captains pursuing privateers in waters beyond their assigned sectors.

74. Wellington to Collier, 22 April 1813, WD, 10:318.

75. Wellington to Collier, 6 May 1813, WD, 10:360–61.

76. Ibid.

77. Collier to Wellington, 9 June 1813, Perrin and Lloyd, *Keith Papers*, 3:291–92.

78. Collier to Keith, 21 June 1813, ibid., 3:292.

79. Wellington to Bathurst, 24 June 1813, WD, 10:458–59.

80. Wellington to Bathurst, 2 July 1813, WD, 10:495.

81. Wellington to Bathurst, 10 July 1813, WD, 10:522–23.

82. Keith to Wellington, 3 July 1813, Perrin and Lloyd, *Keith Papers*, 3:293–94.

83. Collier to Keith, 19 July 1813, ibid., 3:294; The French used small local craft called *trincadores*, manned by two or three skilled seamen, or smaller *chaloupes* to evade the larger British warships and smuggle supplies into the city. For more on how the French circumvented the British blockade, see McCranie, *Lord Keith*, 361–62.

84. Wellington to Bathurst, 10 July 1813, WD, 10:522–23.

85. Wellington to Graham, 20 August 1813, WD, 11:19–20.

86. Bathurst to Melville, no date, contents printed in Melville to Keith, 24 August 1813, Perrin and Lloyd, *Keith Papers*, 3:300–301.

87. Wellington to Collier, 22 July 1813, WD, 10:561–62.

88. Wellington to Bathurst, 1 August 1813, WD, 10:576. Wellington reported that from 7 to 27 July, the allies had suffered over a thousand casualties at San Sebastián.

89. Wellington to Bathurst, 8 August 1813, WD, 10:615.

90. Keith to Collier, 31 August 1813, Martin, *Letters and Papers*, 2:329–30.

91. Keith to Croker, 15 July 1813, ibid., 2:338–39.
92. For examples of Wellington's complaints, see Croker to Keith, 21 May 1813, and Keith to Croker, 23 June 1813, ibid., 2:331–34; See also Thompson, *Earl Bathurst*, 68.
93. Melville to Wellington, 28 July 1813, WP 1/372.
94. Ibid.
95. Wellington to Bathurst, 19 August 1813, WD, 11:17–19.
96. Melville to Wellington, 3 September 1813, WSD, 8:223–26.
97. Wellington to Melville, 21 August 1813, WD, 11:26–28.
98. Melville to Keith, 24 August 1813, Perrin and Lloyd, *Keith Papers*, 3:300–301.
99. Melville to Wellington, 3 September 1813, WSD, 8:223–26.
100. Captain Charles Adams to Pellew, 4 April 1813, *Naval Chronicle*, 78–79.
101. AFY to the Editor, 6 August 1813, *Naval Chronicle*.
102. AFY to the Editor, 2 September 1813, *Naval Chronicle*.
103. Melville to Keith, 3 September 1813, Martin, *Letters and Papers*, 2:365. See also Wellington to Bathurst, 24 September 1813, WSD, 8:272–75. In his letter to Bathurst, Wellington stated that the private letters of Admiralty were forwarded to Sir Thomas Graham, who in turn informed Wellington of their contents.
104. Croker to Keith, 3 September 1813, Melville to Wellington, 3 September 1813, WSD, 8:226–27, 223–25.
105. Bathurst to Wellington, 9 October 1813, WP 1/378.
106. Wellington to Wellesley-Pole, 2 December 1813, Wellington A/66, RP.
107. Wellington to Bathurst, 27 January 1813, WD, 10:48–49.
108. Wellington to Bathurst, 10 February 1813, WD, 10:104–105.
109. Wellington to Bathurst, 27 June 1813, WD, 10:464.
110. Bathurst to Wellington, 22 July 1813, WSD, 8:109.
111. Torrens to Wellington, 19 August 1813, WSD, 8:198–99.
112. Wellington to Bathurst, 1 August 1813, WD, 10:576.
113. Wellington to Bathurst, 11 August 1813, WD, 10:630–31.
114. Napoleon to Soult, 1 July 1813, Napoleon, *Correspondance Ier*, 20208, 25:447–48; Wellington to Bathurst, 1 August 1813, WD, 10:576–78. Wellington learned of Soult's appointment from a captured copy of Marshal Soult's proclamation to his soldiers. In an attempt to demonstrate the confidence the emperor invested in him, Soult was given the title *lieutenant de l'empereur*.
115. Memorandum on the Operation to be carried on the Eastern Coast of the Peninsula, Wellington to Murray, 14 April 1813, WD, 10:297–301. For more on Murray's operation, see Krajeski, "British Amphibious Campaigns," 125–30.
116. Napoleon to Soult, 1 July 1813, Napoleon, *Correspondance Ier*, 20208, 25:447–48; Charles Clerc, *Campagne du Maréchal Soult*, 19–26. During the previous campaign, the French minister of war, Gen. Henri Clarke, had promised Joseph a month's rations but failed to deliver them.
117. Murray to Cole, 2 July 1813, WSD, 8:114.

118. Wellington to Murray, 1 July 1813, WD, 10:488; Muir, *Britain and the Defeat of Napoleon*, 266–68.

119. Napoleon to Caulaincourt, 29 July 1813, *Correspondance Ier*, 20317, 25:603–604.

120. Muir, *Britain and the Defeat of Napoleon*, 266–68; for a detailed account of the action, see Clerc, *Campagne du Maréchal Soult*, 45–66.

121. Wellington to Graham, 25 July 1813, WD, 10:566.

122. Wellington to Bathurst, 1 August 1813, WD, 10:576–88.

123. Return of the killed and wounded from 25 July to 2 August 1813, Wellington to Bathurst, 1 August 1813, WD, 10:599; Clerc, *Campagne du Maréchal Soult*, 45–66. Soult's casualty figures were 12,563 casualties and 2,710 prisoners.

124. Wellington to Bentinck, 5 August 1813, WD, 10:602.

125. Wellington to Wellesley-Pole, 3 August 1813, Wellington A/56, RP.

126. Wellesley-Pole to Wellington, 1 September 1813, Wellington B/121, RP.

127. Wellington to Bathurst, 8 August 1813, WD, 10:615.

128. Casualty estimates from the siege of San Sebastián from 28 July to 31 August 1813, Wellington to Bathurst, 2 September 1813, WD, 11:66.

129. Soult to Clarke, 31 July 1813, as printed in Clerc, *Campagne du Maréchal Soult*, 404–405. See also, Vidal de la Blache, *L'Evacuation de l'Espagne*, 1:286, 289, 300.

130. Wellington to Bathurst, 2 September 1813, WD, 11:67–70. Freire deployed his troops in a manner similar to Bussaco and Sorauren. He screened his primary defensive line with light troops and concealed his primary defensive line on the reverse slope. For a detailed account of the allied defense at San Marcial, see Vidal de la Blache, *L'Evacuation de l'Espagne*, 1:300. See also Herzog, "Once More Unto the Breach," 149–55.

131. Wellington to Bathurst, 2 September 1813, WD, 70.

132. Wellington to Henry Wellesley, 3 September 1813, WD, 11:74.

133. Wellington to Bathurst, 2 September 1813, WD, 11:61–71; Soult's casualty figures are listed in Clerc, *Campagne du Maréchal Soult*, 382–83. Vidal de La Blache, *L'Evacuation de l'Espagne*, 1:305–306.

134. Graham to Rey, 3 September 1813, Rey to Graham, 3 September 1813, Wellington to Graham, 5 September 1813, WSD, 8:229–32.

135. Wellington to Bathurst, 2 September 1813, WD, 11:61. On 9 September, Rey surrendered 1,378 men. In addition, he left 481 wounded men in the castle; Herzog, "Once More Unto the Breach," 155–57.

136. Croker to Keith, 3 September 1813, enclosed in Melville to Wellington, 2 September 1813, WSD, 8:226–27. Martin to Melville, 14 September 1813, Martin, *Letters and Papers*, 2:385.

137. Martin to Keith, 21 September 1813, Martin, *Letters and Papers*, 2:406–407.

138. Wellington to Martin, 16 September 1813, ibid., 2:393.

139. Martin to Wellington, 17 September 1813, Martin, *Letters and Papers*, 2:397–98.

140. Ibid.

141. Wellington to Bathurst, 24 September 1813, WSD, 8:272–75.
142. Wellington to Wellesley-Pole, 18 August 1813, Wellington A/57, RP.
143. Wellington to Wellesley-Pole, 24 September 1813, 2 December 1813, Wellington A/59, 66, RP.
144. Wellington to Bathurst, 23 August 1813, WD, 11:34–35.
145. Grenville to Lord Grenville, 4 October 1813, HMC *Fortescue*, 10:349.
146. Wellington to Bathurst, 7 August 1813, WD, 10:611.
147. Lord Grey to Grenville, 27 October 1813, HMC *Fortescue*, 10:351–55.
148. *Morning Chronicle*, 17 August 1813.
149. Melville to Keith, 3 September 1813, Martin, *Letters and Papers*, 2:359–71.
150. Wellington to Bathurst, 9 July 1813, WD, 10:519; Wellington to Bathurst, 2 September 1813, and Casualty estimates from the siege of San Sebastián from 28 July to 31 August 1813, WD, 11:66. The final assault alone cost the allies 2,400 casualties of which 856 were killed.

CHAPTER 9. THE FINAL ACT

1. Wellington to España, 20 October 1813, Wellington to Bathurst, 19 September 1813, WD, 11:210–11, 122–23; Jones, *Journal of Sieges*, 2:350–51. The Royal Navy blockaded Santoña, which eventually fell in March 1814. Unlike San Sebastián, Pamplona guarded the major inland road, Cul de Maya, and therefore could not be resupplied from the sea. In June, Wellington dispatched Sir Rowland Hill to invest the fortress. In July, Gen. Henry O'Donnell and his Andalucian brigade relieved Hill and the majority of British troops. The command of the siege was passed to a Spanish general, Marshal Carlos de España, in September. Because Wellington had only one siege train (employed at San Sebastián), he directed that the fortress not be formally besieged. Instead, he instructed España to isolate the fortress in the hope that the French garrison would surrender without a fight. Despite Wellington's attempts, the French garrison conducted a series of successful forage operations though the Spanish lines. By the end of September, however, the garrison was on half-rations and was forced to eat roots, dogs, cats, and mice. On the barren countryside with no relief in sight, The garrison surrendered on 31 October.
2. Wellington to Henry Wellesley, 3 September 1813, 16 September 1813, WD, 11:74–75, 114–15. Wellington referred to the peace negotiations at Prague in which Napoleon, through Armand Caulaincourt, rejected Klemens Metternich's outlandish demands to keep Austria out of the war. Wellington cited a 7 September copy of the French newspaper *Moniteur*, which was printed in Bayonne. It claimed the French had lost six thousand troops, thirty cannon, and three hundred carriages under the command of Gen. Dominic Vandamme in Bohemia. Wellington felt little inclination to believe the reproduced copy, which were "improvements upon the lies even of the *Moniteur*."
3. Wellington to Bathurst, 19 September 1813, WD, 11:123–24.

4. Ibid.

5. Wellington to Bentinck, 5 September 1813, WD, 11:85–87.

6. Clerc, *Campagne du Maréchal Soult*, 121–23.

7. Ibid., 123–141. See also Dumas, *Neuf Mois de Campagnes à la suite du Maréchal Soult*, 214–16.

8. Soult to Clarke, 19 October 1813, cited in Clerc, *Campagne du Maréchal Soult*, 143. For Soult's numbers, see page 123.

9. Arrangements connected with a Forward Movement of the Left of the Army, to take place on [7 October], 5 October 1813, WSD, 8:285–92.

10. Wellington to Bathurst, 9 October 1813, WD, 11:176–79. The Bidassoa River was a tidal river, which made determining its depth difficult. British casualties during the crossing were 127 killed and 674 wounded. The allies captured more than 500 French troops and three cannon.

11. Palmerston to Wellington, 14 July 1813, WSD, 8:73. The date of rank of Wellington's promotion was 21 June 1813.

12. Wellington to Bathurst, 9 October 1813, WD, 11:176–79. Hope served in the peninsula during Sir John Moore's campaign of 1809. Upon Moore's death, Hope assumed command of the British army and returned with it to England. Promoted to lieutenant general, Hope commanded a portion of the British forces during the failed Walcheren invasion. For more on the overall implications of Sir John Hope's arrival and his contributions to Wellington's invasion of France, see Reese, "In Defense of the Crown."

13. Wellington to Hope, 8 October 1813, Hope to Wellington, 10 October 1813, WSD, 8:298–99, 302. Sir Thomas Graham returned to England on convalescent leave. In less than a month's time, he was offered and accepted command of the British expedition to Holland.

14. Wellington to Bathurst, 24 August 1812, WD, 9:378.

15. Wellington to Bathurst, 10 October 1813, WD, 11:182–83.

16. Ibid. Sir John Hope was also in financial stress. Prior to departing for the peninsula, he had purchased a winter home and was concerned about making payments. He told his wife that as long as he did not have to purchase new horses in France, his expense account would not exceed his military salary. See Reese, "In Defense of the Crown," 63–65.

17. Wellington to Bathurst, 10 October 1813, WD, 11:182–83; Bathurst to Wellington, 30 October 1813, WP 1/378.

18. Wellington to Wellesley-Pole, 17 September 1809, Wellington A/22, RP; Wellington to Wellesley-Pole 27 January 1812, Wellington A/45, RP.

19. Stuart to Wellington, 2 October 1813, WP 1/378; De La Fuente, "Forjaz," 346–431.

20. Wellington to Liverpool, 25 July 1813, WP, 6:628.

21. For a detailed description of Marshal Beresford's actions as commander of the Portuguese army and of his efforts to raise, equip, and train Portuguese troops, see Vichness, "Marshal of Portugal," 467–80. Unfortunately, Beresford suffered from wounds received at Albuera and played a diminished role in supervising the Regency Council. In his absence, Beresford was aided by Charles Stuart, who took over much of the supervision of the Regency Council and ensured that troops were being recruited and sent to Wellington's army.

22. Stuart to Wellington, 30 October 1813, WP 1/378.
23. Wellington to Stuart, 11 October 1813, WD, 11:183–85.
24. Ibid.
25. Wellington to Stuart, 8 November 1813, WP 1/381.
26. Wellington to Stuart, 11 October 1813, WD, 11:183–85.
27. For an example of Wellington's gratitude for the services of the Portuguese forces, see Wellington to Forjaz, 3 September 1809, WD, 5:113. For a discussion related to the Portuguese subsidy, see Wellington to Forjaz, 8 March 1810, WD, 6:114. For more on the Portuguese subsidy, see De La Fuente, "Forjaz," 379–81.
28. For complete analysis of the Portuguese budget shortfall, see Fryman, "Charles Stuart," 2:373–75.
29. Wellington to Stuart, 1 October 1812, Wellington to Bathurst, 17 October 1812, WD, 9:461–63, 497–501. To combat smuggling and to ensure that the wealthiest Portuguese paid a true proportion of their income in tax, the *décima*, which had traditionally only included 10 percent of the income of a class, was amended in the summer of 1812 to include wealthy merchants. The new laws, which were pushed through the Regency Council by Stuart and Forjaz, forced the merchants to pay 20 percent tax as individuals. The effect was a dramatic increase in tax income and decreased burden on the poor. Furthermore, despite the relocation of Lisbon as the primary supply point to the northern Spanish coastal ports of Coruña, Santander, and Pasajes, the customs revenue increased by nearly £160,000 in 1813. Total revenue grew by almost £600,000 to £2.9 million. See De La Fuente, "Forjaz," 379–81, and Fryman, "Charles Stuart," 478–83.
30. Wellington to Stuart, 1 December 1813, WP 1/381.
31. Stuart to Wellington, 29 October 1813, WP 1/378. Included in Stuart's dispatch was a letter from Forjaz. Wellington forwarded Forjaz's letter to the British government. See Wellington to Stuart, 8 November 1813, WD, 11:263–64. See also Oman, *History of the Peninsular War*, 7:145–46.
32. Stuart to Wellington, 2 October 1813, WP 1/378; Wellington to Stuart, 18 October 1813, WP 1/377. See also De La Fuente, "Forjaz," 376–78. In the fall of 1812, the Portuguese and Spanish reached an agreement, hoping to minimize the costs of the war. Both sides agreed to maintain a running account of the supplies consumed by each country in one another's territory. The Portuguese would be supplied, meat, bread, and forage from Spanish depots, and the Portuguese would pay the Spanish with vouchers, which would be settled at the end of the war. By 1813 the account was considerably in Portugal's favor; however, Spain could not afford to supply the Portuguese troops. Wellington could not afford grievances between the two governments, so he declared that the British commissary would draw supplies from the Spanish, and that the supplies would be credited against British payments already made to Spain. Wellington also decided which portions of the supplies provided by the Spanish would go to the Portuguese troops, and therefore, he would personally settle the accounts between the two countries.
33. Stuart to Wellington, 26 August 1813, WSD, 8:210–11; Stuart to Wellington, 2 October 1813, Stuart to Wellington, 27 November 1813, WP 1/378, 1/379. See also Fryman, "Charles Stuart," 2:354–55.

34. Castlereagh to Strangford, 11 October 1813, WSD, 8:347.
35. Prince of Wales to both houses of Parliament, 4 November 1813, *Parliamentary Debates*, 27:1–21.
36. Wellington to Beresford, 6 November 1813, WD, 11:256–57.
37. Stuart to Wellington, 19 January 1814, WSD, 8:523–24.
38. Wellington to Stuart, 28 January 1814, WD, 11:485–86.
39. Stuart to Wellington, 23 October 1813, WP 1/378.
40. Wellington to Collier, 4 September 1813, WD, 11:78. Charles Stuart was much more effective than Beresford in remedying the crisis. In fact, throughout the entire period, Stuart never mentioned Beresford in his official correspondence. See Vichness, "Marshal of Portugal" 476–77.
41. Wellington to Stuart, 2 January 1814, WP 1/395.
42. Wellington to Bathurst, 16 January 1814, WD, 11:458–59. See also De La Fuente, "Forjaz," 426–28.
43. For more on the strain in Anglo-Portuguese relations, see De La Fuente, "Forjaz," 428–30; Fryman, "Charles Stuart," 2:352–60.
44. *Morning Chronicle*, 1 November 1813.
45. Henry Wellesley to Wellington, 5 October 1813, WSD, 8:292.
46. Henry Wellesley to Wellington, 2 November 1813, WSD, 8:334–35; Esdaile, *Duke of Wellington*, 155–56.
47. Henry Wellesley to Wellington, 5 October 1813, WSD, 8:292.
48. Wellington to Henry Wellesley, 23 October 1813, WD, 11:214–15.
49. Wellington to Henry Wellesley, 11 October 1813, Wellington to Henry Wellesley, 16 October 1813, WD, 11:185–86, 199–200.
50. Wellington to the Magistrates of San Sebastián, 2 November 1813, WD, 11:246.
51. *Morning Chronicle*, 29 October 1813.
52. Ibid.
53. *Times*, 4 November 1813.
54. *Morning Chronicle*, 1 November 1813.
55. Bathurst to Wellington, 5 November 1813, WSD, 8:337.
56. Graham to Bathurst, 10 October 1813, as cited in Bathurst to Wellington, ibid.
57. Ibid.
58. Bathurst to Wellington, 5 November 1813, WSD, 8:337.
59. Bathurst to the House of Lords, 8 November 1813, *Parliamentary Debates*, 27:45–47; Castlereagh to the House of Commons, 8 November 1813, *Parliamentary Debates*, 27:64–67.
60. Bathurst to the House of Lords, 8 November 1813, *Parliamentary Debates*, 27:46–47; *Times*, 9 November 1813. Mercy toward a garrison was rarely granted during the Napoleonic Wars.
61. Earl Darnley to the House of Lords, 8 November 1813, *Parliamentary Debates*, 27:48.
62. Bathurst to House of Lords, 8 November 1813, ibid., 27:47; *Times*, 9 November 1813.
63. Instead of employing the Spanish in one large force, Wellington preferred dividing them into smaller units and attaching them to Anglo-

Portuguese units. For more on the command and control relationship of the Spanish troops in the Pyrenees, see Esdaile, *Duke of Wellington*, 136-40.

64. Wellington to Bathurst, 19 September 1813, WD, 11:123-24.

65. Wellington to Hope, 9 October 1813, WD, 11:169-70.

66. General order, 9 July 1813, WD, 11:169; Proclamation of Abisbal, 16 June 1813, as cited in Esdaile, *Duke of Wellington*, 160.

67. Hope to Wellington, 8 October 1813, WSD, 8:298-99. Hope told Wellington, "Much plunder has been carried out by the Spaniards in this quarter. They cross the Bidassoa River from Fuenterrabia and Irun in great numbers."

68. Wellington to Hope, 8 October 1813, WD, 11:168-69. In his dispatch, Wellington concurred with Hope in his observation of a group of Spanish soldiers who had returned from Olague "drunk and loaded with plunder."

69. Wellington to Bathurst, 13 November 1813, Wellington to Smith, 14 November 1813, WD, 11:279-85, 289.

70. Wellington to Wimpffen, 12 November 1813, WD, 11:277-78.

71. Wellington to Girón, 12 November 1813, Wellington to Bathurst, 13 November 1813, WD, 11:277, 279-85.

72. Freire to Wellington, 13 November 1813, WP 1/382.

73. Wellington to Freire, 14 November 1813, WD, 11:287-88.

74. Wellington to Bathurst, 21 November 1813, WD, 11:303-307.

75. Ibid.

76. Wellington to Henry Wellesley, 24 November 1813, WD, 11:315-16.

77. Henry Wellesley to Wellington, 10 December 1813, WP 1/380; deletions not contained in WSD, 8:418-19.

78. Wellington to Girón, 12 November 1813, WD, 11:277.

79. Wellington to Morillo, 23 December 1813, WD, 11:390-91.

80. Wellington to Dalrymple, 23 December 1813, Wellington to Freire, 25 December 1813, WD, 11:393, 399-400.

81. Wellington to Freire, 24 December 1813, WD, 11:395-96.

82. O'Donoju to Wellington, 19 July 1813, WP 1/372; Wellington to Henry Wellesley, 24 July 1813, WD, 10:564-66. Wellington removed Gen. Javier Castaños, a long-time opponent of the British, and Gen. Pedro Girón from command.

83. Wellington to Henry Wellesley, 9 August 1813, WD, 10:623. For more on Wellington's problematic relations with the Spanish in 1813-14, see Esdaile, *Duke of Wellington*, 143-60; see also Muir, *Britain and the defeat of Napoleon*, 274-75.

84. The assertion was made on 18 September by the newspaper *El Redactor General*. Wellington responded by calling the men responsible for the story fools. See Wellington to Henry Wellesley, 16 October 1813, WD, 11:199-200.

85. Wellington to Bathurst, 1 November 1813, WD, 11:238-40.

86. Wellington to Bathurst, 20 October 1813, WD, 11:211-12.

87. Wellington to Bathurst, 25 October 1813, WD, 11:218.

88. Wellington to Bathurst, 1 November 1813, WD, 11:240-41.

89. Melville to Wellington, 15 October 1813, WP 1/378.

90. Wellington to Bathurst, 1 November 1813, WD, 11:238–41.

91. Ibid. Wellington acknowledged that, weather permitting, these convoys should sail from Lisbon, Coruña, and Santander only on Sunday and Thursday. He hoped reducing the number of days would mean fewer convoys would be necessary and therefore fewer escorts to provide security and supplies.

92. Wellington to Penrose, 1 February 1814, WD, 11:491. Penrose arrived to take command on 28 January 1814.

93. Collier to Wellington, 2 February 1814, WSD, 8:560.

94. For the remainder of the war, the navy continued transporting supplies to Wellington's army. The navy was also responsible for assisting the siege of Bayonne, and in February 1814, it assisted in the construction of a bridge over the Adour River. Wellington's relations with Penrose were cordial as well. See Penrose to Wellington, 24, 27 February 1814, WSD, 8:591–92, 605–606; Wellington to Penrose, 1 March 1814, WD, 11:533.

95. Wellington to Bathurst, 14 December 1813, Wellington to Bathurst, 21 December 1813, WD, 11:365–70, 384–87. The allies suffered over four thousand casualties during the fighting from 9 to 13 December.

96. Bathurst to Wellington, 10 December 1813, WSD, 8:413–15.

97. Bathurst to Wellington, 31 December 1813, WSD, 8:450–52.

98. Wellington to Bathurst, 21 December 1813, WD, 11:384–87. Wellington gained his intelligence on the reported number of French soldiers that opposed him from French newspapers.

99. Ibid.

100. Thompson, *Earl Bathurst*, 69–70. For more on the British expedition to the Low Countries in 1814, see Muir, *Britain and the defeat of Napoleon*, 306–10, and Fortescue, *History of the British Army*, 10:33–59.

101. Wellington to Farington, no date, as published in Farington, *Diary*, June 10, 1811, to December 18, 1814, 255.

102. Returns for Wellington's Army 31 December 1813, WP 1/439

103. Herries to Kennedy, 18 June 1813, as printed in Herries, *Memoir*, 2:232. The opening of the Baltic trade to England after Napoleon's withdrawal from northern Germany in the summer of 1813 made it possible for Britain to obtain grain at a less expensive rate. From July 1813 onwards, the majority of foodstuffs were shipped directly from England, not Lisbon. Herries remarked that this saved "considerable public economy."

104. Some of the supply to these forward bases was obtained by "on the spot" transactions. For an example, see Bathurst to Wellington, 21 April 1814, WSD, 8:531.

105. Wellington to Bathurst, 8 January 1814, WD, 11:425–26.

106. Wellington to Wellesley-Pole, 9 January 1814, Wellington A/67, RP.

107. Farington, *Diary*, June 10, 1811, to December 18, 1814, 194.

108. Wellington to Bathurst, 22 February 1814, WD, 11:525–26.

109. Wellington to Bathurst, 1 March 1814, WD, 11:533–40. The allies suffered more than two thousand casualties at Orthez. See also Oman, *History of the Peninsular War*, 7:358–59.

110. Napoleon to Decres, 12 March 1814, Napoleon *Correspondance Ier*, 21,471, 27:358.

111. Wellington to Beresford, 7 March 1814, WD, 11:556–57.
112. Wellington to Liverpool, 4 March 1814, WD, 11:546–47.
113. Wellington to Beresford, 4 March 1814, WD, 11:550.
114. Wellington to Bathurst, 21 November 1814, WD, 11:303–307.
115. Wellington to Liverpool, 4 March 1814, WD, 11:546–47.
116. Wellington to Beresford, 2 March 1814, WD, 11:541. Wellington instructed Beresford to encourage demonstrations in support of Louis XVIII, but if they occurred, he was not to take part in them. For more on Beresford's actions in Bordeaux see Vichness, "Marshal of Portugal," 484–88.
117. Wellington to Liverpool, 4 March 1814, WD, 11:546–47.
118. Wellington to Bathurst, 12 April 1814, Colville to Wellington, 14 April 1814, WD, 11:632–38, 661. The allies suffered nearly five thousand casualties at Toulouse and another seven hundred to eight hundred casualties at Bayonne. However, the greatest loss was the prestige of Sir John Hope, who was wounded and captured by the French during the fighting. The French later released him. For an excellent account of the fighting at Bayonne, see Reese, "In Defense of the Crown," 144–62.
119. Convention of Toulouse, 18 April 1814, WD, 11:653–56.
120. Bathurst to Wellington, 28 April 1814, WSD, 9:53.
121. Bathurst to Wellington, 23 April 1814, WSD, 9:29–30. The officers to be made peers were generals Sir John Hope, Thomas Graham, Rowland Hill, and Stapleton Cotton, and Marshal William Carr Beresford.
122. Wellington to Castlereagh, 21 April 1814, WSD, 11:668–69.

Bibliography

ARCHIVAL SOURCES

British Library, London

Colonel James Gordon Papers, Additional MSS. 49477, 49473
John C. Herries Papers, Additional MSS. 57393
William Huskisson Papers, Additional MSS. 37416, 38737
Liverpool Papers, MS Loan 72, vol. 20, Additional MSS. 38244, 38325, 38326
George Rose Papers, Additional MSS. 31237
Wellington Papers, Additional MSS. 38246

Public Record Office, Kew Gardens

Foreign Office, Austria, 1809
War Office, Letters from War Department to Wellington 1809–11

Hartley Library, University of Southampton

Correspondence of Sir Arthur Wellesley the Duke of Wellington, Bundles
Palmerston Papers, MS 62
Wellington Papers, MS 61

Gwent County Record Office, Cwmbrân, Wales

Raglan Papers:
Wellington A: 89 letters from Wellington to his brother William Wellesley-Pole (1807–1817)

Wellington B: 40 copies of letters from William Wellesley-Pole to Wellington (1808–1816)

PUBLISHED PRIMARY SOURCES

Arbuthnot, Charles. *The Correspondence of Charles Arbuthnot*. Edited by A. Aspinall, Camden Third Series, vol. 65. London: 1941.
Bell, George. *Soldier's Glory: Rough Notes of an Old Soldier*. London: 1867.
Croker, John Wilson. *The Croker Papers: The Correspondence and Diaries of John Wilson Croker, From 1809–1830*. Edited by Louis J. Jennings. 3 vols. London: John Murray, 1884.
Dyneley, Thomas. *Letters Written by Lieutenant General Thomas Dyneley while on Active Service Between the Years of 1806–1815*. Arranged by Colonel F. A. Whinyates. Ken Trotman Military History Monographs 4. London: Lionel Leventhal, 1984.
Farington, Joseph. *The Farington Diary*. Edited by James Grieg. 10 vols. New York: George Doran, 1927.
George III, King of Great Britain. *The Later Correspondence of King George III*. 5 vols. Edited by A. Aspinall. London: Cambridge University Press, 1962–1970.
George IV, King of Great Britain. *The Letters of King George IV*. 3 vols. Edited by A. Aspinall. London: Cambridge University Press, 1938.
Great Britain, Board of General Officers appointed to inquire into the Convention of Cintra. *Copy of the Proceedings upon the inquiry relative to the armistice and convention, made and concluded in Portugal, August 1808, between the commanders of the British and French Armies; held at Royal Hospital at Chelsea, on Monday the 14th of November; and continued by adjournments until Tuesday the 27th of December, 1808*. London: 1809.
Great Britain, Parliament. *Cobbett's Parliamentary Debates*. First Series. London: T. C. Hansard, 1808–1812.
Herries, Edward. *Memoir of the Public Life of the Rt. Honorable J. C. Herries*. 2 vols. London: J. Murray, 1880.
Historical Manuscripts Commission. *Report on the Manuscripts of Earl Bathurst*. London: H.M.S.O., 1923.
——. *Report on the Manuscripts of J. B. Fortescue, Esq. Preserved at Dropmore*. 10 vols. London: H.M.S.O., 1892–1927.
——. *Report on the Manuscripts of Reginald Rawdon Hastings*. 22 vols. London: H.M.S.O., 1928.
Holland, Henry Richard Vassall. *Further Memoirs of the Whig Party, 1807–1821, with some Miscellaneous Reminiscences*. London: John Murray, 1905.
Huskisson, William. *The Huskisson Papers*. Edited by Lewis Melville. 2 vols. London: Constable, 1931.
Jones, John T. *Journals of Sieges Carried on by the Army under the Duke of Wellington, in Spain, During the years 1811 to 1814; With Notes and Addition: Also Memoranda Relative to the Lines Thrown up to Cover Lisbon in 1810*. 3 vols. London: J. Weale, 1846.

Markham, David. *Imperial Glory: The Bulletins of the Grande Armée, 1805–1814*. London: Greenhill Books, 2003.
Martin, Thomas Byam. *Letters and Papers of Admiral of the Fleet Sir Thomas Byam Martin*. Edited by Sir Richard Vessey Hamilton. 3 vols. London: Navy Records Society, 1903.
Maxwell, W. H. *Peninsular Sketches: By Actors on the Scene*. 2 vols. London: H. Colburn, 1845.
Moore, James. *A Narrative of the Campaign of the British Army in Spain*. London: John Nichols and Son, 1809.
Moore, Sir John. *The Diary of Sir John Moore*. Edited by Sir J. F. Maurice. 2 vols. London: Edward Arnold, 1904.
Murray, George. *Memoir Annexed to an Atlas Containing the Plans of the Principal Battles, Sieges, and Affairs of the British Army during the War in the Spanish Peninsula*. London: James Wyld, 1841.
Napier, William F. P. *A History of War in the Peninsula and in the South of France, 1807–1814*. 6 vols. New York: A. C. Armstrong and Son, 1882.
Napoleon I, Emperor of the French. *The Confidential Correspondence of Napoleon Bonaparte with his Brother King Joseph*. 2 vols. New York: D. Appleton, 1856.
———. *Correspondance De Napoleon Ier; Publiee Par Ordre De L'Empereur Napoléon III*. 32 vols. Paris: Imprimerie Imperiale, 1858–1869.
Perrin, W. G., and Christopher Lloyd, eds. *The Keith Papers: Selected from the Papers of Admiral Viscount Keith*. 3 vols. London: Navy Records Society, 1927–1955.
Rose, George. *The Diaries and Correspondence of the Right Honorable George Rose*. 2 vols. London: Richard Bentley, 1860.
Schaumann, August Ludolf Friedrich. *On the Road with Wellington: The Diary of a War Commissary in the Peninsular Campaigns*. London: William Heinemann, 1827.
Stanhope, P. H. *Notes of Conversations with the Duke of Wellington*. London, 1998.
Swabey, William. *Diary of the Campaigns in the Peninsula for the Years 1811, 12, and 13*. Ken Trotman Military History Monographs 4. London: Lionel Leventhal, 1984.
Tomkinson, James. *The Diary of a Cavalry Officer in the Peninsular War and Waterloo Campaign, 1809–1815*. London: Swan Sonnenschein, 1895.
Vance, Charles, ed. *Correspondence, Dispatches, and Other Papers of Viscount Castlereagh, Second Marquis of Londonderry*. 12 vols. London: William Shoberl, 1851.
Vassall, Henry Richard, Third Lord Holland. *Further Memoirs of the Whig Party, 1807–1821, With Some Miscellaneous Reminiscences*. London. John Murray, 1905.
Wellesley, Henry. *The Diary and Correspondence of Henry Wellesley, First Lord Cowley, 1790–1846*. Edited by his grandson Colonel F. A. Wellesley. London: Hutchinson, 1930.
Wellesley, Richard Colley, Marquess, *The Wellesley Papers: The Life and Correspondence of Richard Colley Wellesley*. 2 vols. London: Herbert Jenkins, 1914.

Wellington, Arthur Wellesley, Duke of. *The Dispatches of Field Marshal the Duke of Wellington: During His Various Campaigns in India, Denmark, Portugal, Spain, the Low Countries, and France, from 1799 to 1812.* 13 vols. Compiled by Colonel Gurwood. London: John Murray, 1837.

———. *A Memoir of Field Marshal the Duke of Wellington with notices of his Associates in Council and Companions and Opponents in Arms.* London: A. Fullerton.

———. *Personal Reminiscences of the First Duke of Wellington.* Edited by George and Mary Gleig. London: William Blackwood and Sons, 1904.

———. *Some Letters of the Duke of Wellington to His Brother William Wellesley-Pole.* Edited by Sir Charles Webster. Camden Miscellany vol. 18. London: Offices of the Royal Historical Society, June 1948.

———. *Supplementary Dispatches, Correspondence, and Memoranda of Field Marshal Arthur, Duke of Wellington.* 14 vols. Edited by the 2nd Duke of Wellington. London: John Murray, 1863.

Wilson, Sir Robert. *General Wilson's Journal, 1812–1814.* Edited by Antony Brett-James. London: William Kimber, 1964.

Wrottesby, George. *Life and Correspondence of Field Marshal Sir John Burgoyne.* 2 vols. London: Bentley and Son, 2873.

BOOKS, ARTICLES, AND PAPERS

Aspinall, Arthur. *Politics and the Press, 1780–1850.* London: Home and Thal, 1949.

Bass, Robert D. *The Green Dragoon: The Lives of Banastre Tarleton and Mary Robinson.* Orangeburg, S.C.: Sandlapper Publishing, 1973.

Black, Frederick H. "Diplomatic Struggles: British Support in Spain and Portugal, 1800–1815." Ph.D. diss., Florida State University, 2005.

Bond, Gordon. *The Grand Expedition—The British Invasion of Holland in 1809.* Athens: University of Georgia Press, 1979.

Bruno, Michael D. "The Military and Administrative Career of Sir John Craddock, 1762–1814." Master's thesis, Florida State University, 1972.

Chandler, David G. *The Campaigns of Napoleon.* New York: Macmillan, 1966.

———. *Marlborough as Military Commander.* London: Scribner, 1973.

Clarke, John. *British Diplomacy and Foreign Policy, 1782–1865: The National Interest.* London: Unwin Hyman, 1989.

Clerc, Charles. *Campagne du Maréchal Soult dans les Pyrénées occidentals en 1813–1814 d'après les archives françaises, anglaises et espagnoles.* Paris, Libraire Militaire de L. Baudoin, 1894.

Clode, Charles M. *Military Forces of the Crown: Their Administration and Government.* 2 vols. London: J. Murray, 1869.

Cornell, Thomas. "The Duke of Wellington and the Transformation of Warfare: The Peninsula Campaigns of 1808–1809." Master's thesis, Florida State University, 1993.

Corti, Egon. *The Rise of the House of Rothschild.* New York: Cosmopolitan, 1928.

De La Blache, Vidal. *L'Evacuation de l'Espagne et l'Invasion Dans le Midi de la France (Juin 1813–April 1814)*. 2 vols. Paris: Berger-Levrault, 1914.
De La Fuente, Francisco. "Dom Miguel Pereira Forjaz: His Early Career and Role in the Mobilization and Defense of Portugal during the Peninsular War, 1807–1814." Ph. D. diss., Florida State University, 1980.
DeToy, Brian. "'A Busy Meddling Folly': Wellington, Berkeley, and the Sieges of Badajoz." In *Consortium on Revolutionary Europe 1750–1850, Selected Papers*, 2002, 184–95. Tallahassee: Florida State University, 2004.
———. "Wellington's Admiral: The Life and Career of George Berkeley, 1753–1818." 2 vols. Ph.D. diss., Florida State University, 1997.
Dumas, Jean-Baptiste. *Neuf Mois de Campagnes à la suite du Maréchal Soult*. Paris: H. Charles-Lavauzelle, 1907.
Esdaile, Charles. *The Duke of Wellington and the Command of the Spanish Army, 1812–14*. New York: St. Martin's Press, 1990.
———. *Fighting Napoleon: Guerillas, Bandits, and Adventurers in Spain 1808–1814*. New Haven, Conn.: Yale University Press, 2004.
———. *The Peninsular War: A New History*. New York: Macmillan, 2003.
Fortescue, John W. *The British Army 1783–1802. Four Lectures Delivered at the Staff College and Cavalry School*. London: MacMillan 1905.
———. *A History of the British Army*. 10 vols. London: Macmillan, 1910.
Fryman, Mildred. "Charles Stuart and the Common Cause: The Anglo-Portuguese Alliance, 1810–1814." Ph.D. diss., Florida State University, 1974.
Galpin, W. Freeman. "The American Grain Trade to the Spanish Peninsula, 1808–1814." *American Historical Review* 28 (1923): 24–45.
Gates, David. *The Spanish Ulcer: A History of the Peninsular War*. Cambridge, Mass.: Da Capo Press, 1986.
Glover, Michael. *Britannia Sickens: Sir Arthur Wellesley and the Convention of Cintra*. London: Leo Cooper, 1970.
———. *Peninsular War: 1807–1814: A Concise Military History*. Hamden, Conn.: Archon Books, 1974.
———. *Wellington as Military Commander*. London: B. T. Batsford, 1968.
———. *Wellington's Peninsular Victories*. London: B. T. Batsford, 1963.
Glover, Richard. *Peninsular Preparation: The Reform of the British Army, 1795–1809*. Cambridge: Cambridge University Press, 1963.
Gray, Daniel. "The Services of the King's German Legion in the Army of the Duke of Wellington." Ph.D. diss., Florida State University, 1970.
Hall, Christopher D. *British Strategy in the Napoleonic War, 1803–15*. Manchester: University Press 1992.
———. *Wellington's Navy: Sea Power and the Peninsular War, 1807–14*. London: Chatham Publishing, 2004.
Herson, James P. "The Siege of Cadiz, 1810–1812: A Study in Joint and Combined Operations during the Peninsular War." Ph.D. diss., Florida State University, 1998.
Herzog, Richard T. "Once More Unto the Breach: Military and Naval Operations around San Sebastián, June–September 1813." Master's thesis, Florida State University, 1991.

———. "The Royal Marine and Insurgent Operations in the Salamanca Campaign, 1812." In *Consortium on Revolutionary Europe, 1750–1850, Proceedings 1992*. Tallahassee: Florida State University, 1993.
Holmes, Richard. *Wellington: The Iron Duke*. London: Harper Collins, 2003.
Horward, Donald D. "Admiral Berkeley and the Duke of Wellington: The Winning Combination in the Peninsula (1808–1812)." In *New Interpretations in Naval History*, edited by William B. Cogar, 105–20. Annapolis, Md.: United States Navy Institute, 1989.
———. *The Battle of Bussaco: Masséna vs. Wellington*. Tallahassee: Florida State University Research Council, 1965.
———. "British Seapower and Its Influence upon the Peninsular War (1808–1814)." *Naval War College Review* 31, no. 2 (1978): 54–71.
———. *The French Campaign in Portugal, 1810–1811: An Account by Jean-Jacques Pelet*. Minneapolis: University of Minnesota Press, 1973.
———. "Logistics and Strategy in the Peninsula: A Case Study, 1810–1811." In *Consortium on Revolutionary Europe, 1750–1850. Proceedings 1999*, 355–63. Tallahassee: Florida State University Press, 2000.
———. "Masséna and Wellington on the Lines of Torres Vedras." In *New Lights on the Peninsular War: International Congress on the Iberian Peninsula Selected Papers, 1780–1840*, edited by Alice D. Berkeley, 119–29. Carcavelos: The British Historical Society of Portugal, 1991.
———. *Napoleon and Iberia: The Twin Sieges of Ciudad Rodrigo and Almeida, 1810*. London: Greenhill Books, 1994.
———. "Portugal and Anglo-Russian Naval Crisis (1808)." *Naval War College Review* 34, no. 4 (1981): 48–74.
———. "Wellington and the Defense of Portugal." *International History Review* 11 (1989): 46, 50–51.
———. "Wellington as a Strategist, 1808–1814." In *Wellington: Studies in the Military and Political Career of the First Duke of Wellington*, 87–116. Manchester: Manchester University Press, 1990.
———. "Wellington, Berkeley, and the Royal Navy: Seapower and the Defense of Portugal (1808–1812)." *British Historical Review of Portugal*, Report 18 (1991): 92–93.
———. "Wellington's Peninsular Strategy, Portugal, and the Lines of Torres Vedras." *Portuguese Studies Review*, 2 (1992–93): 46–59.
James, W. M. *The Naval History of Great Britain During the French Revolutionary and Napoleonic Wars*. 10 vols. Mechanicsburg, Penn.: Stackpole Books, 2001.
Jupp, Peter. *Lord Grenville, 1759–1834*. Oxford: Clarendon Press, 1985.
Knight, George D. "Lord Liverpool and the Peninsular War, 1809–1812." Ph.D. diss., Florida State University, 1976.
Krajeski, Paul. "British Amphibious Operations during the Peninsula War, 1808–1814." Master's thesis, Florida State University, 1995.
———. *In the Shadow of Nelson: The Naval Leadership of Admiral Sir Charles Cotton, 1753–1812*. Westport, Conn.: Greenwood Press, 2000.
Latimer, Jon. *1812: War with America*. Cambridge, Mass.: Belknap Press of Harvard University Press, 2007.

Longford, Elizabeth. *Wellington: The Years of the Sword*. New York: Harper and Row, 1969.
Markham, J. David. *Imperial Glory; The Bulletins of the Grande Armée, 1805–1814*. London: Greenhill Books, 2003.
McCranie, Kevin D. *Admiral Lord Keith and the Naval War against Napoleon*. Gainesville: University Press of Florida, 2006.
Meyer, Jack. "Wellington and the Sack of Badajoz: A 'Beastly Mutiny' or Deliberate Policy?" In *Consortium of Revolutionary Europe, Proceedings, 1991*, 251–57. Tallahassee: Florida State University Press, 1992.
Middleton, Charles M. *The Administration of British Foreign Policy, 1782–1846*. Durham, N.C.: Duke University Press, 1977.
Moon, Joshua. "The Duke of Wellington and the British Government: Problems during the Peninsular War, 1808–1811." Master's thesis, Florida State University, 2003.
Muir, Rory. *Britain and the Defeat of Napoleon, 1807–1815*. New Haven, Conn.: Yale University Press, 1996.
———. *Salamanca, 1812*. New Haven, Conn.: Yale University Press, 2001.
Muir, Rory, and Charles Esdaile. "Strategic Planning in a Time of Small Government: The Wars against Revolutionary and Napoleonic France, 1793–1815." In *Wellington Studies I*, edited by Christopher M. Woolgar, 1–90. Southampton: Hartley Institute, Southampton University, 1996.
Officer, Lawrence. *Between the Dollar-Sterling Gold Points: Exchange Rates, Parity, and Market Behavior*. Cambridge: Cambridge University Press, 1996.
Oman, Charles W. "The French Losses in the Waterloo Campaign." *The English Historical Review* 19 (1904): 681–693.
———. *A History of the Peninsular War*. 7 vols. Oxford: Clarendon Press, 1902.
———. *Wellington's Army, 1809–1814*. London: Edward Arnold, 1912.
Popham, Hugh. *A Damned Cunning Fellow: The Eventful Life of Rear Admiral Sir Home Popham, 1762–1820*. Cornwall: Old Ferry Press, 1991.
Redgrave, Toby Michael Ormsby. "Wellington's Logistical Arrangements in the Peninsular War, 1809–14." Ph.D. diss., Kings College, London, 1979.
Reese, Paul. "In Defense of the Crown: General Sir John Hope's Campaign in Southern France, 1813–1814." Master's thesis, Florida State University, 2000.
Robertson, Ian. *Wellington Invades France: The Final Phase of the Peninsular War, 1813–1814*. London: Greenhill, 2003.
Rosselli, John. *Lord William Bentinck and the British Occupation of Sicily, 1811–1814*. Cambridge: Cambridge University Press, 1956.
Sarramon, Jean. *La Bataille des Arapiles, 22 Juillet 1812*. Toulouse: Association des publications de l'Université de Toulouse-Le Mirail, 1978.
———. *La Bataille de Vitoria: La fin de l'aventure napoléonienne en Espagne*. Paris: J. C. Bailly, 1985.
Schneer, Richard M. "Arthur Wellesley and the Cintra Convention: A New Look at an Old Puzzle." *Journal of British Studies* 19, no. 2 (1980): 97–98.
Severn, John K. *Architects of Empire: The Duke of Wellington and His Brothers*. Norman: University of Oklahoma Press, 2007.

———. *A Wellesley Affair: Richard Marquess Wellesley and the Conduct of Anglo-Spanish Diplomacy, 1809–1812*. Tallahassee: Florida State University Press, 1981.

Sherwig, John W. *Guineas and Gunpowder: British Foreign Aid in the Wars with France, 1793–1815*. Cambridge, Mass.: Harvard University Press, 1969.

Silberling, Norman J. "Financial and Monetary Policy of Great Britain during the Napoleonic Wars." *Quarterly Journal of Economics* 38, no. 2 (1924): 214–33.

Six, Georges. *Dictionnaire Biographique des Généraux & Amiraux Francais de la Révolution et de l'Empire* (1792–1814). Paris: Librairie Historique et Nobiliaire, 1934.

Smith, E. A. *Lord Grey, 1764–1845*. Oxford: Clarendon Press, 1990.

Stephen, Leslie, and Sidney Lee. *The Dictionary of National Biography from the Earliest Times to 1900*. 24 vols. London: Oxford University Press, 1917.

Teffeteller, Gordon. *The Surpriser: The Life of Rowland Hill*. Newark: University of Delaware Press, 1983.

Thompson, Neville. *Earl Bathurst and the British Empire, 1762–1834*. South Yorkshire: Leo Cooper, 1999.

Vichness, Samuel E. "Marshal of Portugal: The Military Career of William Carr Beresford, 1785–1814." Ph.D. diss., Florida State University, 1976.

Walpole, Spencer. *The Life of the Rt. Honorable Spencer Perceval*. London: Hurst and Backett, 1874.

Ward, Stephen G. P. *Wellington's Headquarters: A Study of the Administrative Problems in the Peninsula, 1809–1814*. Oxford: Oxford University Press, 1957.

Weller, Jac. *Wellington in the Peninsula, 1808–1814*. London: N. Vane, 1962.

Woolgar, Christopher. "Writing the Dispatch: Wellington and Official Communication." In *Wellington Studies II*, edited by Christopher M. Woolgar, 1–25. Southampton: Hartley Institute, Southampton University, 1999.

Index

Abercrombie, Gen. Sir Ralph, 25
Admiralty Board, 79, 81
Alba de Tormes, 55, 60
Albuera, 93, 95, 100
Almeida, 71–72, 93, 241nn3–4
Alten, Gen. Charles von, 159
Angoulême, Duc d' (Louis Antoine de Bourbon), 211
Annual Mutiny Act, 5
Antwerp, 206–208
Arbuthnot, Charles, 94
Army, British: artillery, 7, 24, 126–27, 129, 181, 232n11; budget and expenditures, 5–6, 45, 76, 237n27; bureaucratic structure of, 5–11, 213–14, 219, 232n19; casualties, 38, 49–50, 93, 96, 127, 146, 154, 179–80, 236n5, 242n7, 245n43, 261n10, 265n95; cavalry, 24, 143–44, 155–56, 158, 250n37; command and control, 5–11, 18, 33–34, 158; commissary general of, 9; defensive fortifications of, 56, 59, 61, 72–73, 238n8; desertions from, 39, 74, 137, 146; diversionary operations by, 102, 124, 130, 151, 162, 250n30, 255n47; evacuation from Spain (1808), 27; expedition to Holland (1809), 26, 31–32, 50–52, 57, 62, 215, 238nn48–49; expedition to Holland (1814), 206–208; growth of, 5, 74; home army, 143, 252n77; horses, 23–25, 157; indiscipline and insubordination in, 39, 42, 137–40, 163–64; infantry, 157, 233n11; joint operations with navy, 124, 216; logistics and supply of, 22–23, 25, 38, 40, 123, 204, 209, 220–21; losses from disease, 5, 38, 144, 146–47; militia, 31, 74; modernization of, 219; monetary procurement efforts by, 105–108, 110–11, 216, 245–46n49; money shipments to, 40, 46, 107, 150, 236n12, 247n68, 247n79; money shortages, 40–41, 43–44, 46, 106–107, 208–10, 216; morale, 20, 40, 73, 151; outnumbered in Iberia, 101, 108, 122, 128, 151, 178; paying of troops, 38–39, 43, 46, 64, 107, 111, 151; plundering and looting by, 41–43, 102, 163, 181, 194–98, 220, 244n36; political patronage system in, 14–15, 214; Portuguese army commanded by, 28, 32, 190–91, 213,

Army, British (cont.)
236n2, 261n21; provisional units in, 154–55, 158; recruitment, 74, 242n12; reinforcements in, 32, 38, 74, 97, 121, 143–44, 146, 181; requisitioning of troops for Iberia, 145–46; rivalry with navy, 8; seniority system in, 12, 14–15, 22, 33, 133–35, 214; supposed acts of mercy by, 198–99, 263n60; troop strength in Iberia, 54, 128, 146; troop strength in southern France, 209; Wellington's disdain for troops in, 39, 42–43, 64, 74–75, 163, 236n8. See also Officers, British army; Peninsular War; Peninsular War battles and sieges
Artillery, Royal, 7, 24, 126–27, 129, 181, 232n11
Auckland, Lord (William Eden), 104, 121, 140
Austria, 27, 29–30, 46; British subsidies to, 30, 36, 235n11; re-entry into war, 184, 186

Badajoz, 54, 92–93; British army sacking of, 102, 244n36; siege and capture of, 93, 101
Bank of England, 104, 112–13, 150
Barrow, Sir John, 80
Bathurst, Lord Henry (3rd Earl of Bathurst), 118, 145, 158, 162–63, 189, 212, 220; added to War Office, 120, 147; helps obtain money for Wellington, 112–14, 150, 217; on Holland expedition, 206–207; on King's German Legion, 159; on looting charges against army, 197, 198–99; on restoring discipline in army, 164; on Transport and Ordnance Boards, 177; and Wellington's relations with Admiralty, 115, 171, 176
Bay of Biscay, 124–25, 182
Bayonne, 206, 212, 265n94, 266n118
Bentinck, Gen. Sir William, 102, 145, 160–61, 253n8
Beresford, Marshal William Carr, 93, 96, 266n121; as commander of Portuguese army, 28, 191, 236n2, 261n21; as Wellington second-in-command, 94, 134–35
Bergen-op-Zoom, 206, 208
Berkeley, Adm. George Cranfield, 80, 82, 115, 123; as Wellington ally, 8–9, 78–79, 216; Wellington's initial lack of faith in, 35, 77–78, 115
Bidassoa River, 188, 261n10
Bissett, John, 110, 246n66
Bonaparte, Joseph, 55, 122, 128, 162, 165; ineptitude of, 178; installed as Spanish king, 3, 27
Bonaparte, Napoleon. See Napoleon Bonaparte
Bourdeaux, 210
Britain: Austrian subsidy of, 30, 36, 235n11; dependency on American markets, 62, 115, 166, 221; embargo of, 3, 45, 46, 62, 106, 166; financial crisis in, 104, 217, 246n50; gold and silver reserves of, 62, 112–14, 121, 150, 218; government credibility in, 20, 30; issuing of treasury notes by, 104–105, 108–109, 114, 236n9, 245n48; Portuguese subsidy of, 31–32, 45, 61–62, 97–99, 111, 192, 194, 217, 239–40n31, 240n35; public opinion in, 48, 52, 94–95, 214; relations with Portugal, 23, 27, 191; relations with Spain, 23, 26, 28–29, 36, 141–42; Russian subsidy of, 104, 107, 144; Spanish subsidy of, 45, 120, 201–202, 217; taxes in, 45; trade expansion by, 150, 221, 265n103; war expenditures of, 73, 76, 98–99, 104–11, 114, 215–16, 247n79; war with United States, 104, 106, 145, 148, 167, 219–20. See also Army, British; Navy, Royal
British army. See Army, British
British East India Company, 153
Brunswick Oels Jäger, Duke of, 74
Buckinghamshire, Earl of, 33

Bunbury, Col. Henry, 81, 145, 161
Burgos: British retreat from, 137–39; French abandonment of, 162, 176, 255n48; siege of, 124, 126–27, 129–31, 176, 218
Burgoyne, John, 126–27
Burrard, Sir Harry, 13, 15–18, 233n11; and Convention of Cintra, 18–20
Bussaco, 72–73, 241n7, 242n8

Cadiz: British troops and, 64–66, 240n43; French siege of, 55, 122–23
Caffarelli, Gen. Marie-François, 122, 124, 126–28, 151
Canning, George, 57, 214, 235n11; rivalry with Castlereagh, 30, 32, 57; Wellington relations with, 14, 25
Cape Verde Islands, 80
Castaños, Gen. Javier, 264n82
Castlereagh, Viscount (Robert Stewart, 2nd Marquess of Londonderry), 15–16, 24–25, 48, 212; assists Wellington, 46, 215; names Wellington to head Portugal expedition, 32–33, 214; and Peninsular War strategy, 31–36; returns to Foreign Office, 120, 147; rivalry with Canning, 30, 32, 57; support for Portuguese government by, 192, 193; Wellington relations with, 11, 14, 25
Catalonia, 187
Catholic emancipation, 116, 119, 232n16, 248n86
Cato, 222
Caulaincourt, Armand, 260n2
Cavalry, British: horses, 23–25, 157; proposed provisional units of, 155–57; reinforcements, 144, 158; shortage of officers in, 250n37; used to quell civil disturbances, 143–44, 250n37; Wellington efforts to obtain, 143
Chancellor of the Exchequer, office, 8–9

Chatham, Lord, 24
Chowne, Gen. Christopher, 252n67
Chronicle. See *Morning Chronicle*
Ciudad Rodrigo, 93; British army sacking of, 102; British capture of, 101; French siege of, 71–72, 241n3
Ciudad Rodrigo, Spain, 152
Clarke, Gen. Henri, 258n116
Clarke, Mary Ann, 30
Clausel, Gen. Bertrand, 254n10
Collier, Adm. George, 168–71, 205–206, 257nn70–71
Command and control: fragmented nature in British army, 5–10, 158; Wellington on, 18, 33–34
Commander in chief, office, 6–7, 10, 30
Commissary, office, 105–106, 246n66
Consisco, 195
Continental System: collapse of, 150; establishment of, 3; impact on British economy and trade, 45–46, 106, 167
Convention of Cintra, 18–20, 214; public outrage over, 20–22, 25; Wellington and, 18–22, 25, 52, 216
Cordoba, 55
Coruña, 27–29
Cotton, Adm. Sir Charles, 8–9, 25, 35, 216
Cotton, Gen. Sir Stapleton, 134, 266n121
Craddock, Lt. Gen. Sir John, 27, 32–33, 35, 236n12
Crimean War, 219
Croker, John Wilson, 176, 183
Cuesta, Don Gregorio, 38

Dalhousie, Gen. Lord James, 252n63
Dalrymple, Sir Hew, 15–16, 233n9; and Convention of Cintra, 18–20, 22
Delaborde, Gen. Henri-François, 233n1
Desertions, 39, 74, 137, 146
Disease: among British troops, 5, 38,

Disease (cont.)
144, 146–47; among French POWs, 81; "Walcheren fever," 74, 82, 238n48
Douglas, Sir Howard, 126–27
Douro River, 38
Drovet, Gen. Jean-Baptiste, 254n10
Duende de los Cafés, El, 195–97
Duff, Sir James, 105, 245n49
Dundas, David, Sir, 6, 30
Dundas, Robert. *See* Melville, Lord

Egypt, 25
Engineers, Royal, 7, 10, 233n11
Erskine, Maj. Gen. Sir William, 131–32, 243n2, 251n38
España, Marshal Carlos de, 141, 245n44, 260n1

Ferguson, Gen. Henry, 62
First lord of the Admiralty, office, 8, 10
Forced requisitioning, 23, 64
Foreign secretary, office, 8–10, 57
Forjaz, Dom Miguel, 190, 194, 216, 262n29; calls for separate Portuguese units, 191, 193; and Portuguese subsidy, 62–63, 192, 239n31
Fortescue, John W., 244n36
France, southern: atrocities by Spanish troops in, 200–203, 264nn67–68; British army misconduct in, 198; British invasion of, 158–59, 162–63, 188, 204–205, 210–11, 220, 261n10; British troop strength in, 209; royalists in, 210–11; Wellington calls for invasion of, 158–59, 179–80, 183–84, 187
Freire, Gen. Manuel, 180, 201, 203, 259n130
French army: Army of Portugal, 71, 73, 122, 124, 241n1, 254n10; Army of Spain, 27, 101, 178, 186, 258n114; Army of the Center, 254n10; Army of the North, 124–26, 254n10; Army of the South, 151, 254n10; artillery shortages of, 178; builds defensive lines along Spanish border, 187–88; camp followers of, 256n53; casualties, 13, 38, 73, 93, 103, 179–80, 236n5, 242n7, 245n43; cavalry, 72, 143, 241n6; commanders, 178, 233n1, 254n10; composed of inexperienced recruits, 178; fortresses in Portugal, 92–93, 124; invasion of Portugal by, 28, 54, 71–72, 214; invasion of Russia by, 106, 121, 166, 216; in Italy, 160; lack of reinforcements, 73, 181, 242n9; naval forces, 170, 182, 257n83; outnumbers British, 101, 108, 122, 128, 151, 178; reconquest of Madrid by, 128–29; reorganization of forces in Spain, 178; retreat from central Europe by, 150, 184, 186, 260n2; retreat from Russia by, 145, 149–50, 185, 217, 220–21; siege of Cadiz by, 55, 122–23; strategic deployment of, 56, 152, 178–79, 187; supply and logistics system, 39, 56; troop rations of, 178, 180, 258n116; troop strength in Iberia, 14, 54, 122, 128–29, 151–52, 178; troop strength in southern France, 207, 265n98; Wellington outflanking of, 162, 188, 255n48; withdrawal from Spain of, 162, 165, 180–81. *See also* Peninsular War battles and sieges
Frere, John Hookham, 234n1
Fuentes d'Oñoro, 82, 93, 95–96, 242n24

Gazan, Gen. Theodore, 152, 254n10
George III, King, 30, 33, 45–46, 57, 232n16
Germany, 159–60
Gibraltar, 240n42
Girón, Gen. Pedro, 201, 264n82
Gold and silver: Bank of England reserves of, 112–14, 150, 218; British shortage of, 62, 121; global shortage of, 106, 114, 215–17; prices of, 106, 110; Rothschild

help surrounding, 114; Wellington need of, 39, 45, 109
Gordon, Col. James Willoughby, 6
Graham, Gen. Sir Thomas, 134, 170, 181, 255n48, 266n121; given command of northern wing, 162, 255n46; heads expedition to Holland, 206, 208; and looting of San Sebastián, 195, 197–98; replacement of, 189, 261n13
Grenville, Lord (1st Baron William Wyndam), 9, 98, 101, 183, 232n16
Grey, Lord Charles, 100–101, 111–12; and army command structure, 10–11, 232–33n19

Harrowby, Charles, 113
Hazlitt, William, 234n27
Herries, John, 106, 108–109, 113–14, 150, 218
Hill, Gen. Sir Rowland, 134, 189, 266n121; as battlefield commander, 133, 241–42n7, 260n1; ordered to remain in Madrid, 123, 220
Holland and Low Countries, 23; British expeditions to (1793, 1799), 3; British expedition to (1809), 26, 31–32, 50–52, 57, 62, 215, 238nn48–49; British expedition to (1814), 206–208; Wellington command of troops in, 233n23
Hope, Gen. Sir John, 261n16, 266n121; joins Iberia expedition, 133, 261n12; in southern France campaign, 188–89, 210, 266n118
Horse Guards, 136, 164, 214; about, 6; and officers' leave requests, 137; and seniority system, 14–15, 133; Wellington clashes with, 11–12, 73, 133, 135–36, 144, 218–19
Horses, 23–25, 157
Howarth, Brig. Gen., 50
Huskisson, William, 40, 43–45, 57, 67, 236n11

India, 3, 11, 233n11, 233n23
Ireland, 11, 22, 74, 119, 211
Italy, 160–61

Joseph. *See* Bonaparte, Joseph
Jourdan, Marshal Jean-Baptiste, 152, 162, 178
Junot, Gen. Jean-Andoche, 14, 18, 233n1, 241n1

Keith, Adm. Lord George, 125, 128, 171
Kellermann, Gen. François, 18
Kennedy, Robert, 246n66
King's German Legion, 74, 143, 245n44; debate over sending to Hanover, 159–60; structure of, 252n80

Lamb, Charles, 234n27
La Merchant, Gen. John, 245n43
Lawrence, Sir Thomas, 210
Leipzig, 198
Lines of Torres Vedras, 59, 61; aims and value of, 56, 72–73; described, 238n8; secrecy around, 67–68, 216
Lisbon, 14; defense of, 55–56, 73, 92; as logistics base, 37, 65; strategic situation of, 31, 65–66
Liverpool, Lord (Robert Banks Jenkinson, 2nd Earl of Liverpool), 57, 70, 118, 218, 251n39; conservative fiscal policy of, 217; demands money savings, 75–76, 98, 107–108; gives Wellington authority for offensive operations, 97; inconsistency of, 75; named prime minister, 112; on Napoleon defeat in Russia, 149–50; on Parliamentary opposition, 154; on Peninsular War strategy, 58–60, 64–65, 73, 158, 215, 240n43; on Portuguese subsidy, 63; and press, 68–69, 153; support to Wellington by, 99, 102, 215, 218; and Wellesley-Pole, 119; Wellington relations with, 70, 220
Loison, Gen. Henri, 233n1
Longa, Gen. Francisco, 200–201, 254n9
Löw, Gen. Sigismund, 252n67
Low Countries. *See* Holland and Low Countries
Lynch, Jean Baptiste, 211

Madrid, 122–23, 129
Maida, 3
Maitland, Lt. Gen. Frederick, 129, 135, 160, 250n30
Marines, Royal, 125, 127–28, 175, 233n11
Marmont, Marshal Auguste, 101, 121, 124, 218
Martin, Adm. George, 115, 168–69
Martin, Adm. Sir Thomas, 181–82, 205
Masséna, Marshal André, 71–72, 218
Master general of the ordnance, office, 7, 10, 24. *See also* Ordnance Board
McGregor, Dr., 146
Medical Board, 146–47
Melville, Lord (Robert Dundas, 2nd Viscount Melville), 125, 205, 239n14; correspondence with Wellington, 115–16, 171–75, 219
Metternich, Klement, 260n2
Military secretary, office, 6
Milton, Sir Edward, 51–52
Miña, Espoz, 254n9
Moira, Lord, 248n86
Monarchy, British, 5–7. *See also* George III, King
Moniteur, 260n2
Moore, Gen. Sir John, 17, 24, 39, 64, 69; death of, 26–27; denied command of Portugal expedition, 14–15
Morillo, Gen. Pablo, 200, 202
Morning Chronicle, 61; about, 20, 234n27; on atrocities by British troops, 196–97; on rapprochement with Napoleon, 184
Mulgrave, Lord, 50, 77–78, 135–36, 183
Murat, Marshal Joachim, 161
Murray, Gen. Sir George, 162, 255n47
Murray, Gen. Sir John, 151, 253n8
Mutiny Act, 164

Napoleon Bonaparte, 66, 178, 186, 210, 213, 242–42n27; abdication of, 211; alliance with Russia, 46; debate over rapprochement with, 67, 184, 239n12; defeat in Russia of, 140, 149–50, 185, 216–17, 220–21, 253n1; establishes Continental System, 3; invasions of Spain and Portugal by, 27, 71; leadership qualities of, 135–36; misestimates by, 152, 254n11; Peninsular War as bleeding ulcer for, 213; retreat from central Europe by, 150, 184, 186, 260n2; strategic conceptions of, 54, 56, 179; at Waterloo, 222
Naval Chronicle, 175
Navy, Royal: amphibious raids by, 124–26; army's rivalry with, 8; blockades and sieges by, 115, 125–26, 165, 167, 169–70, 175, 181–82, 184; budget of, 5; bureaucracy of, 8; cooperation with Wellington by, 8–9, 25, 125–27; diminished role in Peninsular War, 205–206; joint operations with army, 124, 216; payment of sailors in, 46; and privateers, 115–16, 166–68, 172, 204; recruitment challenges of, 167, 172; seniority system in, 174; shipping of supplies to army, 123, 152–53, 165, 169, 182, 186, 188, 204–205, 265n91, 265n94; shortage of ships, 167–69, 171–72, 257n73; as strategic problem for Napoleon, 78, 151; strength in Bay of Biscay, 182; supplying of Spanish guerillas by, 125, 130, 151; and U.S. Navy, 167, 172, 256n67; and war with America, 145, 148, 167, 220; Wellington compliments to, 126, 182; Wellington conflicts with, 8, 114–16, 121, 124, 165–76, 181–83, 204–206, 219; Wellington failure to credit, 123, 130; women employed by, 171
Ney, Marshal Michel, 241n1
Nive and St. Pierre, 206, 265n95

Ocaña, 55, 60
O'Donnel, Gen. Henry, 260n1

O'Donoju, Gen. Juan, 195
Officers, British army: dismissal of, 139, 252n67; incompetence of, 95, 131–33, 135–36, 214, 251n38; leave requests by, 136–37; pay of, 137, 189, 261n16; and seniority system, 12, 14–15, 22, 33, 133–35, 214; shortage of, 136–37, 250n37
Ordenanza, 56, 61, 63
Ordnance Board, 5, 7, 176–77, 184–85
Oswald, Gen. John, 252n63

Paget, Sir Edward, 135, 251–52n63
Palmerston, Viscount (Henry John Temple), 7, 232n11
Pamplona, 181, 187; British siege of, 153, 178, 186, 260n1
Parliament, 6, 33, 95; attacks on Wellington in, 51–52; civil control of military by, 5, 7; and Duke of York scandal, 30; opposition to war in, 111; on Portuguese subsidy, 62–63, 98, 240n35; votes of thanks to Wellington, 49, 99–100, 102, 199
Pasajes, 124
Payne, General, 41
Pelet, Col. Jean-Jacques, 72–73
Pellew, Adm. Sir Edward, 175
Peninsular War battles and sieges: Alba de Tormes (1809), 55, 60; Albuera (1811), 93, 95, 100; Almeida (1810), 71–72, 241n4; Badajoz (1811–12), 93, 101; Battle of the Pyrenees (1813), 179; Bayonne (1814), 206, 212, 265n94, 266n118; Burgos (1812), 124, 126–27, 129–31, 176, 218; Bussaco (1810), 72–73, 241–42nn7–8; Cadiz (1809–11), 55, 122–23; Ciudad Rodrigo (1810), 71–72, 241n3; Ciudad Rodrigo (1812), 101; Coruña (1808), 27–29; Fuentes d'Oñoro (1811), 82, 93, 95–96, 242n24; Nive and St. Pierre (1814), 206, 265n95; Ocaña (1809), 55, 60; Pamplona (1813), 153, 178, 186, 260n1; Porto (1809), 37–38; Roliça (1808), 13, 214, 233n1; Salamanca (1812), 103, 121, 245n43; San Marcial (1813), 180, 259n130; San Sebastián (1813), 166–67, 169–70, 173–78, 180–81, 184; Sorauren (1813), 179; Talavera (1809), 38, 49–51, 236n5; Toulouse (1814), 210, 212, 266n118; Vimeiro (1808), 13, 17–18, 214, 233n1; Vitoria (1813), 162, 185, 256n49
Penrose, Rear Adm. Charles, 205–206, 265n94
Perceval, Lord Spencer, 57, 108, 217; assassination of, 112, 118, 218
Perry, James, 234n27
Picton, Gen. Sir Thomas, 250n37
Pitt, William, 45, 99, 235n11
Pole, William. *See* Wellesley-Pole, William
Ponsonby, William, 98
Popham, Adm. Sir Home, 124–26, 128, 176, 257n70
Portland, Duke of, 50, 57, 232n16
Porto, 28, 37–38
Portugal: Britain's relations with, 23, 27, 191; budget deficit of, 192; French invasions of, 28, 54, 71–72, 214; government corruption in, 63–64, 97; as key to Wellington's strategy, 31–32, 60, 214, 239n26; Napoleon's strategy in, 54; Regency Council in, 27, 61, 97, 190–94; taxes in, 192, 262n29; tensions with Spain, 192–94, 262n32. *See also* Army, British; French army; Peninsular War battles and sieges
Portuguese army: British command of, 28, 32, 190–91, 213, 236n2, 261n21; conscription and recruitment for, 194; fights bravely, 74, 190; *ordenanza* militia of, 56, 61, 63; payment arrears to, 192; politicians' disregard for, 62–63; Wellington praise for, 55, 190, 193
Portuguese subsidy, 194, 217; Parlia-

Portuguese subsidy (*cont.*)
ment on, 62–63, 98, 240n35; size of, 45, 98–99, 192, 239n31; Wellington on, 31–32, 61–62, 97–98, 111

Press, 28–29, 49, 187; on Convention of Cintra, 20, 22; Liverpool and, 68–69, 153–54; manipulation of information by, 69; reports on British atrocities by, 102, 194–95; undermining of British war effort by, 28, 215; Wellington battles with, 21–22, 47–48, 68, 190–92, 195–97, 213; Wellington duplicity toward, 67–68, 95, 216; Wellington mistrust of, 68–69, 241n56; Wellington utilization of, 67–70, 96, 215. See also *Morning Chronicle*; *Times*

Prime minister, office, 9

Prisoners of war, French: debate over sending to Britain of, 79–82; disease among, 81; numbers of, 79, 103, 261n10; troops needed for guarding, 144; Wellington opposition to parole for, 81–82

Privateers, 183, 204; naval protection from, 115–16, 204; Wellington concern about, 115, 123, 166–67, 169

Rape, 102
Rawlings, John, 43
Reille, Gen. Charles, 254n10
Rey, Gen. Louis-Emmanuel, 180–81, 195
Reynier, Gen. Jean Louis, 241n1
Robinson, Gen. Frederick, 252n67
Roliça, 13, 214, 233n1
Rose, George, 62
Rothschild, Nathan, 114, 150
Russia: British subsidies for, 104, 107, 144; French alliance with, 3, 46; Napoleon's invasion of, 106, 121, 166, 216
Russian retreat by Napoleon, 145, 217; impact on Peninsular War of, 185, 220–21; Liverpool on, 149–50

Salamanca, 103, 121, 245n43
Sampaio, Enrique, 105
Sánchez, Julian, 141, 254n9
San Marcial, 180, 259n130
San Sebastián: blockade of, 166, 169–70, 173, 176, 180–81, 184; British failures at, 167, 170, 174–75, 177–78; British looting of, 181, 194–98; French fortifications at, 153, 165–66
Santander, 124–26, 130, 165, 204
Santarém, 73
Santoña, 165, 181–82, 186
Scorched earth policy, 56
Secretary at war, office, 7, 10
Secretary for war and colonies, office, 8–10, 57
Seniority system, 15, 134–35; adverse effects of, 22, 214; Horse Guards and, 14–15, 133; in navy, 174; Wellington and, 12, 14, 33, 133
Sepoy Mutiny, 219, 233n23
Seville, 55
Sicily, 145–46, 160–61
Silveira, Gen. Francisco, 191
Skerrett, Gen. John, 146
Somerset, Capt. Lord Fitzroy, 96, 232n18
Sorauren, 179
Souham, Gen. Joseph, 128, 131
Soult, Marshal Nicholas, 27, 37, 55, 93, 101, 218; and Cadiz siege, 122–23; replaced, 151–52; and southern France defense, 187–88, 204; takes command of Army of Spain, 178, 258n103
Spain: appreciation for Wellington in, 103–104; Britain's relations with, 23, 26, 28–29, 36, 141–42; British 1808 defeat in, 27; British 1812 return to, 102–103; British subsidy to, 45, 120, 201–202, 217; Cortes in, 141–42, 147, 202–203; French conquest of, 3, 27; French withdrawal from, 162, 165, 180–81; guerillas in, 102, 124–25, 151, 221, 254n9; as key concern for

Napoleon, 54; liberals in, 141; revolt against French in, 3; tensions with Portugal, 192–94, 262n32; as unpredictable ally, 55, 221. *See also* Army, British; French army; Peninsular War battles and sieges

Spanish army: in battle, 55, 180, 221; in invasion of France, 199–204, 263n63; looting by, 200–203, 264nn67–68; Wellington command over, 140–42, 147, 203, 213; Wellington on, 55, 140, 180, 201–202; Wellington unhappiness with, 103, 140, 200–201

Spencer, Gen. Sir Brent, 13, 133–35, 231n2

Stanhope, Lord, 96

Stewart, Brig. Charles, 68

Stewart, General, 138, 251n63, 252n67

Stewart, Robert. *See* Castlereagh, Viscount

Stuart, Charles, 63–64; and Portugal political-economic stability, 192, 216, 246n50, 262n29; and Portuguese troops, 190, 194, 261n21, 263n40

Stuart, Sir John, 74

Suchet, Marshal Louis Gabriel, 101, 122, 151, 187

Swabey, Lt. William, 130–31, 137–38

Tagus River, 38

Talavera, 38, 49–51, 236n5

Tarleton, Gen. Banastre, 52, 98

Tarragona, 151, 253n8

Taxes: in Britain, 45; in Portugal, 192, 262n29

Taylor, Lt. Col. Herbert, 240n43

Times, 22, 49, 69, 143–44; on British war reverses, 28–29; criticisms of Liverpool by, 153; criticisms of Wellington by, 47–48

Torrens, Col. Henry, 6, 132–33, 156, 177

Tory Party, 9, 57

Toulouse, 210, 212, 266n118

Transport Board, 176–77, 183–85, 204

Treasury notes, 104–105, 108–109, 114, 236n9, 245n48

United States: Britain's war with, 104, 106, 145, 148, 167, 219–20; British dependency on markets in, 62, 115, 166, 221; Navy of, 167, 172, 256n67; privateers from, 115–16, 123, 166–67

Valladolid, 152

Vandamme, Gen. Dominic, 260n2

Vansittart, Nicholas, 113

Vega, Andrés de la, 142

Victor, Marshal Claude, 37–38

Villiers, John, 28, 41, 63, 105, 245n49

Vimeiro, 13, 17–18, 214, 233n1

Vitoria, 162, 185, 256n49

Von Bernewitz, Gen. J. H. C., 252n67

Wagram, 54, 56

Walcheren Expedition (1809), 26, 52; described, 238n48; effects of, 32, 50–51, 57, 62; inquiry into, 57, 238n49; "Walcheren fever" from, 74, 82, 238n48

Wales, Prince of, 193

War Office, 7, 147, 219, 232n11

Waterloo, 12, 222

Weller, Jac, 245n36

Wellesley, Arthur. *See* Wellington, 1st Duke of

Wellesley, Henry, 103–104, 118, 120, 194–95, 247n68; becomes minister plenipotentiary to Spain, 70; efforts for political stability in Spain, 203, 216; works for British command of Spanish army, 140–42

Wellesley, Richard, (Marquess Wellesley): career, 32; declining political fortunes of, 120, 218; named foreign secretary, 57; personal and political conduct of,

Wellesley, Richard (*cont.*)
116–18; resigns as foreign secretary, 116, 247n86; sent to Spain, 32, 36, 54; tries to form ministry, 118, 144; Wellington's lack of defense of, 118, 218

Wellesley-Pole, William, 48–49, 67, 95, 100; advises public relations work by Wellington, 50, 76; on Beresford, 94, 100; political career of, 119, 218, 239n14; on press abuse of Wellington, 47, 50; on public support for Wellington, 50, 179; on Richard Wellesley, 117; selects title for Wellington, 49

Wellington, 1st Duke of (Arthur Wellesley), biography and character: as aristocrat, 52, 214; becomes ambassador to Paris, 212; Catholicism conversion accusation, 203, 264n84; on central Europe, 184, 186–87, 260n2; as chief secretary to Ireland, 11, 22; combat record before Portugal, 12–14, 233n23; commands troops in Low Countries, 233n23; elevated to dukedom, 212; elevated to earldom, 118; elevated to peerage, 49; in India, 3, 11; life following Peninsula War, 219; as member of Parliament, 11, 22; military leadership abilities, 77, 82, 221–22; optimism, 47, 93–94; pay and pensions of, 118, 189–90; as political general, 9–11, 14, 25, 58, 120, 153; pragmatic nature of, 119–20, 218; promoted to field marshal, 188, 220, 261n11; promoted to lieutenant general, 14; temper of, 135, 176

Wellington, 1st Duke of (Arthur Wellesley), Peninsular War commander: on battle of Vimeiro, 17–18; on Battles of the Pyrenees, 179; battles with press, 21–22, 47–48, 68, 190–92, 195–97, 213; on being relieved of command in Iberia, 15–16; on Berkeley, 77–79;

on British casualties, 50, 96; budget for, 40; on cavalry and horses, 23–24, 143; on command and control, 18, 33–34; compliments navy, 126, 182; conflicts with navy, 8, 114–16, 121, 124, 165–76, 181–83, 204–206, 219; and Convention of Cintra, 18–22, 25, 52, 216; cooperation with navy, 8–9, 25, 125–27; on creation of provisional units, 155–58; defense of Lisbon by, 55–56, 73, 92; disdain for British troops, 39, 42–43, 236n8; doesn't defend brothers, 118–20, 218; efforts to obtain naval support, 127–28, 165; efforts to procure money, 41–42, 105–108, 110–11, 216, 245n49; efforts to restore discipline, 43, 64, 163–65; fails to credit navy, 123, 130; forbids forced requisitioning, 23; given command of Spanish army, 140–42, 147, 203, 213; granted authority for offensive operations, 97, 217; on his second-in-command, 133–34; on Holland expeditions, 31, 207–208; and invasion of southern France, 158–59, 162–63, 179–80, 183–84, 187–88, 261n10; on Italian aid plan, 161–62; on lack of government support, 11, 67, 73–74, 76, 112, 209–10; logistics efforts by, 123, 165, 180, 205, 265n91; Memorandum of Operations by, 59, 239n20; on military indiscipline, 139, 163–64; military mistakes by, 123, 129–31, 216, 218, 220; named Portugal commander, 3, 5, 26, 32–33, 35–36, 231n2; on need for money, 46, 76–77, 99, 112, 150–51, 208–10; on officer incompetence, 131–32, 136, 138–39, 252n67; Parliamentary votes of thanks to, 49, 99–100, 102, 199; on party politics, 57–58; on payment of troops, 39, 43, 64, 107, 111, 151; on Perceval, 118; political opposition to, 46, 47, 51–52, 69, 93–94, 154; as popular hero, 49, 96, 141, 212; on Portugal's defensibility, 59, 65–67; on Portuguese army, 55, 190–91, 193; on Portuguese subsidy, 31–32, 61–62, 97–98, 111; on prisoners of war, 79–82; on privateer threat, 166–67, 169, 183; public relations efforts by, 52, 95–96; pursuit of Masséna by, 92–93, 101–103, 120–21; on reinforcements, 74, 121, 143–45; relations with Castlereagh, 11, 14, 25; relations with Liverpool, 70, 220; requests for money by, 40–41, 43–44, 59, 64, 107–108, 216; on Richard Wellesley, 117; on royalist support in France, 211; secrecy and duplicity by, 67–70, 75, 95–96, 100, 216, 244n11; sees Portugal as key, 31–32, 60, 214, 239n26; and seniority system, 12, 14, 33, 133; on shortage of officers, 136–37; on siege of Burgos, 129–30; on siege of San Sebastián, 170, 173, 178; on Spanish army, 55, 140, 180, 201–202; and Spanish-Portuguese tensions, 193, 262n32; on Spanish subsidy, 201–202; staff of, 10; strategic deployments by, 37, 66, 122, 124–25, 152–53, 162, 179, 217; strategy in Peninsular War, 31–32, 34, 55–56, 59, 214, 215; on Transport and Ordnance Boards, 176–77, 183; uses press, 67–70, 96, 215; on war with America, 148, 167, 219–20; withdraws Spanish troops from France, 202, 204; wounded in battle, 103, 210

Whig Party: attacks war policies, 52, 57–58, 104, 111–12, 215, 239n12; on Convention of Cintra, 20; as opposition party, 9; pessimism on war by, 100–101, 111–12, 154, 183–84; and Portuguese subsidy, 98; praise for Wellington from, 99–100; on rapprochement with Napoleon, 184, 239n12; Richard Wellesley approaches, 118; shift in stance on war, 97

Women: raped by British troops, 102; as ship navigators, 171

York, Duke of (Frederick Augustus), 6, 49–50; on army indiscipline, 164; political scandal of, 30; on seniority system in army, 134–35; on troop rotation and reinforcement, 154–56

www.ingramcontent.com/pod-product-compliance
Lightning Source LLC
Chambersburg PA
CBHW022105150426
43195CB00008B/281